OXFORD ENGLISH MONOGRAPHS

General Editors

JOHN CAREY   STEPHEN GILL
DOUGLAS GRAY   ROGER LONSDALE

af w

Coleridge, Wordsworth
and the
Language of Allusion

LUCY NEWLYN

OXFORD
UNIVERSITY PRESS

OXFORD

UNIVERSITY PRESS

Great Clarendon Street, Oxford OX2 6DP

Oxford University Press is a department of the University of Oxford.
It furthers the University's objective of excellence in research, scholarship,
and education by publishing worldwide in

Oxford New York

Athens Auckland Bangkok Bogotá Buenos Aires Calcutta
Cape Town Chennai Dar es Salaam Delhi Florence Hong Kong Istanbul
Karachi Kuala Lumpur Madrid Melbourne Mexico City Mumbai
Nairobi Paris São Paulo Shanghai Singapore Taipei Tokyo Toronto Warsaw

and associated companies in Berlin Ibadan

Oxford is a registered trade mark of Oxford University Press
in the UK and in certain other countries

Published in the United States
by Oxford University Press Inc., New York

© Lucy Newlyn 1986

The moral rights of the author have been asserted
Database right Oxford University Press (maker)

First published 1986

First published in paperback 2001

All rights reserved. No part of this publication may be reproduced,
stored in a retrieval system, or transmitted, in any form or by any means,
without the prior permission in writing of Oxford University Press,
or as expressly permitted by law, or under terms agreed with the appropriate
reprographics rights organization. Enquiries concerning reproduction
outside the scope of the above should be sent to the Rights Department,
Oxford University Press, at the address above

You must not circulate this book in any other binding or cover
and you must impose this same condition on any acquirer

British Library Cataloguing in Publication Data

Data available

Library of Congress Cataloging in Publication Data

Data available

ISBN 0–19–924259–3

1 3 5 7 9 10 8 6 4 2

Printed in Great Britain
on acid-free paper by
Antony Rowe Ltd., Chippenham

For Mags, Jacob and Amy
In memory of Pete

Preface to the Second Edition

'Not so fast with your lecture', said Charlotte. 'Let me prove I am keeping up. Have we not already come to relationships and affinities?'

'We have indeed', the Captain replied, 'and let us at once get to know them in what they are and in what they do. We say of those natures which on meeting speedily connect and inter-react that they have an affinity for one another. This affinity may be very remarkable. Alkalis and acids, although opposed to one another and perhaps precisely because they are so opposed, will in a most decisive way seek out, take hold of, and modify one another and form, in so doing, a new substance together. We have only to think of lime, which manifests towards all acids a strong inclination, a decided wish for union. As soon as our chemistry cabinet arrives we shall show you various experiments which are very entertaining and which will give you a clearer idea than words, names, and technical terms may do.'

'I must confess', said Charlotte, 'that when you speak of these wondrous entities as related they seem to me not so much blood relations as related in spirit and in the soul. In precisely this way true and important friendships may come about between people: opposing qualities make an intenser union possible . . .'

(Goethe, *Elective Affinities* (1809), ch. 4)

Even if there are more than two of them, the model will almost always be furnished by a twosome, by some great couples of friends. Always men. Well, more often than not, and that is what counts; it is of *them* that one speaks—the *two of them*, it is the *twosome* that is kept in memory and whose legend is archived. Our culture, our school, our literature are the theatre of these couples—and the posterity of these great friends.

(Jacques Derrida, *Politics of Friendship* (1997), ch. 4)

I

Like all friendships, Coleridge's and Wordsworth's was unique. Unlike most others, it has had an after-life of 200 years. Posterity has seen it as a marriage of minds—an instance of what Goethe, following contemporary scientists, called 'elective affinities'. But that is because it bore fruit in a collaboration of almost unprecedented importance for the history of European literature. In human terms, the story is very different. It was a friendship which began well and ended badly, with damaging consequences on both sides. This book examines the course of the friendship alongside the literary collaboration it generated. On the one hand it explores the beneficial effects that mutual influence had on Wordsworth's and Coleridge's writing. On the other, it considers the emotional harm each inflicted as the relationship went wrong. I have tried to disentangle two threads in what is quite a complicated narrative; but to do this effectively I have needed to show how they came to be entangled. The two writers contributed to the myth of their own literary friendship, by idealizing and romanticizing it through poetry. It is a compelling myth, but it should be read sceptically.

In broad outline, the story goes as follows (I will complicate it later). The two men met in the 1790s, during the period of political unrest which followed the French Revolution. Their immediate sense of affinity was strengthened by a shared vision of what the future might be. Excitement, energy, a spirit of optimistic experimentation, characterised the culture of dissent in which the first phase of their friendship thrived. The *Lyrical Ballads*, published jointly and anonymously in 1798, laid the foundations for English Romanticism. Its polemical advertisement announced a new kind of poetry, stripped of elevated diction and close to the prosaic language spoken by ordinary, uneducated people. In and around this publication, as well as congruent with its revolutionary agenda, there emerged the 'conversation' poem. This was a species of occasional verse, carefully crafted but informal in register, which Coleridge is credited with inventing. The two poets used this idiom to explore their shared enthusiasm for the possibilities of political change, human companionship, and the ennobling reciprocity of nature and imagination. Their belief in themselves as poet-prophets, who might discover the basis for society's future evolution and happiness, emerged in a sequence of poems written to and for each other between 1797 and 1807. Amongst these are some of the most philosophically profound contributions to the English Romantic canon.

At the end of 1798 the two writers set off on a trip to Germany, accompanied by Wordsworth's sister Dorothy. Once there, they separated. Coleridge read widely in the latest works of Continental philosophy and science. He absorbed the implications of a vitalistic understanding of the organic world, and began to refine the concept of imagination as a transforming faculty of mind. His friends, meanwhile, retreated to the small town of Goslar, where Wordsworth (somewhat homesick) began his autobiographical poem, *The Prelude*. This was a work as densely packed with philosophy as Coleridge's Notebooks of this time. But in it, Wordsworth showed a continuing interest in the British associationist David Hartley, whose epistemology Coleridge would soon reject. He also showed a fascination with the psychology of Edmund Burke, whose theory of the sublime and the beautiful he began to apply to his own early life. His allegiance to British philosophical tradition was counterbalanced by Coleridge's eclecticism, his openness to Continental thought. The trip to Germany proved decisive in confirming these intellectual differences. It was a short, but crucial, interlude in their friendship.

When the Wordsworths returned to England, they chose to live in Cumbria, where they had been born. Not in the West Country, where Coleridge had lived as a child, and where the friends had lived as neighbours. This move was consistent with Wordsworth's hunger to revisit his origins. (He wanted to understand how his own imagination had been fostered by an upbringing among the lakes and mountains.) Coleridge joined them soon afterward, but for him this was neither a homecoming nor a return to the place in which their friendship was rooted. His was a cosmopolitan temperament. He thrived when he was in London or on his travels, and never settled in the Lakes with the same deep sense of contentment and belonging achieved by his friend. This sense of rootlessness, of displacement, may have contributed to (and in turn been intensified by) his steadily deteriorating mental and physical health. He became unhappy in his marriage, desperate in his unrequited love for Sara Hutchinson, dependent on but excluded from the intimacy of Wordsworth's household, and increasingly addicted to opium as a stimulus for his creative writing.

During the years 1800–1804 which saw the beginnings of this decline, there emerged a sequence of major works which were later to establish the reputations of both writers. These works could not have existed had their dialogue not occurred, or had it taken a course other than the one it took. The second edition of *Lyrical Ballads* in 1800 was published under Wordsworth's name only: Coleridge's minimal presence in its pages signalled an intellectual divergence between the two friends. Coleridge was committed to the 'supernatural', Wordsworth to the 'natural'. Their disagreement with respect to language and poetics was to prove foundational for the development of English Romanticism. But it contributed to the growing emotional distance between them. Other differences came sharply into focus in 1802–4, when the two poets wrote elegies (*Dejection* and *Intimations*) lamenting the loss not only of their imaginative power, but of their shared political vision, and their belief in a beneficent universe animated by a divine principle of love. They built solace for themselves through their verse, and in doing so demonstrated fundamental divergences, of a kind that were never to be resolved. Intellectually, these divergences can be seen with hindsight as highly productive, because the separate identities of the two writers emerged through them. Creatively, too, they made up the substance of a dialogue which has come to be valued. But for the two human beings involved, that is not how they were experienced and felt.

The Prelude, expanded from the two-part version which Wordsworth had begun in Germany, brought their dialogue to its culmination. The poem focuses on the interanimation of mind and world, the presence of evil and suffering in the natural scheme of things, and the active part played by imagination in seeking an egalitarian society. Both writers had needed to justify the role of the poet in a climate that was utilitarian, antipathetic to the idea of creative genius. Wordsworth's autobiographical epic continued this process of justification by celebrating 'the growth of a poet's mind', and showing how 'love of nature' could lead to 'love of mankind'. Examining his own life before his meeting with Coleridge, Wordsworth folded him into his vision of human progress and perfectibility. Unpublished until 1850, *The Prelude* was known until then by family and friends as 'the poem to Coleridge'. Their friendship is invoked throughout—both positively, as a source of sustenance to the author, and negatively, as an anxiety or threat to his self-sufficiency. Coleridge's answering poem, 'To William Wordsworth' (1807) was the last of the sequence of 'Conversation Poems' begun in 1797. In it, Coleridge abased himself before Wordsworth's genius, seeing his own poems as offshoots or tributaries of his friend's *œuvre*. A similar theme was amplified in *Biographia Literaria* (1817), which devoted its second volume to Wordsworth as the exemplar of a unique kind of 'philosophical poetry'. Here Coleridge was defining for the first time a species of 'practical criticism'. In tacitly making the claim that critics were in their own way just as creative as poets, he was competing with his friend.

Both writers paid generous tribute to each other, drew on each other's writings for their terms of reference, and defined their own poetic and critical contributions in relation to works published (or awaiting publication) by the other. For ten years, they may be said to have occupied one another's minds. But although on the surface they each made an ideal audience for the reciprocal exchange of ideas, they also had major differences—temperamental, imaginative, intellectual—which pointed to a fundamental incompatibility. These led ultimately to the breakdown of communication and trust. Some of these preceded the relationship itself, arising out of the their differing backgrounds and upbringings. Others emerged in the course of the first ten years of intellectual exchange, and were brought the more sharply into focus through discussion. Coleridge's interest in the supernatural, as against Wordsworth's in the natural; Coleridge's theocentric vision contrasted with Wordsworth's faith in the human heart; Coleridge's investment in a symbolic understanding of the natural world and poetic form, as distinct from Wordsworth's prosaic literalism; Coleridge's interest in abstractions as against Wordsworth's 'clinging to the palpable'; and Coleridge's belief that poetry was elevated, Wordsworth's that it need not be. All of these contrasting views have proved to be important constituents of Romanticism as we currently know it. They make up the system of oppositions (albeit crudely and formulaically summarized here), through which subsequent generations of poets and critics have understood literature. To trace these fundamental divisions back to their origins is to perform an archaeological search which has implications for the way we view English poetic tradition.

II

In all evolving relationships, external conditions are in flux and the internal balance of power is constantly shifting and being shifted. Not only that, but the ways in which the relationship is seen by those involved is often very distinct from how it seems to those outside it. In the case of Wordsworth and Coleridge, this process is especially complicated, not just because the shape they retrospectively gave their friendship was a stylized version of what actually happened, but because their investment in the idea of life lived as an experiment led them to comment with abnormal frequency and self-consciousness on its unfolding pattern. No biographer approaching their friendship could ever succeed entirely in separating fact from fiction, since every surviving piece of evidence is heavily mediated by the hopes and fears, the aspirations and disappointments, of its participants.

These difficulties are further compounded by the overwhelming volume of material available for interpretation. If one were to list the poems written during the most important years of this relationship, these would stand out only as the most visible markers in a terrain which is criss-crossed by multiple intersecting and diverging paths. Letters, notebooks, and journal entries help to give a fuller picture of how the relationship developed, of the tensions within it, and of the strains which led to communication breaking down. But even these are only the tip of the iceberg; for beyond the materials to which a biographer turns, there are also the less straightforward materials of quotation, echo, allusion, and revision—all of which offer the potential for a more nuanced and inflected sense of what is going on, as it were behind the scenes, in a literary dialogue of great richness and complexity. Such materials invite acts of interpretation or judgement, as well as a set of presuppositions about the psychology of literary relationships. They belong partly to the arena of biography, partly to hermeneutics.

I am no biographer. Nonetheless my aim has been to understand not only how the friends described and theorized their relationship, but how they experienced it, as an ontological process. I have given a chronological account of the similarities, and also of the fundamental differences, between the two sides of a literary partnership. These differences have proved difficult to reconstruct, because disagreements are so often played down, both in critical accounts of the relationship and in the scattered retrospective comments made by the poets themselves. Coleridge's retrospective account of the *Lyrical Ballads* project, for instance, flattens the two poets' contributions, making their collaboration sound as though it involved a neat and tidy division of labour that was decided in advance: 'it was agreed that my endeavours would be directed to persons and characters supernatural—Mr Wordsworth, on the other hand, was . . . to give the charm of novelty to things of every day' (*Biographia*, ch. xiv). In practice, *Lyrical Ballads* had come into being by a very different creative dynamic. Begun as a collaboration in which the writers had shared aims and objectives, it became only in the process of composition a thoroughfare for two distinct (and ultimately rivalrous) voices. Conversely, these comforting words from the closing lines of the *Two-Part Prelude* seek to resolve what is perceived as a deep dissimilarity between the two friends. They do so, firstly, by simplifying it in symbolic terms into a city/country opposition, a poetic trope that is recognizably formulaic. Secondly, they claim that differences of origin have been resolved by a similarity of direction and an ultimate convergence of paths. The result is transparently a form of wish-fulfilment, but not the less tender and deeply affectionate for that:

> Thou, my friend, wast reared
> in the great city, mid far other scenes,
> But we by different roads at length have gained
> The self-same bourne.

> (*1799*, ii. 496–9)

It is even more difficult to separate fact from fiction during the period around 1802, when intellectual differences came strongly to the fore, and were complicated by personal conflicts. Is it true that Coleridge at this time came to acknowledge his poetic inferiority to Wordsworth? Or was something more complicated going on? 'If I die', he commented with typical depressiveness in a letter to William Godwin, 'and the Booksellers will give you anything for my Life, be sure to say— Wordsworth descended on him . . . by shewing to him what true poetry was, he made him know, that he himself was no Poet' (Griggs, ii. 714). So persistently did Coleridge present himself as a failed poet, and so strongly was this construction confirmed by his friend, that it is hard to resist his account. We need to remember what Thomas McFarland calls Coleridge's 'masochism', but also the rhetorical investment, the self-dramatization, that lay behind all the estimates he gave of his achievements.

What method do we adopt to describe the interweaving of literary and emotional strands in a relationship so complex? What word do we have for a friendship which was at once productive and destructive? 'Literary friendship' or 'literary partnership' are too bland, too general. 'Collaboration' and 'mutual influence' deal only with literary and intellectual content. 'Symbiosis' is inaccurate, given that both writers were in so many ways an emotional liability to each other. 'Affinity' does not account for the important differences which emerged as the relationship unfolded. 'Duet' is too choreographed, too organized, and mutually enhancing. 'Duel' plays too much on antagonism. 'Dialogue' is too circumscribed, given that more than two voices can be heard during the process of any intellectual and emotional exchange. 'Competitive/collaborative relationship' is accurate, but cumbersome.

When this book first appeared, more than one of my friends told me that in it I had written (unconsciously, of course) about my first marriage. After the first shock of recognition, there came a stage of wondering which of its two main characters I was identified with in their minds. This rather painful process of self-examination proved ultimately fruitless, because of course I was both and neither. Doubtless the critical act involves sympathetic identification, often more apparent to one's readers than to oneself. But, looking back from the safe distance of fifteen years, I realize the truth of my friends' observation in a more general, less autobiographical sense. This is a book about two writers who defined themselves in relation to each other. Their creative identities were closely bound together. Their public and private roles (for better and for worse) assumed the shape they did by a kind of tacit mutual agreement. I had described the struggle of their personalities within and against the restrictions of those roles. I had also shown how this was counterbalanced by the need to create a shared self. In doing both these things, I had unwittingly offered an account of how I saw marriage, mine included. Marriage, after all, is an intense version (or paradigm) of many kinds of significant friendships. As J. R. Watson put it in a review:

Like all deep and enthusiastic friendships, [Wordsworth and Coleridge's] brought with it immense rewards and correspondingly difficult demands and fallings-short: it produced a collaboration and a mutual re-inforcing of ideas, but it also, and more lastingly, involved an ultimate self-definition, an awareness which developed into an incompatibility. . . . The reader may reflect that friendship is often like this, an initial enthusiasm followed by a later discovery that everything is not perfect, and can never be so. (*Review of English Studies*, 1987)

As to the vexed question of whom this book presents as the 'dominant' partner in the Wordsworth–Coleridge relationship, there has been little agreement amongst readers and reviewers. I was surprised to read a review by Norman Fruman, whose critical acumen I deeply respect, claiming that I had found Coleridge 'the decisively dominant partner in . . . the crucial first six months of his close association with Wordsworth, and *the more original and powerful intellect at all times*' (*Choice*, 1986; my italics). I believe, on the contrary, that my account presents the relationship in terms of an intellectual and creative equality; but one that is complicated by an emotional imbalance. Coleridge emerges as weak, dependent, self-destructive, and Wordsworth as strong, productive, self-reliant. In particular, my understanding of their relationship during the tense and involved dialogue of 1802 is strongly coloured by Coleridge's self-immolation.

Paul Magnuson, alluding to my book in *Coleridge and Wordsworth: A Lyrical Dialogue* (1988), seemed closer to the mark than Fruman. He claimed I had 'examined the relationship between Coleridge and Wordsworth as a dialogue of public and private allusions in which private disagreement is masked by public declarations of fraternal agreement'.: 'In her account there is little unanimity of mind and no threat of amalgamation. The two poets are unique individuals, and Wordsworth, she argues, frees himself from Coleridge's influence in the spring of 1798 and becomes the autogenous poet' (p. 7 n.). To say that I see 'no threat of amalgamation' is very nearly right. But it would be truer to say that I see no threat *in* amalgamation. What I have tried to show is the way in which Wordsworth and Coleridge retrospectively mythologized the early part of their relationship. They wanted it to fulfil an ideal of merged identities, interchangeable voices, despite the fact that these had at all times been quite distinct. They clung to this ideal of amalgamation, even when to do so was to fly in the face of facts. Which tends to confirm my hypothesis that they saw 'amalgamation' as a state devoutly to be wished, not as a threat to be avoided. In a Notebook entry of 1805, for instance, Coleridge confided to Wordsworth a longing 'that my Spirit purged by Death of its Weaknesses, which are alas! my *identity* might flow into *thine*, & live and act in thee, & be thou' (*Notebooks*, ii. 2712).

The poets' construction of their relationship could be described, in Stephen Greenblatt's terminology, as a form of 'self-fashioning'. It involved misrepresentation, both public and private, as well as make-believe. Its strategies were, variously, deliberate and open, wishful and concealed. In uncovering these strategies, as well as the critical myths to which they have given rise, my aim has been to present difference as the incompatibility it increasingly was, as well as the means of self-definition it turns out to have been. The key to this interpretation comes in a sceptical, at times deconstructive, approach to the poets' allusive language; for it was in and through this language that their opposition emerged. My contention is that an acknowledgement, quotation, or allusion which appears on the surface to express affinities can register, on a more submerged level, disparity, aggression, and unease. By reading between the lines, we can move towards a clearer understanding of the split between theory and practice which made this friendship both a failed experiment and a fascinating historiographical puzzle.

III

As far as critical method is concerned, this book is indebted to Harold Bloom's theory of the 'anxiety of influence'. However, as the first in a sequence of revisionary moves I have made in relation to Bloom's work, it shows that anxieties are just as apparent in the relationship between contemporaries as they are between writers and their precursors. Literary dialogue has as one (but only one) of its aspects a kind of sibling rivalry. The twin impulses towards competition and towards collaboration are often simultaneously present, both in the creative process and in the resulting literary artefact. Furthermore, these impulses can be detected within the workings of literary language itself—that is, in echoes and allusions, rather than behind their screen. Allusions imply a double bond: with the initiated reader, who is allowed access to hidden meanings, and with the writer whose works are being quoted or revised. The vocabulary and grammar of a literary dialogue is private, in that it depends upon personal association. But it is also public, in its reference to a literary text which has circulated amongst more readers than its author. Hidden meanings, for those overhearing the dialogue, become accessible through familiarity with the speakers and their relationship, and with the texts themselves.

Tracking the story of the Wordsworth–Coleridge friendship through all the published and unpublished writings of both writers would have been the task of a lifetime. This book confines itself to the years 1797–1807. It takes as its two centrepieces the crucial collaborative 'annus mirabilis' of 1797–8 and the pivotal year of 1802, in which differences of opinion came to the fore. My aim has been to make sense of the available biographical information, but also to offer an account of the allusive language in which the dialogue emerged, and of the psychodynamics of the relationship. At the time I wrote this book, neither Stephen Gill's biography of Wordsworth nor Richard Holmes's biography of Coleridge's early years had yet appeared. The *Cornell Wordsworth* was just emerging, as was the *Collected Coleridge*. I drew on the scholarship of Mary Moorman, Mark Reed, and Jonathan Wordsworth for the details of Wordsworth's and Coleridge's interaction. This enabled me to piece together a chronological account of how each phase in the dialogue took place, and what were the surrounding factors affecting it. In addition to McFarland's essay, 'The Symbiosis of Wordsworth and Coleridge' (1972; repr. 1987), a number of major scholarly books provided different perspectives which helped me in formulating my own: H. M. Margoliouth, *Wordsworth and Coleridge, 1795–1834* (1953), Jonathan Wordsworth, *The Music of Humanity* (1969), William Heath, *Wordsworth and Coleridge: A Study of Their Literary Relations in 1801–1802* (1970), Jared Curtis, *Wordsworth's Experiments with Tradition: the Lyric Poems of 1802* (1971), Norman Fruman, *Coleridge: The Damaged Archangel* (1971), Stephen Parrish, *The Art of the Lyrical Ballads* (1973), Mary Jacobus, *Tradition and Experiment in Wordsworth's Lyrical Ballads* (1976), and Jonathan Wordsworth, *The Borders of Vision* (1982).

Since 1986, when *Coleridge, Wordsworth, and the Language of Allusion* was first published, a sequence of monographs about the Coleridge–Wordsworth dialogue have appeared. From all of these I have learnt something new about how to read its changing dynamic. Paul Magnuson's study came out two years after my own, but independently of my research. (It is ironic to think that we had both been working in the same field without knowing it, and have only recently come to know each other.) *Coleridge and Wordsworth: A Lyrical Dialogue* had a great deal in common with my book, but it was framed as a theoretical enquiry and an experiment in Bakhtinian methodology. Magnuson examined the interaction of the two poets 'dialogically', as a collaborative enterprise in which their two voices could be discretely heard. He emphasized that each stage in the chronological unfolding of this dialogue was both a departure from the previous stage, and part of a steadily emerging whole. In its organic complexity, its sudden shifts of theme, mood, and argument, the overall pattern of the dialogue resembled an ode, and Magnuson argued that it should be understood as such. These were the generic terms that would have made most sense to the poets themselves:

> Their dialogic poetic sequence proceeds by the abrupt transitions that are characteristic of the ode, the turns that are the tropes of form. The eytmological origin of *verse* is, of course, *versus* and indicates, quite simply, a turn from what has preceded. The origin of a verse is in its turn from a previous one. In general, the dialogue proceeds by opposition, a later poem or fragment turns from a preceding one. (p. 18)

The persuasiveness of this argument depended quite heavily on the restricted scope of the enquiry. It would have been tendentious to treat the thirteen-book *Prelude* as though it were a sub-section in an Ode, whereas it is not difficult to see it as part of an ongoing 'dialogue' in the more general sense. Magnuson took the subject forward most emphatically in his assertion (and its substantiation through 300 pages of empirical investigation) that

> the Coleridge-Wordsworth canon includes, not only what are usually considered completed and separate poems, but also early versions, fragments, canceled drafts, and poems in progress. . . . All are parts or fragments of a poetic dialogue or poetic dialectic . . . Each poem or fragment in the dialogue takes its significance from its surrounding context. (p. 18)

Magnuson's book gave scholars a way of responding to the vast influx of new information which was reaching them through the *Cornell Wordsworth*. It was now possible to see how the individual components in a continuous dialogue might be viewed not just as 'fragments of a ruined past' or 'pieces of an unreachable ideal', but as 'parts of a poetic canon evermore about to be, as parts of a generative process'. Magnuson also helped us to move beyond a Bloomian conception of poetic influence. He emphasized the formal (as opposed to the psychic) aspect of poetic tropes. And he played down the idea of a competitive struggle in the creative process. He was, however, concerned with the 'threat of amalgamation' which collaboration involves, and keen to prove that both poets needed to avoid the 'complete merging of voices' if they were to preserve distinct identities. In some respects then, a psychoanalytic approach to poetic collaboration underpinned Magnuson's Bakhtinian methodology.

Gene Ruoff's *Wordsworth and Coleridge: The Making of the Major Lyrics, 1802–1804* was published a year later, in 1989, and took a stage further the analysis of manuscript data. Ruoff focused on the cluster of major lyrics which made up the poets' dialogue at its crucial turning-point in 1802–4. Those years saw (among other writings) the beginning of Wordsworth's *Intimations* in 1802, and Coleridge's answering *Verse Letter to Sara Hutchinson*, also in 1802. These were followed by *The Leechgatherer* and its finished version, *Resolution and Independence* (1802), then finally Coleridge's *Dejection* (the *Verse Letter to Sara* revised for publication that same year) and, in 1804, Wordsworth's completed *Intimations*. The great virtue of Ruoff's study was that the tightness of its textual focus allowed for a microscopic attention to details of chronology and interconnection. It also enabled a study of the wider literary context of the dialogue. Wordsworth and Coleridge were shown speaking to each other, but also including Milton, Chatterton, Burns, etc. in their conversation through echo and allusion. The result was a strengthened sense of 'triangulation' in their poetic language. This allowed a sharper awareness of the indistinct line between 'public' and 'private' reception. Ruoff's was in some ways a more Bakhtinian study than Magnuson's, because it allowed for a multiplicity of voices. Assorted genres were acknowledged to coexist within the poetic dialogue. But Ruoff did not flag his method as Bakhtinian. Instead, he saw it as an attempt to define what an 'adequate genetic criticism' might be:

Any text has strong connections to its immediately preceding versions and to the prior body of a writer's work. It also has connections to a surrounding literary climate . . . A text's origins also must be seen in its relations to several different, overlapping canons: a canon of relatively recent writing, against which a text will often attempt to demonstrate its individuality; a canon of classic writers and texts, in relation to which it can display a complete Bloomian repertoire of reflexive attitudes, as well as the non-Bloomian attitude of piety; and a canon of forms or kinds, which it will, often simultaneously, incorporate and transcend, or even repudiate. (p. 16)

Rightly, Ruoff pointed out that 'the individual strands of genetic commentary are frequently carried out in isolation from each other'. This is almost inevitable, given the complexity of intertextual genesis. His own book, on the other hand, brought together the various strands in a way that was exemplary.

A new departure in the study of mutual influence came in 1997 with Richard E. Matlak's *The Poetry of Relationship: The Wordsworths and Coleridge, 1797–1800*. This book built on reconfigurations of the Romantic canon which had taken place over the preceding decade. It included Dorothy Wordsworth's voice as part of the ongoing dialogue between the poets. Matlak's methodology was indebted to McFarland's 1972 essay for its application of psychobiography to poetic relationship. He also drew on Magnuson's book for its formal and intertextual analysis. He grafted on to these two strands of enquiry a careful account of Dorothy's biographical and textual unfluence on her brother's poetry. He also presented a 'macro-context' for the poetry in the political scene of the 1790s, rather than in the field of literary influences from the seventeenth century onwards. The result was twofold: Matlak's book offered a considerably more nuanced group psychobiography than had hitherto proved possible. He also succeeded in shifting the focus away from intertextuality towards a more experiential analysis of poetic relations. The primary determinants of Wordsworth's and Coleridge's relationship were, in Matlak's view, the constant triangulation caused by Dorothy's hold on Wordsworth's psyche, and 'the tensions and uncertainties of powerfully contested world views' during the first decade after the French Revolution. In effect, Matlak succeeded in *politicizing* the study of poetic dialogue in ways that brought it into line with new-historicist and feminist agendas. He did this without sacrificing an awareness of poetic form. The resulting synthesis was bold and arresting.

A number of other books published since 1986 have been formative in redirecting the way that scholars think about the Wordsworth–Coleridge relationship. I mention here only the ones that stand out as landmarks. Nicholas Roe's *Wordsworth and Coleridge: The Radical Years* (1988) provided a detailed account of both writers' changing responses to political events during the 1790s. Implicitly, this study was also an anlysis of the ideological differences between Wordsworth and Coleridge, some subtle and some much more divisive. Stephen Gill's *William Wordsworth: A Life* (1989) provided not only a definitive biography of the poet himself, but a detailed contextualization of his relationship with friends, publishers, and the reading public. Tim Fulford, in *Coleridge's Figurative Language* (1991), analysed the pattern of Coleridge's dependence on the words of friends and collaborators, finding this to be a sign of strength rather than weakness. He showed that

Coleridge's poetic allusions succeeded in uniting around him 'a public readership transformed into a listening community which incorporates the texts of nature and scripture in its shared experience of spiritual intimacy' (pp. 60–1). Susan Eilenberg's *Strange Power of Speech: Wordsworth, Coleridge and Literary Possession* (1992) opened up a new way of thinking about the issue of collaborative and single poetic identities by seeing these in the context of the themes of possession and property. Michael Baron's book, *Language and Relationship in Wordsworth's Writing* (1995), broadened our understanding of what relationship meant to the Lake poets, and gave us a much more community-oriented Wordsworth than had previously emerged. Richard Holmes in his portrait *Coleridge: Darker Reflections* (1998) described a writer victimized by Wordsworth, and always struggling, but nonetheless re-emergent after long silence. Seamus Perry, in *Coleridge and the Uses of Division* (1999), folded the Wordsworth–Coleridge dialogue into his study of Coleridge's dialectical patterns of thought.

Thanks to these and other books in the field, my own views on the Wordsworth-Coleridge dialogue have changed in a number of substantial ways. I am now less inclined to see it as a struggle for mastery, in which Wordsworth (aided and abetted by Coleridge's self-destructive idolization) emerged uppermost. Indeed, I no longer believe that it was a dialogue impelled primarily by rivalry. As John Beer pointed out in a review (*Times Higher Educational Supplement*, 1986), it is not enough to read the poetry in purely psychological terms. That leaves out of count its importance as a medium for debating such questions as the status of fiction, the revelatory power of nature, the best form of education, the workings of memory, and the role of imagination. Also, recent work on reception has made me acutely aware of the hostile climate in which these two writers struggled for recognition. They were drawn together in an alliance against the periodical critics. The first stage of their relationship, mutually supportive and exclusive, allowed them for a while to sidestep the tastes of the reading public and the reviewers. Their choice to address each other (and others within their coterie), their recognition of each other as 'joint-labourers', and their nurturing of a shared project of poetic prophecy were all as important as the singularities which drew them ultimately into conflict.

It follows that my reading of *The Prelude* has altered. In 1986 I focused almost exclusively on the egotistical dimension of Wordsworth's poem, seeing his addresses to Coleridge as disingenuous expressions of friendship, masking an underlying sense of hostility. The poet, I contended, was searching ultimately for an autonomous identity, a communion between himself and the natural world which excluded even the nearest and dearest of his family and friends. Now I see a poem in which the quest for autonomy makes up only a single strand of Wordsworth's complicated relation to others. I have recently been struck by the extraordinary strength with which the poet held on to the idea of himself and Coleridge as joint-labourers. His early political idealism, and the sense of this as a commitment shared with his friend, went on exerting a hold over his poetic imagination long after he had lost faith in political activism and Godwinian rationalism. The closing lines of *The Prelude* address Coleridge with an intensity and conviction all the more moving for one's sense that they honour a past self, a vision of human perfectibility which had at one time been the prime motive for writing poetry:

> Prophets of nature, we to them will speak
> A lasting inspiration, sanctified
> By reason and by truth . . .

> (*1805*, xiii. 442–4)

Wordsworth's and Coleridge's need to integrate their past with their present now seems to me an important component of their elegiac sense that they had lost their youthful selves. Equally, their shared allegiance to the idea of an elect community of poet-prophets was just as significant as the tugging of their individual voices in different directions. They both believed in something that corresponded closely to the idea of a 'Republic of Letters'. When other ideals (such as pantisocracy) failed to materialize, the political excitement they had experienced during the 1790s became redirected towards this alternative form of ideal community. A Republic of Letters, like a canon, is transhistorical: 'The truly Great | Have all one Age, and from one visible space | Shed influence' (*To William Wordsworth*, 50–2). Both poets believed themselves and each other to belong to this alternative community. Wordsworth's claim in *The Prelude* that 'There is one great society alone on earth | The noble living and the noble dead' (*1805*, x. 968–9) was greeted in 1807 by Coleridge's acknowledgement that in writing his great autobiography Wordsworth had placed himself in the 'choir | Of ever-enduring Men' (*To William Wordsworth*, 48–9). The bond between these two writers was only one component of the vast intertextual network of affinities which *The Prelude* set out to celebrate. Wordsworth's personal canon of friends and sympathizers included on the poetic side Milton and Cowper; on the prose side Bunyan, Rousseau, Godwin, and Paine.

If I were given the opportunity to re-write this book, I would now expand the chronological scope of my enquiry. As the argument stands here, Coleridge is left diminished and depleted by Wordsworth's great achievement. But were the study of their relationship to be continued up till 1815–17, it would include the crucial turning-point in Coleridge's life. After a long period of dormancy, he had suddenly re-emerged as a productive writer. The crucial publications that belong to this period are 'Christabel' (his longest single poem), *Kubla Khan* (arguably his most original poetic contribution, aside from *The Ancient Mariner*), and *The Pains of Sleep*. More importantly, this was also the time when Coleridge published his *Lay Sermons* and *Biographia Literaria*, the works that were to establish his reputation as a major prose-writer and critic. In a remarkable essay of 1985, entitled 'Imagining Wordsworth: 1797–1807–1817', Richard Gravil opened up many of the important questions which surround this later stage of mutual influence. There is, however, enough material here for an entire monograph.

It is now apparent to me that the competitive/collaborative relationship between poetry and prose was of inestimable significance to Wordsworth and Coleridge, and that the preference for one or other of these two media was often influenced by the pattern of their relationship at a given time. At the core of their intellectual difference was a disagreement about poetry's kinship (or otherwise) with prose. When he wrote his contributions to *Lyrical Ballads* in 1797–8 and their Preface in 1800, Wordsworth was convinced that poetry could be genuinely prosaic, and the more powerful for being so. Coleridge, on the other hand, thought that poetry aspired (and should aspire) to something higher. Choosing to focus on this disagreement in *Biographia Literaria*, Coleridge had a number of complicated motives, which included his resentment that *Christabel* had not been included in *Lyrical Ballads* (1800), and his envy for Wordsworth's superiority as a poet. It is of crucial significance, I think, that he conducted this debate in prose. Although he celebrated Wordsworth's achievement as a poet, he took his friend to task as a critic and theorist. Coleridge used prose in this instance as a means of establishing a new identity for himself, as herald of poetic genius and ideal listener, but also as the great critic of his age. That his prose style in this work is so often elevated (aspiring, perhaps, to the condition of prose-poetry?) bolstered his argument as well as his credentials. It is no wonder that the *Biographia* was lambasted by contemporary reviewers. Amongst them were Hazlitt and Jeffrey, who felt safer thinking of Coleridge as a failed poet than as, potentially, a prose-writer of equivalent stature to themselves. The rivalry was intensified by political animosity.

I have described above a number of changes in my thinking about Wordsworth and Coleridge. Although these are substantial, they are as nothing compared with a bigger shift in the methodology I would adopt were I to re-write this book. What was of primary interest to me when I first published my research—namely the 'private language' in which two friends addressed each other—now seems of less importance than the dynamics of friendship itself. What did the word 'friendship' mean in England during the early 1790s, when these two men met? How was it different from the 'brotherhood' or 'fraternité' championed in Revolutionary France? Did a strong revolutionary sympathy predispose these men (or indeed others of their ilk) to any specially intense understanding of what a friend was, or might be? What were the pressures exerted on this particular relationship by different childhood experiences, by shared political disappointments, by changing family commitments, by literary rivals, and by anxieties of reception? In the light of impressive recent scholarship in the field, and in the wake of Derrida's profound meditation on the subject of friendship, it should be possible to answer some at least of these important questions. But they are matter for another song. In the final two sections of this preface, I will offer some tentative hypotheses, which I hope might contribute to the theoretical side of future discussion.

IV

In his seminal essay, 'The Symbiosis of Wordsworth and Coleridge' Thomas McFarland described a development of attitude in the two writers 'so dialogical and intertwined that in some instances not even the participants themselves could discern their respective contributions' (*Romanticism and the Forms of Ruin*, 57). The technical term 'symbiosis' has crossed over from biology into popular vocabulary, and is often used to describe a marriage. It suggests the compatible cohabitation of two organisms, each of which feeds off the other without causing harm. A symbiotic relationship is the opposite of a parasitic one: McFarland seized on it as an apt analogy for the mutually beneficial complementarity of Wordsworth and Coleridge, whose intellectual differences were (as he saw them) productive of an intensely creative synthesis.

The term has a satisfying neatness if what we are considering is the literary side of the relationship. But I have explained already my reservations about applying it to a human interaction which proved in the end to be emotionally damaging. My interest here is in looking more closely at what was involved in McFarland's definition of symbiosis, what work it performed in his (tacitly understood) theory of literary friendship, and how we might move beyond it. Let me take as a starting-point the following sentence: 'The structure of symbiosis', McFarland claimed, 'presupposes a principle of opposition or polarity as the very condition of the urge toward submersion and oneness' (p. 69). That is a very interesting statement.

Biologists of the twenty-first century would not agree that polarity is necessarily involved in a symbiotic relationship; but Coleridge would surely have done so. Dialectical thinking, the view that opposites interact to generate a synthesis, is to be found in every branch of enquiry—scientific, philosophical, metaphysical—on which his mind was engaged. He was driven by the search for an overarching unity, or system, which would transcend the compulsion to think in terms of dichotomies; and in this sense he might be seen as a dualist with monist cravings. It was his fascination with the principle of polarity (the idea that opposites attract) that underlay his interest in contemporary experiments in magnetism and electrolysis. His thinking about sexuality, and particularly androgyny, was motivated by the need to find an underlying affinity between apparent opposites. He was drawn to David Hartley's theory of associationism because it offered a model of the world and the human mind as a system of progressive linkages. This, in its turn, led to his immersion in German *Naturphilosophie*. His Unitarianism, and later his belief in the Logos as a unifying principle, were impelled by a longing for 'One Life' that subsumed all the manifold disparates. The eccentric theory of history he developed in *The Friend* dwelt on a choreographed sequence of pairings between historical figures as intellectually diverse as Erasmus, Luther, and Munster on the one hand and Voltaire, Rousseau, and Robespierre on the other (*Friend*, i. 129–34). His eclecticism, his interdisciplinary patterns of thinking, were of a piece with his commitment to syncretism.

Wordsworth, too—though less systematically, and more in the domains of psychology, epistemology, and ethics than in those of science and metaphysics—was intrigued by the possibility of an underlying unity between things apparently disconnected. He was an associationist by temperament, and for much longer than Coleridge. In *The Prelude*, he ascribed the 'creative agency' of his youthful imagination to the 'observation of affinities | In objects where no brotherhood exists | To common minds'. He affirmed a vital spirit, 'coercing all things into sympathy', which he believed to be 'the great social principle of life', at work both in the natural world and in human relationships (*1805*, ii. 400–10). In the following lines we can see an anthropomorphic impulse which is typical of Romantic science, alongside an interest in the ethical potential of sympathetic identification which goes back through Hume and Hutcheson to Shaftesbury. The combination is distinctly Wordsworthian:

> To every natural form, rock, fruit, or flower,
> Even the loose stones that cover the high-way
> I gave a moral life, I saw them feel,
> Or linked them to some feeling: the great mass
> Lay bedded in a quickening soul, and all
> That I beheld respired with inward meaning.
>
> (*1805*, iii. 124–9)

Intermittently, too, Wordsworth felt a profound sense of reverence towards the more inscrutable processes of unity in which Coleridge believed. He was less inclined to ascribe this to a divine spirit; but he nonetheless recognized a 'dark invisible workmanship' which 'reconciles discordant elements', making them 'move in one society'.

McFarland's idea of a symbiosis founded in polarity may be evidence of his saturation in what Jerome McGann calls 'Romantic Ideology'. But this makes it no less interesting or probable as a starting-point for investigating the mutual influence of Wordsworth and Coleridge. The notion that 'EXTREMES MEET' taps into a fundamental urge towards the synthesis of dualities which underpins Romantic science, philosophy, and literature. McFarland's particular slant on symbiosis is therefore as relevant to the two writers' intellectual paradigms as are the beliefs voiced in Blake's *Marriage of Heaven and Hell* that 'Opposition is true friendship', and that 'Without contraries is no Progression'. There was, however, a more relevant model than that of symbiosis, that McFarland might have employed. The technical term that was available in the Romantic period to describe the attraction of opposites was 'elective affinity'. Drawn from chemistry, not biology, this term provides a scientific analogy for human relationships which would have been known by Wordsworth and Coleridge in the 1790s. So far as I am aware, neither writer ever used the term. But the concept was widely available and part of current vocabulary in the intellectual milieu in which they moved.

The concept of 'affinities' between differing substances had a prehistory in alchemy, and was later developed into a theory of gravitational attraction and repulsion. Newton refined this theory so as to explain the chemical likes and dislikes that individual substances displayed towards one another, which he attributed to the presence of ether. He suggested that there were very strong attractive powers between the particles of bodies, which extended only a short distance from them and varied from one chemical species to another. This concept of short-range force (as opposed to the long-range attraction between planets and stars) led to speculation amongst early eighteenth-century chemists about *gradations* of attractive power among substances. The French chemist Etienne Geoffroy (1672–1731) and the Swedish chemist Torbern Bergman (1735–84) produced tables of affinities to explain these attractions, and in 1785 Buffon identified the laws of affinity with gravitation. François Jacob accounts for the importance of this post-Newtonian model of the universe as follows:

What maintained . . . particles in place and bound them together to form a coherent universe was the force of attraction. This was not a component of the universe. It had no part in its construction but between all the constituent atoms of the universe it wove a network of dependencies giving cohesion to the world. It was the concept of gravitation that provided chemists with a force to replace the astral influences which, for the alchemists, had linked stars to planets. When substances were blended, they did not remain inert but displaced one another. Thus between different bodies relations could be found which made them combine more or less readily. According to Geoffroy, when two substances with 'some disposition to join together' were united, if a third appeared which had more affinity for one of them, it united 'by making the other loose its hold'. (*The Logic of Life*, ch. 1)

The theory of chemical affinity had a long-established history in eighteenth-century France and England, before being given a new impetus by its confluence with *Naturphilosophie*. This German philosophy stressed the world's underlying oneness, and 'laid upon its adherents the necessity for looking at connections between natural phenomena that had hitherto been regarded quite separately' (C. A. Russell, *The Theory of Valency* (1971), 17).

   The term 'elective affinities' was, at least in the first instance, associated with natural science, and it arose as an explanation of the fact that some compounds mixed more readily than others. The *Oxford English Dictionary* defines elective affinity as 'the tendency of a substance to combine with certain other particular substances in preference to others'. This theory came into question when the French chemist Claude Berthollet accompanied Napoleon on his expedition to Egypt, and noticed large deposits of soda on the shores of the Egyptian salt-lakes. Concluding that these came about from a reaction between salt and limestone, he attributed the phenomenon to an abnormally high concentration of sodium chloride in the lakes. According to the historian of science C.A. Russell, it was from this beginning that Berthollet

> developed the idea (nascent in the work of earlier writers) that mass could be a determinative factor in all compositions and decompositions produced by 'elective affinity'. . . . This realization of the importance of mass in chemical reactions was incompatible with any view of absolute 'elective affinities' and led, in time, to the enunciation of the law of mass action. (*Theory of Valency*, 17)

That was in 1798, coincidentally the year in which *Lyrical Ballads* was published. Eleven years after Berthollet's experiment, Goethe used the term 'elective affinities' as the title for one of the most famous and controversial novels of the time, *Die Wahlverwandtschaften*. In a densely allusive scene of this novel, which is staged as a scientific tutorial (and this proves crucial to its unfolding emotional plot), one of the four central characters explains the theory of affinities as follows:

> Alkalis and acids, although opposed to one another and perhaps precisely because they are so opposed, will in a most decisive way seek out, take hold of, and modify one another and form, in so doing, a new substance together. We have only to think of lime, which manifests towards all acids a strong inclination, a decided wish for union. (p. 32; quotations are from the translation by David Constantine)

The word 'Verwandtschaft' means a relationship (or affinity) in science and in human affairs, and Charlotte's reply to her friend plays on its double meaning: 'I must confess . . . that when you speak of these wondrous entities as related they seem to me not so much blood relations as related in spirit and in the soul.' The tutorial is self-reflexively significant because of the attraction between its participants, who go on to discuss the combining and separating powers of chemical substances in ways that have an intricate applicability to their own lives. As Tony Tanner puts it, 'In the long discussion about the various experiments conducted in contemporary chemistry, the characters themselves are effectively creating the experiment in which they will be the materials' (*Adultery in the Novel* (1979), 209). Especially crucial to their discussion is the question of whether the term 'elective affinity' is appropriate to the process it describes. Since they themselves are drawn into relationships 'as inexorably as if they were substances in a chemical equation', Goethe's implication must be that the word 'elective' is a misnomer. Just as the reactions between chemical substances are involuntary, so too among human beings attraction is purely a matter of what nowadays would be called 'chemistry'.

It is difficult to trace the point at which the term 'elective affinities' passed over from science into literature, becoming in the process a metaphor for human relationships. This is partly because the prehistory of the term throws up a number of synonyms, which criss-cross between the domains of science and social/political interactions. In a specifically scientific context, The *Oxford English Dictionary* records 'elective attraction' (1766), 'elective affections' (1794), and then 'Tables of elective affinity' (1800). Edmund Burke used the term 'elective affections' in a political context: 'Sympathetick attraction discovers our elective affections' (*Thoughts on the Prospect of a Regicide Peace*, 1796). Tony Tanner's claim that Goethe's novel initiated the term's metaphorical application to human relationships is unlikely to be accurate. It was probably only after the publication of Goethe's novel in 1809 that the term gained a very wide currency. But that it had already done so in England, before the novel had been translated into English, is attested by a reference of Hazlitt's in his essay 'On Genius and Common Sense' (1821), which plays on the sexual connotations Goethe had given it: 'The imagination gives out what it has first absorbed by congeniality of temperament, what it has attracted and moulded into itself by elective affinity, as the loadstone draws and impregnates iron.' Later in the nineteenth century, and partly as a result of Berthollet's findings in 1798, the idea of 'elective affinities' was to be replaced by the atomistic theory of 'valency'. This word, which stands for the general phenomenon of chemical binding or linking, came into scientific discourse not through the Latin word *valere*, which means 'to be strong or well', but through a shortening of the technical word 'quantivalence' (see Russell, pp. 81–91). The concept of valency offered a more scientifically robust explanation for the combining power of chemical substances than 'elective affinity'. But it was less attractive to the Romantic temperament precisely because it did away with the fanciful notion that matter was endowed with sympathy, volition, intelligence, and free will.

Meanwhile, however, Romantic science offered a compelling model of the natural world, not as a static collocation of disparate entities ('a universe of little things', as Coleridge put it), but as an organic web of interconnections, energized by a life-force that draws opposites into unity. Answering the needs of both writers, this vision was what attracted Coleridge and Wordsworth to *Naturphilosophie*. They responded with excitement to the idea that everything in the universe—animate and inanimate, organic and inorganic—was linked to everything else through forces of attraction. They were predisposed to sympathize with the idea that apparently inanimate substances appear to possess human volition. They were also inclined to share the view expressed by Goethe's heroine that 'in precisely this way true and important friendships may come about between people: opposing qualities make an intenser union possible' (p. 32). The theory of 'elective affinities' lays special emphasis on the attraction of opposites. And in the same way, it is the principle of polarity which lies at the centre of a Romantic conception of friendship.

V

How does a scientific concept become absorbed as an intellectual paradigm that has emotional significance? Can a term such 'elective affinities', even when it is equally relevant in the domains of science and human relations, apply to the conduct of a specific friendship? How does a theory translate into practice? How, in other words, do we get from the idea of 'elective affinities' to Wordsworth and Coleridge—two men, with human desires and foibles, who met, interacted, sustained an intense friendship, then grew apart?

During the 1790s and early 1800s, these two writers moved in a circle of intellectuals, among whom were a number of distinguished chemists. Humphry Davy was a close friend. They attended the lectures in Bristol at which Davy experimented on his audience with nitrous oxide, in order to test its effects as a creative stimulus. They also knew Davy's teacher, Thomas Beddoes. He was well acquainted with the theory of elective affinities, since in the 1780s he had translated into English a work published by Bergman, in which tables of elective affinity are included. Neither Wordsworth nor Coleridge made a contribution to science in the way that Goethe did. But they were intensely concerned with the progressive claims of science, and its possible collaboration with poetry. In 1802, when Wordsworth revised the Preface to *Lyrical Ballads*, the following important new passage was included:

If the materials of Science should ever create any material revolution, direct or indirect, in our condition, and in the impressions which we habitually receive, the Poet will sleep then no more than at present, but he will be ready to follow the steps of the Man of science, not only in those general indirect effects, but he will be at his side, carrying sensation into the midst of the objects of the science itself. . . . If the time should ever come when what is now called Science . . . shall be ready to put on, as it were, a form of flesh and blood, the Poet will lend his divine spirit to aid the transformation, and will welcome the Being thus produced, as a dear and genuine inmate of the household of man. (Brett and Jones, 259–60)

Wordsworth and Coleridge were passionately committed, in the early phase of their friendship, to the idea of an evolving society in which science and poetry might play a mutually enlightening role. Their friendship with Davy accentuated this commitment. In *Elective Affinities*, Goethe was later to experiment with the idea of a collaboration between science and literature in the very title he chose for the novel, and in his intricate mapping of chemical terminology onto its unfolding plot. In much the same way, Wordsworth and Coleridge experimented with the metaphorical application of scientific terminology to people, processes, and relationships. Coleridge's description of Dorothy Wordsworth, in a letter of July 1797, is a case in point: 'her information various—her eye watchful in minutest observation of nature—and her taste a perfect electrometer—it bends, protrudes, and draws in, at subtlest beauties & most recondite faults' (Griggs, i. 330–1).

The intellectual climate in which Wordsworth and Coleridge found themselves in the 1790s was one of experimentation. The two writers made themselves the subject of a number of practical experiments, as well as planning yet more which never came to fruition. When the Wordsworths were charged with looking after Basil Montagu's son, they used this as an opportunity to try out different kinds of teaching and discipline, as well as to observe how Hartley's theory of association worked in the mind of a young child. Later, Coleridge and Wordsworth were jointly invited by the entrepreneurial Tom Wedgwood to set up a school so they might test the efficacy of Rousseau's educational theory as a means of transforming ordinary children into creative genii. The Wedgwood scheme was never implemented, but it had important practical repercussions: Coleridge accepted an annuity from Wedgwood which enabled him to write poetry rather than joining the ministry, and (perhaps out of obligation) his verse focused on educational theory and practice for a while. In *Frost at Midnight*, an ideal Rousseauian upbringing is projected for his own son, Hartley, whose behaviour later became the subject of numerous notebook entries. (The very name Hartley had been chosen with the associationist philosopher in mind, so it is perhaps not surprising that the child was expected to live up to theoretical expectations.) The Wedgwood episode had yet further implications for Wordsworth, whose interest in education lasted a lifetime. *The Prelude* focused on his own childhood as a test-case for the hypothesis that a childhood nurtured by the sublime and beautiful in Nature ensures 'the growth of a poet's mind'.

An experimental approach was also present in the kinds of political vision the writers applied to their private lives. Together with his friend Robert Southey, Coleridge made detailed plans for living in a Utopian community on the banks of the Susquehanna. Here they and their families intended to put into practice their avowed commitment to the abolition of property. The plans for pantisocracy fizzled out, due to lack of unanimity among the organizers; but there survived, in Coleridge's conception of domestic life, a desire that it might fulfil those early political ideals. His marriage to Sara Fricker, integral to the pantisocratic scheme, went ahead even when the scheme itself was abandoned. In due course—and perhaps inevitably, given these pressures—the marriage collapsed.

Just as friendship provided the raw materials for examining the efficacy and durability of the domestic affections, so too it was a testing-ground for many other kinds of psychological and philosophical enquiry. More was at stake, in the models of domesticity and friendship these two writers shared, than personal happiness. The French Revolution was a large-scale experiment in which they could participate only as enthusiastic witnesses, and which they later came to see as a failure. In its wake, they conceived of family life as an arena in which the slow process of human perfectibility might begin. Close friendships moved like satellites around the family nexus, and were seen as the focus for a more disinterested spirit of fraternity. Godwin, whose influence on Wordsworth's (and, to a lesser extent, Coleridge's) early thought was profound, was sceptical about the political utility of familial bonds, and suspicious that they might interfere with genuine benevolence. But he believed in friendship, which 'requires that the hearts of the persons should, as it were, be amalgamated into one substance, that their thoughts should be transparent to each other, and their communications entire' (*Enquirer*, 1797). It is interesting to note that Godwin here uses a chemical metaphor to describe a human process. He draws on contemporary scientific theory in describing friendship in terms of an amalgamation of substances, a forming of compounds.

The idea of an intimacy founded on deep affinity and equality was emotionally, philosophically, and politically crucial to Wordsworth and Coleridge, especially during the years which saw the waning of their revolutionary sympathies. The expectations they had of friendship might be seen as closely corresponding not only to the Godwinian ideal of mutual transparency and equality, but to the spiritual beliefs which underpinned their vision of an egalitarian future. They longed for a community united by the principle of love rather than the principle of property. The affection and sympathy felt by one friend towards another was, they thought, like an echo of the love felt by human beings towards the divine principle. In this condition, the self aspired to a condition of selflessness, in which it merged with the other: 'SELF, spreading still! oblivious of it's own, | Yet all of all possessing!' (*Religious Musings*, 170–1). The concept of self or identity as a species of property is here dissolved. The self finds itself by losing itself in God.

Even from the very brief outline I have given here, we can see that the two writers brought to their understanding of friendship a highly charged baggage of emotional, psychological, and philosophical expectations. Most people do so; but not with such intensity and self-consciousness. Nor with such a desire to put theoretical ideas to the test. The readiness of these two writers to use themselves, as well as family and friends, as guinea-pigs for Hartleyan, Rousseauian, and Burkean experiments suggests, I think, a peculiarly strong investment in the idea that life should be lived as a form of scientifically motivated *praxis*. This was an attitude characteristic of dissenting culture in England at the time, but it also bears a close resemblance to the more aristocratic life of leisure led by the four characters in *Elective Affinities*, who 'create the experiment in which they will be the materials', and enter into 'a kind of play and experimentation, not only with the composition and arrangement of the garden and landscape but in the composition and arrangement of themselves' (Tanner, 209, 182). One of the novel's many ironies lies in the fact that the characters, despite being aware of the paradigms within which they are conducting their own experiment, are blind to its implications. As Tanner acutely observes,

We become aware of the meaning that they inhabit. We are not interpreters; rather we are forced into a realization of the hermeneutics within which the characters move, and have their being. What we might, as readers, consider too obvious, too significant, is a projection of the significances by which the characters define their existence and beyond which they cannot see. (p. 180)

We can, I think, learn much from this observation that is applicable to Wordsworth and Coleridge, if not to the way they 'conducted' their friendship, then certainly to the way they retrospectively viewed it.

The scientific, political, and spiritual beliefs which I have described above came together to form an ideological model of literary friendship, which influenced the unfolding shape of Wordsworth's and Coleridge's interaction, because it predetermined its parameters. The theory of 'elective affinities' was part of their mental world in much the same way that Freud's theory of the unconscious is a part of ours. It was a Romantic paradigm. It offered an overarching design, against which the plot of their friendship unfolded. This design was peculiarly appealing, in that it confirmed the interconnectedness of science, human relationships, and poetic endeavour. It also had a strong imaginative appeal, in suggesting that temperamental opposition and intellectual disgreement might be subsumed in a larger pattern of unity.

More often than not, the two poets presented themselves as joint labourers even while they were moving apart. Their divisions, when they acknowledged them, tended either to be rationalized as compatibility or transcended by the ideal of a shared vision. In this way, the messiness of lived experienced was converted into evidence of the unity that underlies opposites. Even when recognizing the failure of life to match up to their ideals, they turned to the paradigm of elective affinity. 'The Styles of myself and Coleridge', Wordsowrth once said, 'would not *assimilate*'. The poet is here using a chemical metaphor to describe an ideal synthesis. When the merging or 'compounding' of opposite styles proves impossible, collaboration is figured as an experiment that has gone wrong.

The notion that opposites attract (or, as Coleridge put it, that 'EXTREMES MEET') was both a theory that the two writers put to the test, and an ideological pressure which influenced and distorted the ways in which they saw themselves. I believe that it *overdetermined* the retrospective narratives used by the poets themselves to explain the dynamic of their unfolding literary partnership. In particular, that it distorted the way they looked back on their early collaboration, which they needed to see in terms of opposites attracting and being amalgamated. This, in its turn, has had repercussions for the critical reception of their friendship, its afterlife in the hands of critics, scholars, and historians.

Which brings us back to the methodological difficulties involved in describing a relationship whose immense historical importance lay partly in its inability to fulfil unrealistic expectations. McFarland's adaptation of the term 'symbiosis', so that it includes the idea of polarity, is indeed symptomatic of 'Romantic ideology'. It is a word whose meaning he has adapted to fit the case of literary friendship we have before us. In using it thus, McFarland shows that he has absorbed at a deep level the concept of 'elective affinity'. He has also responded to the subtle pressures of Wordsworth's and Coleridge's mythologizing language. Like them, he wants to see literary friendship in terms of the reconciliation of opposites. At some deep level, this may be a model of friendship which is necessary (or even inevitable) to post-Romantic consciousness. Perhaps it is a paradigm that has survived beyond and despite Freud. Doubtless Freudian theory would have something interesting to say about its survival. But if we are to be true as readers to the untidiness of life, we need to read against its grain. Wordsworth's and Coleridge's friendship was as much a collaborative experiment as the *Lyrical Ballads* project of 1798. It was an experiment in 'elective affinities', an experiment in domestic affections, and an experiment in spiritual love. But experiments often fail. They are especially likely to do so when they involve human beings, and when the objects of investigation are also the investigators. In practice, this was a human friendship that turned sour. It was also a literary relationship of lasting significance.

St Edmund Hall Oxford   L.N.
October 2000

Acknowledgements

The second edition of this book gives me the opportunity to re-thank those who contributed to its making in 1986. I am grateful, first and foremost, to Jonathan Wordsworth, not only for his work as a scholar and teacher, but for his personal inspiration and continuing generosity over the years. Roy Park was an admirably supportive and exacting supervisor of the thesis out of which the book later grew. John Bayley and Wallace Robson made some very useful suggestions. The following friends and colleagues played an important part in encouraging, or refuting my ideas: Robert and Pamela Woof, Richard Gravil, Nicky Trott, Tony Brinkley, Duncan Wu. I include in this new edition (as an Appendix) an article originally published by the *Review of English Studies* in 1981, and I am grateful to the editors for permission to do so.

The preface to the second edition of this book could not have been written without the influence of those whose names are mentioned in it. All of them have helped me to rethink the relationship between Wordsworth and Coleridge. I am especially grateful to those with whom I have had conversations over the past ten years: Stephen Gill, Tim Fulford, Seamus Perry, and Paul Magnuson. Neil Vickers has recently helped me with a crucial piece of scientific information. I owe special thanks to Michael Mingos, for his detailed criticism of a first draft of the preface, as well as for his guidance in reading and thinking about chemical theory. I am also grateful to Hermione Lee and Philip Cardinale for their very helpful comments. Matthew Hollis has been a wonderfully tolerant and supportive editor; he and his team have worked with great speed and efficiency to see the book through the Press.

I re-dedicate this book to the family of Pete Laver, librarian of Dove Cottage, who died tragically, on 24 August 1983, aged 36.

L.N.

Contents

ERRATUM

This edition is missing prelim pages xxxix–xliv (A note on texts and Abbreviations). Complimentary copies of these pages can be obtained by writing to Matthew Hollis, Academic Division, Oxford University Press, OX2 6DP, enclosing a return sending address.

Part One

'That Golden Time'

The First Acquaintance of the Poets, 1793–7

Wordsworth and Coleridge were well acquainted before their important meeting at Racedown in June 1797. By this time, they had formed strong impressions of each other's writing, had become aware of shared commitments, and had met on a number of occasions. Coleridge's early impressions of Wordsworth are well documented, but his two most important statements are retrospective, and cause problems. 'During the last year of my residence at Cambridge' he writes, in the fourth chapter of *Biographia Literaria*, 'I became acquainted with Mr. Wordsworth's first publication entitled "Descriptive Sketches;" and seldom, if ever, was the emergence of an original poetic genius above the literary horizon more evidently announced.' (*Biographia*, i. 77) Even taking hindsight into account, this is an exaggerated claim. *Descriptive Sketches* is competently written. It also contains the first versions of the 'Simplon' and 'Snowdon' passages in the 1805 *Prelude*—passages which the Wordsworth of 1804 follows in detail, and which 'anticipate', therefore, his mature writing. But there is little at first sight to raise the poem above the couplets of Goldsmith's *The Traveller*, on which it is based; and nothing that merits Coleridge's grand acclamation. Similar problems arise from his famous and much quoted comment on *Salisbury Plain*:

It was not . . . the freedom from false taste . . . which made so unusual an impression on my feelings immediately, and subsequently on my judgement. It was the union of deep feeling with profound thought; the fine balance of truth in observing with the imaginative faculty in modifying the objects observed; and above all the original gift of spreading the tone, the *atmosphere*, and with it the depth and height of the ideal world around forms, incidents, and situations, of which, for the common view, custom had bedimmed all the lustre, had dried up the sparkle and the dew drops. (*Biographia*, i. 80)

If Coleridge were describing the Wordsworth of *Tintern Abbey* or *The Prelude*, one could not fail to be impressed; but moments of 'deep feeling' and 'profound thought' are rare in the two versions of *Salisbury Plain* that he saw in 1795–6. Qualities in Wordsworth's writing that developed later,

under his own influence, have been allowed to colour his memories of the
past.

Though he describes it in literary terms, the basis of his original
attraction to Wordsworth was of a different kind. When he first
encountered *Descriptive Sketches* at Cambridge in 1793, the consuming
interest in his life was not academic but political. He had come heavily
under the influence of William Frend, whose trial took place in May 1793;
his immediate circle of acquaintances were all radicals; and in summer
1794 he was to write *The Fall of Robespierre* with Robert Southey. It seems
likely that he was attracted to Wordsworth in the first place because of his
radical sympathies; and it is probable that his first reading of *Descriptive
Sketches* occurred amongst a gathering of friends who would have
remembered Wordsworth from two years before.[1]

To such an audience, the poem's political implications must have been
exciting. Wordsworth's republicanism, inspired in the summer of 1792 by
his brief friendship with Michel Beaupuy, is given full expression here in
his vision of Switzerland as an ideal Republic. Drawing on William Coxe's
Travels, which he read in a French translation,[2] Wordsworth contrasts the
lot of the *haut savois*, starving under Austrian oppression, with that of the
Swiss peasant, living an idyllic pastoral existence (ll. 702–39). His
idealism was such that he believed this inequality would come to an end:
'—Yet, hast thou found that Freedom spreads her pow'r/Beyond the
cottage hearth, the cottage door' (ll. 756–7). And the poem breaks into a
millenarian conclusion:

> Lo! from th'innocuous flames, a lovely birth!
> With it's own Virtues springs another earth:
> Nature, as in her prime, her virgin reign
> Begins, and Love and Truth compose her train . . .

(ll. 782–5)

It was to this political optimism that the Coleridge of 1793 chiefly
responded. His literary appreciation of the poem was delayed until a later
date.

Coleridge's first meeting with Wordsworth, which took place in
September 1795, was at a political Debating Society in Bristol. He makes
no reference to the occasion himself, but the Farington Diary for April

[1] Amongst Coleridge's acquaintances at Cambridge was the poet's brother, Christopher,
who records discussions with Coleridge and others on the subject of Wordsworth's poetic
reputation. See Woof, *BWS*, 89.
[2] See Paul D. Sheats, *The Making of Wordsworth's Poetry, 1785–1798* (Cambridge,
Mass., 1973), 61–6.

1810 records that 'on one occasion Wordsworth spoke with so much force & eloquence that Coleridge was captivated by it, & sought to know him'.[3] Robert Woof has suggested that Wordsworth's own recollection, in 1845, of having first met Coleridge (with Sara and Edith Fricker) in a 'lodging in Bristol' refers to an occasion which took place shortly after the political meeting (*BWS*, 78). It must have been in the lodging that Wordsworth so affected Coleridge 'by his recitation of a manuscript poem': *Salisbury Plain*.[4] The version he heard was written in summer 1793. The previous February, war had been officially declared between England and France, and it is on the horrors of warfare that the poem centres:

> Better before proud Fortune's sumptuous car
> Obvious our dying bodies to obtrude,
> Than dog-like wading at the heels of War
> Protract a cursed existence with the brood
> That lap, their very nourishment, their brother's blood.

> (ll. 311–15)

The power of this writing cannot be explained in the literary terms of *Biographia*. It is committed social protest, offering hope, as the conclusion of *Descriptive Sketches* had done, for the defeat of tyranny and the betterment of mankind. *Adventures on Salisbury Plain*, which Coleridge obtained in manuscript from the Pinneys and Cottle in March 1796, and had the time to study, is in most respects more powerful. Wordsworth worked at it in 1795, extending its social and political themes by the addition of the sailor's story. The result, as Stephen Gill has said, is a new preoccupation 'with man in solitude, with the agony such a man as the sailor suffers from his own sense that he has put himself beyond human love'.[5] It is a change largely attributable to Godwin, whose *Political Justice* (1793), had influenced Wordsworth at the time of publication, and whose *Caleb Williams* (1794) he had almost undoubtedly read. *Salisbury Plain* ended with a plea that 'the herculean mace | Of Reason' should be reared 'High o'er the towers of Pride'; and Coleridge, hearing the poem for the first time, would have responded to the word 'Reason' as an allusion. What *Adventures on Salisbury Plain* offers is not an extension of direct Godwinian reference, but a demonstration of society's responsibility for individual actions. The events of the sailor's life speak for themselves: he is

---

[3] *The Farington Diary*, ed. James Greig (8 vols., London, 1922–8), vi. 36.

[4] *Biographia*, i. 78–9.

[5] *Salisbury Plain Poems*, 13.

press-ganged, forced for several years to fight in the war, and released without pay. Then,

> In sight of his own house, in such a mood
> That from his view his children might have run,
> He met a traveller, robb'd him, shed his blood;
> And when the miserable work was done
> He fled, a vagrant since, the murderer's fate to shun.
>
> (*Adventures*, 95–9)

In Godwin's terms, the sufferings of the sailor, before and after his crime, can directly be attributed to society's infringements of his individual liberty. Only reason, guiding man towards a truly benevolent society, might prevent such oppression. For Wordsworth in 1795, optimism of this kind is no longer possible. The address to the 'Heroes of Truth', which had made *Salisbury Plain* such a hopeful poem, is replaced in *Adventures* by an exposure of the penal system, and by the hanging of the benevolent hero. Wordsworth has not quite 'Yielded up moral questions in despair' (*1805*, x. 900), but his confidence in the amelioration of mankind has disappeared.

'I was once and only once in Company with Godwin', Coleridge writes to Thelwall in May 1796: 'He appeared to me to possess neither the strength of intellect that discovers truth, or the powers of imagination that decorate falsehood—he talked futile sophisms in jejune language' (Griggs, i. 215). It is atheism, of course, which explains this rooted antipathy. Coleridge refused to condone any system which gave reason supremacy by ignoring God (see *Religious Musings*, 139–72). What he could not fail to admire was the enquiry Godwin had made into the causes of political injustice. This was the aspect of Godwinian theory he found reflected in *Salisbury Plain*. Hearing the poem in 1795, then reading it for himself a year later, his early hopes were confirmed. He had found in Wordsworth a man who shared his radical views, and who might share more.

Comparatively little is known about Wordsworth's early impressions of Coleridge. On 24 October 1795, three weeks after their first meeting, he wrote to William Mathews, 'Coleridge was at Bristol part of the time I was there. I saw but little of him. I wished indeed to have seen more—his talent appears to me very great.' (*EY*, 153) By the time of their meeting, Coleridge had already written many of his *Poems on Various Subjects* published the following year; but there is no certainty that Wordsworth read them while in Bristol. The impression of Coleridge's talent came no doubt from his conversation, and from the reputation acquired by his political lectures at the beginning of the year. In the same letter, Wordsworth refers to his meeting with Southey, who was 'about publishing an epic poem on the subject of the Maid of orleans' (*EY*, 153). At this stage, Coleridge could not yet have begun the 255 lines of poetry that would form his contribution. But from the first Wordsworth referred to him and Southey in the same breath—'To-morrow I am going to Bristol', he wrote in a letter probably belonging to November, 'to see those two extraordinary young men, Southey and Coleridge' (*EY*, 156)—and it seems likely that by January 1796 he knew of their collaboration.[6]

It seems, then, that Wordsworth first encountered Coleridge's abstruse speculations within the framework of a narrative poem that had much in common with *Adventures on Salisbury Plain*.[7] *Joan of Arc* Book VI was later to provide the source of *The Ruined Cottage*, and there was much in Southey's protests against the evils of contemporary society that Wordsworth would have found impressive. Perhaps in this context he barely noticed the grand Coleridgean declarations—

> For all that meets the bodily sense I deem
> Symbolical, one mighty alphabet
> For infant minds . . .
>
> (*Destiny of Nations*, 18–20)

> 'Glory to Thee, Father of Earth and Heaven!
> All-conscious Presence of the Universe!
> Nature's vast ever-acting Energy!
> In will, in deed, Impulse of All to All! . . .'
>
> (ll. 459–62)

—but presumably they stayed with him, 'Until maturer seasons', and Coleridge's persuasive conversation, 'called them forth | To impregnate and to elevate the mind' (*1799*, i. 425–6). They must, too, have helped to prepare the way for *Religious Musings*, the only Coleridge poem of this period about which a comment from Wordsworth has survived. In May 1796, a month after the publication of *Poems on Various Subjects*,

---

[6] When he wrote to Cottle that month, thanking him for 'the highly acceptable present' of *Joan of Arc*, he added in a postscript 'Best compts to Coleridge, and say I wish much to hear from him.' (*EY*, 163) If Cottle had not already informed him of Coleridge's part in the venture, he must soon after have heard of it from Coleridge himself. The latter's reference to him in May 1796 as 'a very dear friend of mine' (Griggs, i. 215) suggests there was sustained contact between them after January.

[7] Parrish, 64–5, argues that one passage from *Visions of the Maid of Orleans* draws on *Adventures on Salisbury Plain*.

Coleridge asks Thelwall why he is 'so violent against *metaphysics* in poetry?' 'That Poetry pleases which interests' he goes on: '*my* religious poetry interests the *religious*, who read it with rapture—why? because it awakes in them all the associations connected with a love of future existence &c—'. And, invoking Wordsworth, he continues:

A very dear friend of mine, who is in my opinion the best poet of the age (I will send you his Poem when published) thinks that the lines from 364 to 375 & from 403 to 428 the best in the Volume—indeed worth all the rest—And this man is a Republican & at least a *Semi*-atheist.

(Griggs, i. 215–16)

Conspicuously, Wordsworth did not comment on the most political lines in the poem (ll. 352–6) which, to a republican, should have been exciting. And he seems not to have reacted to the passages containing Coleridge's most important scientific beliefs (see, for example, ll. 423–6, later echoed in *Tintern Abbey*). Instead, he singled out two of the most unearthly passages in the poem. The first offers a vision of heaven as it is experienced in life by the elect. The second, written in a higher Miltonic style, and incorporating images from *Revelation*, begins by describing the millennium—'O Years! the blest preeminence of Saints!' (ll. 395 ff.)— then concludes in a passage of solemn, apocalyptic grandeur that outdoes the ending of *Descriptive Sketches*:

> The veiling clouds retire,
> And lo! the Throne of the redeeming God
> Forth flashing unimaginable day
> Wraps in one blaze earth, heaven, and deepest hell.
>
> (ll. 416–19)

Coleridge's lines are supported by views that Wordsworth would later come to share—

> 'Tis the sublime of man,
> Our noontide Majesty, to know ourselves
> Parts and proportions of one wond'rous whole . . .
>
> (ll. 135–7)

—but one suspects that at this stage he was borne along by the rhetoric, rather than finding a serious cause for optimism.

During the second half of 1796 there may have been a gap in the relationship. A letter Coleridge wrote to Cottle the following January, when the 1797 edition of his *Poems* was about to be published, suggests they had been corresponding (Griggs, i. 297), but nothing survives as confirmation. There is no evidence that they met again until March 1797, when Wordsworth visited Coleridge in Stowey on his way from Bristol to Racedown.[8] Here, for the first time, they had an opportunity to talk at length. Doubtless their discussion centred on *The Borderers*, begun the previous autumn. Coleridge had written almost nothing for the last six months, but had been asked by Sheridan in February 'to write a tragedy on some popular subject'.[9] On 10 March he complained to Cottle 'I have no genius that way—Robert Southey has . . . I think, that he will write a Tragedy' (Griggs, i. 313); and at the end of the month, when Wordsworth visited him, he was probably no clearer about his subject. In early April, however, he writes, 'I employ myself now on a book of Morals in answer to Godwin, and on my Tragedy' (Griggs, i. 320). It is likely the new development is due to Wordsworth. Even without hearing *The Borderers* Coleridge could have gathered what it was about. And his sudden renewal of interest in writing the long-projected answer to Godwin[10] implies a detailed knowledge of its ideas. Speculation about this early meeting should not be carried too far, but it does seem likely that for Wordsworth too it had its importance. His *Essay on Rivers*, which explores and clarifies the Godwinian theme, was almost certainly written between March and June.

It was three months later that Coleridge paid his return visit to Racedown. Wordsworth was busy on *The Ruined Cottage*, which he read aloud on the first day.[11] Coleridge must have been aware that its source was a passage in the seventh book of Southey's *Joan of Arc* which he had printed in *The Watchman* the previous year:

[8] On 19 March, Wordsworth had left Racedown on a visit to Bristol which he expected to last a fortnight (Reed, i. 195). On 29 March he transcribed *Written on the Thames near Richmond* in Cottle's Notebook, and on his way back to Racedown he visited Coleridge at Stowey (see Coleridge's letter of early April, Griggs, i. 319). It is known that Coleridge too was in Bristol on 23 March, and there is a possibility that the two poets not only met there, but also accompanied one another on the journey from Bristol to Nether Stowey.

[9] 'Mr Bowles perhaps will be able to inform me', Coleridge writes, 'whether you meant . . . to recommend a fictitious and domestic subject, or one founded on well-known History.' (Griggs, i. 304)

[10] Coleridge had denounced Godwin in his third *Lecture on Revealed Religion* (May 1795) and again in *The Watchman* (*CC*, i. 164–5; *CC*, ii. 98–9, 194–8). The scheme for a book, to compare the systems of Godwin and Jesus, at six shillings octavo, appears in three letters of November–December 1796 (Griggs, i. 253, 267, 293).

[11] Though no manuscript survives, it is possible to determine what he heard. Wordsworth began the story of Margaret at the end, describing the last years and finally the death of his heroine. See Dorothy's transcription for Coleridge, 10 June 1797 (Griggs, i. 327–8).

> At her cottage door
> The wretched one shall sit, and with dim eye
> Gaze o'er the plain, where, on his parting steps,
> Her last look hung. Nor ever shall she know
> Her husband dead, but tortured with vain hope
> Gaze on—then heartsick turn to her poor babe
> And weep it fatherless![12]

Wordsworth, in telling Margaret's story, does not embellish what he has read. Preserving the bareness of Southey's narrative, he leaves unaltered such details as the woman's eagerness to hear news, and her protracted gazing into the distance. Where his account differs is in its attitude to suffering. The woman's tale in *Joan of Arc* is a set piece, intended to make a political point. *The Ruined Cottage* focuses intently on Margaret's state of mind.

When Wordsworth read *The Borderers* aloud the following day (6 June), Coleridge's response to it was unequivocal. 'His Drama', he wrote to Cottle two days later, 'is absolutely wonderful. You know, I do not commonly speak in such abrupt & unmingled phrases—& therefore will the more readily believe me.' '—There are in the piece', he continued, 'those *profound* touches of the human heart, which I find three or four times in "The Robbers" of Schiller, & often in Shakespeare—but in Wordsworth there are no *inequalities*.' (Griggs, i. 325) The second half of his claim seems far-fetched; the first rings perfectly true. *The Borderers* does not just contain these '*profound* touches of the human heart'. It is a revelation of the heart's capacity to be touched—a demonstration of the primacy of human feeling.

To claim that the play is anti-Godwinian would be misleading. It represents (to use one of its own metaphors) 'a *transition* in [Wordsworth's] soul' (II. i. 92), and bears the same relation to *Political Justice* as Godwin's own novel, *Caleb Williams*. What Wordsworth sets out to show is not the damage caused by a misapplication of Godwinian reason, so much as the inevitable tendency of the irrational to pervade human motives. Rivers, the villain-hero of the piece, persuades Mortimer to kill the father of the woman he loves. In the temptation scenes he is ruthless and cynical, arguing with specious logic that murder is no more than its name (II. iii. 230–4), and denying the power of remorse:

---

[12] From the text of *Joan of Arc*, vii. 320–1 printed by Coleridge in *The Watchman*, 1 March 1796 (*CC*, ii. 45).

> It cannot live with thought, think on, think on,
> And it will die.
>
> (III. v. 82–3)

At the climax of the play, he adopts the unmistakeable voice of Godwinian reason:

> To day you have thrown off a tyranny
> That lives but by the torpid acquiescence
> Of our emasculated souls, the tyranny
> Of moralists and saints and lawgivers.
> You have obeyed the only law that wisdom
> Can ever recognize: the immediate law
> Flashed from the light of circumstances
> Upon an independent intellect.
>
> (III. v. 26–33)

Compelling though it is, the speech is undercut by different kinds and levels of irony. Mortimer has been persuaded to commit this crime, not by the 'reason' in Rivers' argument, but by the sequence of lies, which exploit his love for Herbert's daughter. (A Godwinian rhetoric is being used, but it bears no relation to the facts.) Furthermore, as the climactic scene goes on, Rivers unfolds the true motive behind his actions. He himself had been tricked, at the height of his career, into murdering an innocent man. Filled with a remorse he cannot admit, he justifies his actions in the name of reason, and binds Mortimer to him in a repetition of his crime:

> you are my master, and have taught me
> What there is not another living man
> Had strength to teach . . .
> Therefore I'll cleave to you
> In camps and cities, in the wood and mountain,
> In evil, and in solitary pain,
> You still shall find that I will cleave to you.
>
> (III. v. 16–21)

He claims as his goal the enlightenment of humanity—'Henceforth we are fellow-labourers—to enlarge | The intellectual empire of mankind' (IV. ii. 188–9)—but the craving for 'independent intellect' is unfulfilled. All Rivers' actions are determined by his past, and by his invincible compulsion to repeat. He is trapped in the emotions he seeks to deny.

Wordsworth, then, offers two separate critiques of Godwinian philosophy. He shows that when reason is divorced from benevolence, it becomes 'terrifyingly perverted' (Jacobus, 29). And he disputes Godwin's claim that unadulterated reason can exist, proving that it will never be a replacement for emotions, though it can be used as their justification or disguise.[13] The play would have seemed shocking to anyone with Godwinian sympathies. But for Coleridge, alarmed and alienated by atheism, it was a confirmation of deeply held beliefs.

He was impressed by more in the play, however, than the refutation of Godwin. When he described it as 'absolutely wonderful', and referred to its '*profound* touches of the human heart' he had Shakespeare and Schiller in mind. He meant it literally when he implied that Wordsworth was as great as them, but also more consistent. The grandeur of his claim rests on the character of Rivers. In dramatic terms, he is based on Iago, but his alienation is motivated as Iago's never is. Taking a hint from Belial's magnificent anguish in *Paradise Lost*—'for who would lose, | Though full of pain, this intellectual being?' (*PL*, ii. 146–7)—Wordsworth has created a character who seems almost designed to appeal to Coleridge:

> In these my lonely wanderings I perceived
> What mighty objects do impress their forms
> To build up this our intellectual being . . .

> (IV. ii. 133–5)

It is grandeur of intellect that drives him to create a second self, and so be revenged on the world that excludes him. Coleridge must have shared Wordsworth's reverence for such pride. He may also have responded more personally to the sense of alienation. Like Rivers, he believed that pain and guilt were endemic to the human condition: they were the price man had paid, and would continue to pay, for his 'intellectual being'. No price, for the Romantic, could be too high. Suffering cannot be measured; it is experienced by the mind, and shares the endlessness to which the mind aspires (see III. v. 60–5). Through it we know ourselves to be human, yet feel ourselves to be '*greater than we know*'.[14] Creating a second self, Rivers perpetuates all that he has himself endured. In a final speech, Mortimer anticipates not just the obscurity and darkness of his future lot, but the dignity which isolation brings:

> I will wander on
> Living by mere intensity of thought,
> A thing by pain and thought compelled to live,

---

[13] See *1805*, x. 810–13 for Wordsworth's later formulation of this view.
[14] The Duddon 'After-thought' (xxxiv), 14 (*PW*, iii. 261).

> Yet loathing life, till heaven in mercy strike me
> With blank forgetfulness—that I may die.
>
> (V. iii. 271–5)

By the time of his visit to Racedown, he had completed two and a half acts of his own play, *Osorio*, which he read to the Wordsworths on the first day he was there.[15] In an unpublished 'Preface' written at a later stage, he confesses to thinking of it as 'but an embryo' in which 'all is imperfect, and much obscure'. He apologizes for its obvious defect, the omission of a 'long story, which yet is necessary to the complete understanding of the play', and goes on to discuss a much more radical flaw:

Worse than all, the growth of Osorio's character is nowhere explained—and yet I had most clear and psychologically accurate ideas of the whole of it . . . A man, who from constitutional calmness of appetites, is seduced into pride and the love of power, by these into misanthropism, or rather a contempt of mankind, and from thence, by the co-operation of envy, and a curiously modified love for a beautiful female (which is nowhere developed in the play), into a most atrocious guilt. A man who is in truth a weak man, yet always duping himself into the belief that he has a soul of iron. Such were some of my leading ideas.[16]

By implication, Coleridge had his 'leading ideas' from the first, but within the play itself they emerge most clearly in the second half. Wordsworth must in March have discussed the importance of pride and guilt in the character of Rivers, and it is likely their conversation influenced the first two and a half acts. In June, however, Coleridge not only heard the full text of *The Borderers*; he almost certainly read Wordsworth's newly-written Preface, the *Essay on Rivers*:

Let us suppose a young Man of great intellectual powers, yet without any solid principles of genuine benevolence. His master passions are pride and the love of distinction. He has deeply imbibed a spirit of enterprize in a tumultuous age. He goes into the world and is betrayed into a great crime.

That influence on which all his happiness is built immediately deserts him. His talents are robbed of their weight; his exertions are unavailing, and he quits the world in disgust, with strong misanthropic feelings.

(Osborn, 62)

The connections are clear enough. It is not surprising that when looking back over his work Coleridge should use Wordsworth's essay as a model,

---

[15] Dorothy records no impression of the play in her letter to Mary Hutchinson (*EY*, 188–9), but according to Coleridge (Griggs, i. 326) Wordsworth himself thought '*very* highly of it'.

[16] Preface to *Osorio* from MS 1 (*EHC*, ii. 1114).

14   *Introduction*

but the *Essay* seems to have helped him in the actual writing of the play, as
well as in his later summary of its 'leading ideas'.

In the play's first half, Coleridge is more preoccupied by storyline than
by the psychology of guilt. Osorio's character is never allowed to develop:
there is no analysis of motivation, and no sense of being taken into his
mind. But in the second half this is changed. In a scene which vividly
recalls *The Borderers*, Osorio tells his own life-story—'Under the mask of
the third person', as Coleridge points out in MS 2, and 'as in the delusion
of self-justification and pride, it appeared to himself—at least as he wished
it to appear to himself':[17]

OSORIO.
                                              He walk'd alone,
          And phantasies, unsought for, troubled him.
          Something within would still be shadowing out
          All possibilities, and with these shadows
          His mind held dalliance. Once, as so it happen'd,
          A fancy cross'd him wilder than the rest:
          To this in moody murmur, and low voice,
          He yielded utterance as some talk in sleep.

                              . . . Why babblest thou of guilt?
          The deed was done, and it pass'd fairly off.
          And he, whose tale I tell thee—dost thou listen? . . .
          Surveying all things with a quiet scorn
          Tamed himself down to living purposes,
          The occupations and the semblances
          Of ordinary men—and such he seem'd.
                              (IV. i. 92–9; 108–10; 116–19)

What Coleridge learns from Wordsworth is a way of writing about the
mind in states of guilt, suffering, loneliness. The question posed by
Alhadra at the end of Act V is half-way between *The Borderers* and *The
Wanderings of Cain*:

                              is it then
          An enviable lot to waste away
          With inward wounds, and like the spirit of chaos
          To wander on disquietly thro' the earth,
          Cursing all lovely things?
                              (V. ii. 295–9)

The poet of *The Ancient Mariner* is only two months away.

[17] *EHC*, ii. 567.

'I speak with heart-felt sincerity', Coleridge writes in a letter to Cottle of 8 June, '& (I think) unblinded judgement, when I tell you, that I feel myself a *little man by* [*Wordsworth's*] side; & yet do not think myself the less man, than I formerly thought myself.' (Griggs, i. 325). He was of course in the habit of turning his friends into idols. Back in 1795 he had written sadly to Southey, after their quarrel:

You have left a large Void in my Heart—I know no man big enough to fill it. Others I may love equally & esteem equally: and some perhaps I may admire as much. But never do I expect to meet another man, who will make me unite attachment for his person with reverence for his heart and admiration of his Genius!

(Griggs, i. 173)

Chance had provided Coleridge with a larger man sooner than he could have expected, and he was after all right, as well as sincere, when he talked of Wordsworth as 'the greatest Man, he ever knew'.[18] What seems odd in retrospect is not the judgements themselves, exalted and emotional though they are, but the kind of poetry on which they are based. Coleridge had the opportunity at Racedown of responding to very different sides of Wordsworth's genius, but only one attracted him. Despite having just heard *The Ruined Cottage*, which in 1815 he was to call 'the finest Poem in our Language, comparing it with any of the same or similar Length' (Griggs, iv. 564), he gives the poem no mention. He was so impressed by *The Borderers* that he seemed unaware of major developments since March.

Old Man Travelling, written a matter of days before Coleridge's visit, registers the change. Where Mortimer had prophesied for himself a lonely, anguished future—'Living by mere intensity of thought, | A thing by pain and thought compelled to live' (V. iii. 272–3)—the old man travels, in his solitude, with a sense of inward peace:

> every limb,
> His look and bending figure, all bespeak
> A man who does not move with pain, but moves
> With thought . . .

(ll. 4–7)

Nothing is left of the intensity which characterized both the earlier

<hr>

[18] Griggs, i. 325. As late as March 1798 he was referring to 'The Giant Wordsworth' in a letter to Cottle (Griggs, i. 391). There is surely some unconscious aggression when in July 1797 he writes to Southey: 'Wordsworth is a very great man—the only man, to whom *at all times* & in *all modes of excellence* I feel myself inferior' (Griggs, i. 334).

writing and the states of mind it portrayed. Complexities of psychology, too, have disappeared: the old man's movement is more significant than what he is thinking, and his condition seems almost universal. Coleridge could not have known it, but in responding excitedly to *The Borderers* he was admiring a kind of poetry that had already been discarded.

If anything, Wordsworth in June 1798 had less idea of Coleridge's true poetic achievement than Coleridge had of his. He knew and admired *Religious Musings* and the lines in *Joan of Arc*, but was probably aware neither of the more recent work nor of the major short poems of 1795–6, *The Eolian Harp* and *Reflections on Having Left a Place of Retirement*. At Alfoxden in the year following, he would have the chance to get to know these early poems, and to respond both to their formal qualities and to the philosophical positions they contained. The year falls, in fact, neatly in two: six months (July–December 1797) of apprenticeship, during which he writes nothing but learns a great deal; and the period, January–July 1798, in which Coleridge's influence is at its height. It is a strange fact that, despite Wordsworth's very evident subordination during the next stage of their relationship, Coleridge continued to think of himself as the inferior of the two. For some reason, he assumed that the sequence of Wordsworth's poems he had known and admired—*Descriptive Sketches*, *Salisbury Plain*, *The Borderers*—amounted to more than he was capable of himself. Events had conspired, since 1795, to make Wordsworth seem confident and removed; and that was how he stayed, in Coleridge's eyes, 'for the more substantial Third of a Life' (Griggs, iv. 571). As Thomas McFarland has recently said: 'it was almost as though Coleridge simply decreed poetic greatness for Wordsworth, somewhat as Kubla Khan decreed the pleasure dome.'[19] And Wordsworth, it seems, was contented with his role.

[19] McFarland, 221.

Interaction and Influence:
The Early Days at Alfoxden

(i) *The Beginnings of an Allusive Idiom*

Wordsworth's dependence on Southey's *Joan of Arc*, as he begins work on *The Ruined Cottage*, offers a perfect example of source-material used merely for its convenience.[1] With Coleridge and Wordsworth, borrowing is of a different kind. From the first, it implies relationship, and the smallest echo or allusion can bring with it a context that expands and enriches the immediate frame of reference.

As early as 1795, in his *Lines Written at Shurton Bars*, Coleridge uses echo as both public tribute and private bond:

> Nor travels my meandering eye
> The starry wilderness on high:
> Nor now with curious sight
> I mark the glow-worm, as I pass,
> Move with 'green radiance' through the grass
> An EMERALD of Light.
>
> (ll. 1–6)[2]

The quotation is from *An Evening Walk*, and the note acknowledging it contained in its original form an attack on contemporary reviewers for their scornful treatment of the poem.[3] Cottle abridged the note when

---

[1] The lines from *Joan of Arc* are quoted in the Introduction, above. Southey depends on Wordsworth in the same way in his *Idiot* (June 1798), and an English Eclogue called *The Ruined Cottage* (autumn 1798). But for Southey, borrowing amounts to little more than theft. See Mary Jacobus, 'Southey's Debt to *Lyrical Ballads* (1798)', *RES*, New Series 12, 85 (October, 1971), 20–36.

[2] The phrase 'an EMERALD of Light' is based on a line from Samuel Rogers' *Pleasures of Memory* (1792): 'The glow-worm loves her emerald-light to shed' (Part One, l. 143). The poem influenced Coleridge deeply, though he tried on occasion to deny it. (See particularly the long note attached to *Lines on an Autumnal Evening*, where he defends himself against the charge of plagiarism.) Norman Fruman has drawn attention to the deviousness present in Coleridge's borrowings (see Fruman, 73, 99, for instance), and it would seem possible that the public acknowledgement of Wordsworth is there partly because it conceals the debt to Rogers.

[3] See Woof, *BWS*, 88.

preparing Coleridge's volume for the press, but its implications are there in the final version:

The expression 'green Radiance' is borrowed from Mr. WORDSWORTH, a Poet whose versification is occasionally harsh and his diction too frequently obscure: but whom I deem unrivalled among the writers of the present day in manly sentiment, novel imagery, and vivid colouring.[4]

What Coleridge manages to suggest is both Wordsworth's uniqueness and his own discrimination. The note is more than an acknowledgement. It is a public declaration of friendship: a construction of literary myth.[5]

Allusion becomes more complicated as friendship is deepened and enriched. In June 1797, Coleridge arranged for the Wordsworths to live at Alfoxden house, two miles walk from Nether Stowey. *This Lime Tree Bower My Prison*, written in July, is a kind of initiation. It involves the bringing together of old and new friends—the balancing of reference to past poems with allusion to ones more recently composed. Abandoned to an isolation he knowingly exaggerates, Coleridge imagines a journey he cannot share, and by imagining shares it. Or rather, by shaping it in his mind, he makes a recompense for what he has missed, which he wishes to believe in as an act of sharing. Writer and reader alike are dependent on the *'Possession of being well Deceived'*.[6]

The journey he describes is essentially allegorical. Lamb and his companions are seen descending into a dark underworld, emerging into a wider prospect, and climbing to a height from which all can be viewed. They set off together, but Lamb is singled out for peculiar joy, standing Moses-like on the mountain to be visited by God. He is made elect, not just because he has suffered, and shown virtue and resilience in the past—

> In the great City pent, winning [his] way,
> With sad yet bowed soul, thro' evil & pain
> And strange calamity.

(ll. 13–15)[7]

---

[4] *Poems on Various Subjects* (1796), 185–6.

[5] Wordsworth returns the compliment when in November 1796 he publishes *Address to the Ocean*, the first line of which, as his note points out, is borrowed 'from Mr Coleridge'. See Parrish, 63.

[6] See 'A Digression Concerning Madness' in Swift's *Tale of a Tub*, ed. A. C. Guthkelch and D. Nichol Smith (Oxford, 1959), 108.

[7] Compare the passage from *Joan of Arc* describing heavenly Truth 'from Bethabra northward . . . | With gradual steps, *winning her difficult way*' (*Destiny of Nations*, 124–5, my italics). Self-echo enhances meaning, and Lamb assumes for the moment an allegorical role.

—but because he is understudy, and proxy, to Coleridge himself:

> So my friend
> Struck with joy's deepest calm, and gazing round
> On the wide view, may gaze till all doth seem
> Less gross than bodily, a living Thing
> That acts upon the mind, and with such hues
> As cloathe the Almighty Spirit, when he makes
> Spirits perceive His presence!
>
> (ll. 20–6)[8]

The words 'as I have stood' refer one back, not to a previous viewing of the same scene, but to an earlier poem enacting a similar symbolic climb. Coleridge has in mind the landscape of his *Reflections on Having Left a Place of Retirement*: a landscape of 'Dim coasts, and cloud-like hills, and shoreless Ocean' which, under the influence of joy, could seem 'like Omnipresence!' (ll. 37–8) In a later revision, the background presence of *Reflections* is highlighted by correspondences of visual detail which amount almost to a form of allusion.[9] Lamb, at each stage of the poem's development, stands for the continuity of an earlier self. Verbal echo registers the process.

Coleridge's reference to the Quantock landscape as '*a living Thing*' is a reminder that behind both *This Lime Tree Bower* and *Reflections* lies the central belief of Priestleyan Unitarianism in an active universe energized by an immanent God. In the lines that follow, this is fused with Berkeley's more complex view of the natural world as symbolic: God's language, rather than matter activated by His presence. Believing as he did that 'the sublime of man' is 'to know ourselves | Parts and proportions of one wond'rous whole' (*Religious Musings*, 135–7) Coleridge was bound to concern himself with precisely how man, the individual practising Christian, could attain to such knowledge. The answer could not lie solely

---

[8] I refer to the early version of the poem, as published in Griggs, i. 334–6.

[9] Before publishing *This Lime Tree Bower* in *The Annual Anthology* (1800), Coleridge inserted a descriptive passage drawing on the style and language of *Reflections*:

> Now my friends emerge
> Beneath the wide wide Heaven, and view again
> The many-steepled tract magnificent
> Of hilly fields and meadows, and the sea
> With some fair bark perhaps which lightly touches
> The slip of smooth clear blue betwixt two isles
> Of purple shadow!
>
> (ll. 20–6; text from *Annual Anthology*)

in climbing hills and having religious feelings; the sense of omnipresence
had to be explained. God's material presence Coleridge came to think a
dangerous one, for reasons that are set out amusingly but clearly in a letter
written soon after *Reflections*: 'How is it that Dr Priestley is not an
atheist?' he writes:

He asserts in three different Places, that God not only *does*, but *is*, every thing.—
But if God *be* every Thing, every Thing is God—: which is all, the Atheists
assert—. An eating, drinking, lustful *God*—with no *unity* of *Consciousness*—these
appear to me the unavoidable Inferences from his philosophy—Has not Dr
Priestley forgotten that *Incomprehensibility* is as necessary an attribute of the First
Cause, as Love, or Power, or Intelligence?—

(Griggs, i. 192–3)

Berkeley came to the rescue by offering creation (the universe) as an
imaginative act that at once demonstrated God's '*unity* of *Consciousness*',
and preserved His Incomprehensibility:

But chiefly this, him First, him Last to view
Through meaner powers and secondary things
Effulgent, as through clouds that veil his blaze.
For all that meets the bodily sense I deem
Symbolical, one mighty alphabet
For infant minds . . .

(*Destiny of Nations*, 15–20)

This accepted, man's role became clear. Through moments when 'all doth
seem | Less gross than bodily' he was able to read the sign-language that is
the natural world. In understanding God's symbols, man did not merely
sense His omnipresence, but partook of the godhead.

There was a special appropriateness in attributing such experience to
Lamb. He was not impressed by natural landscape, but as a committed
Unitarian he shared Coleridge's most deeply held beliefs, and to some
extent also their recent refinements. 'Are you yet a Berkleyan?' he asked,
in a letter of mid-1797: 'Make me one. I rejoyce in being, speculatively, a
necessarian.—Would to God, I were habitually a practical one. Confirm
me in the faith of that great & glorious doctrine, & keep me steady in the
contemplation of it.' (Marrs, i. 89) It is to Lamb (with this confirming and
steadying purpose in mind) that Coleridge officially dedicates his poem;
and it is to him that pride of place is given. But within and behind the
poet's formal, carefully designed address to his old friend, a different
conversation is taking place. Between April and June 1797 Wordsworth
had written his *Lines Left upon a seat in a Yew Tree*: the source,

companion-piece, and inspiration, for *This Lime Tree Bower*. In the dialogue between these two poems one sees, not the consolidation of an old friendship, based on shared assumptions, but the start of a new one, grounded in significant difference. And one sees also, for the first time, an allusive idiom that is conscious of its power.

The hero of *Lines Left upon a Seat* does not belong to the gothic world of *The Borderers*. But in the spiritual pride which his misanthropy reveals (ll. 18–21) he resembles both Osorio and Rivers. The 'great crime' Wordsworth sees him as committing consists neither in the loftiness of his youth (l. 14) nor in the misanthropy of his later years (both of which, in different guises, the poet himself has manifested, or admired, or condoned)[10] but in his retreat into self-hood. The true recluse, in his 'silent hour of inward thought', might learn to 'suspect' as well as to 'revere' himself (ll. 58–9). This man is shown neglecting the real worth of his environment, just as his own had been neglected by the world.

It is a post-Godwinian, but largely pre-Coleridgean poem;[11] and as yet there is no structure in Wordsworth's thinking to determine what the 'solid principles of genuine benevolence' advocated in the Preface to *The Borderers* might actually consist of. One assumes that *genuine* benevolence is distinct from the Godwinian kind portrayed in *The Convict* and by this time discarded. It follows that there can be no easy solution in plunging back into society to perform 'labours of benevolence' or to fight the 'bloodless fight'.[12] A guideline of sorts is laid down in the poem's concluding lines (44–60), probably written after Coleridge's visit to Racedown. But Wordsworth does not yet have the concept of the 'One Life' to show how the self can be left behind. *This Lime Tree Bower* is a corrective poem: it suggests what 'sacred sympathy' might be,[13] and leads Wordsworth to an understanding of '*genuine* benevolence' in terms that are consciously anti-Godwinian.

---

[10] Pride, as *The Borderers* had shown, could be the sign of intellectual power and romantic solitude, to both of which Wordsworth was drawn. Misanthropy played its part in Wordsworth's own withdrawal—first to Racedown, then to Alfoxden, and finally to Grasmere.

[11] It is likely that the last paragraph was composed after Coleridge's visit to Racedown in June, and before the writing of *This Lime Tree Bower*. See Parrish, 66–70.

[12] Coleridge had left Clevedon, in February 1796, with this determination (*Reflections*, 61–2). Mary Jacobus (31–2) argues that Wordsworth's attitude in *Lines Left Upon a Seat* is analogous, but she depends on the assumption that this is an uncritically Godwinian poem. Wordsworth's position is surely less clear-cut. He is conscious of the potential immorality in being a recluse, but does not regard its social aspect as of paramount importance. The 'crime' he commits is against himself, and the solution, therefore, lies within.

[13] See *Religious Musings*, 152.

Wordsworth's title does not give so much away as Coleridge's. But looked at closely, the description of the yew-tree's setting—'on a desolate part of the shore, yet commanding a beautiful prospect'—nudges us towards a specific reading. Wordsworth is never again to write so emblematically. In these contrasting scenes of desolation and beauty, he evokes opposites which his own eye and mind can reconcile, but which the recluse sees as disparate and unharmonized. As the poem unfolds, we are made aware of the man's wilfulness in choosing between what he wrongly sees as alternative settings. Details of his immediate environment—the wind breathing soft, the curling waves—offset its desolation (ll. 5–7), and the loneliness of the place is potentially relieved by the presence of 'a straggling sheep, | The stone-chat, or the glancing sand-piper' (ll. 23–4). Even the barrenness of the rocks is qualified by signs of life and growth— 'with juniper, | And heath, and thistle, thinly sprinkled o'er'—indicating possible connections with the distant scene. But none of these details is enjoyed, or even noticed. Like Tennyson's Mariana, who 'could not look on the sweet heaven', the solitary refuses to acknowledge that his dreariness might be relieved. The landscape seen from his station looks back at him from an unreachable remove—the object of his envy and yearning, but also an emblem, in his own mind, of the beauty which excludes him:

> And lifting up his head, he then would gaze
> On the more distant scene; how lovely 'tis
> Thou seest, and he would gaze till it became
> Far lovelier, and his heart could not sustain
> The beauty still more beauteous.
>
> (ll. 30–4)

Wordsworth seems at first to be suggesting that the recluse is capable of genuine insight. As the language gathers intensity, one is tricked into believing that visionary experience will be achieved. But, with an intrusion that is appropriately negative, the expected climax is denied:

> Nor, that time,
> Would he forget those beings, to whose minds,
> Warm from the labours of benevolence,
> The world, and man himself, appeared a scene
> Of kindred loveliness: then he would sigh
> With mournful joy, to think that others felt
> What he must never feel: and so, lost man!
> On visionary views would fancy feed,
> Till his eye streamed with tears.
>
> (ll. 34–42)

The weeping is not redemptive, as it might and should be, but self-pitying. The lines 'his heart could not sustain | The beauty still more beauteous' (33–4), rather than implying a heart overwhelmed, punningly suggest one that is unable to give beauty the nourishment it deserves. And the word 'visionary' (used here not as a term of approval, but to evoke delusion) contains all the potential for true sight which the recluse himself denies.[14] Until the final (Coleridgean) paragraph, no outlet is offered. This is a mind that is 'self-closed, all repelling'.[15]

Every ingredient of *This Lime Tree Bower* is strategically corrective. Picking up the themes of envy and exclusion, but writing about them with a degree of self-mockery, Coleridge structures his poem around an experience he has literally missed, but is capable of vicariously enjoying. The poem is a lesson to Wordsworth: it rewrites anticlimax as climax, and supplies what he had been straining toward.

Reusing the tree / prison metaphor, Coleridge tacitly adopts the part of the introverted man, but also (at an ironic distance) watches the workings of the solipsistic mind. Self-parody is there in his inflated Miltonics ('Lam'd by the scathe of fire, lonely & faint') and uneasy exaggeration in 'My friends, whom I may never meet again'. The benign associations called up by lime trees (carefully juxtaposed with those of the yew) already play their part in offsetting introversion. Benignity will develop, of course, in the poem's ending, with the observation of sunshine and shadow on the trees' leaves.

Lamb, as Coleridge's representative, becomes the genuine visionary the recluse could never be. He 'gazes' (and the repetition is allusive)[16] at a landscape which dims before his eyes, revealing God's presence. In one of his revisions for *The Annual Anthology*, the debt to Wordsworth is highlighted: 'Struck with joy's deepest calm, and gazing round | On the wide view' (ll. 21–2) becomes 'Struck with deep joy may stand, as I have stood, | Silent with swimming sense' (ll. 37–9). The word 'swimming' suggests tears—not of self-pity, in this case, but of joy.

As Coleridge brings one back, from hilltop to bower, his staged reversal of the earlier poem becomes at once more obvious and more didactic:

> A Delight
> Comes sudden on my heart, and I am glad
> As I myself were there! Nor in this bower
> Want I sweet sounds or pleasing shapes.

(ll. 26–9)

---

[14] Contrast, for instance, 'visionary power' and 'bleak and visionary sides' (*In Storm and Tempest*, 9, *Pedlar*, 171) and 'visionary dreariness' (*1799*, i. 322).

[15] *Urizen*, Book One, 3.

[16] See *Lines Left upon a Seat*, 30–2.

The lines are a declaration of the poet's capacity to transcend loneliness, not believable in itself, but acceptable as an instructive fiction. Every detail (ll. 29–40) offers reconciliation in place of loneliness. The recluse had trained his yew-tree to shut out the light; Coleridge admits and welcomes the evening sunshine which filters through the leaves. The recluse had been unable to link his own setting with the distant scene; he observes the nearby foliage as it catches the 'deep radiance' of the setting sun (l. 33). Even the 'solitary humble-bee', singing in the bean flower, has an allusive function, filling an absence in the earlier poem's setting ('What if these barren boughs the bee not loves?')[17] just as other absences are filled.

It is on the power of blessing that Coleridge's philosophy of joy depends. Wordsworth's recluse had not even acknowledged his visitants, let alone been able to respond to their presence. Coleridge, on the other hand, welcomes the last rook (despite its dissonant creeking) because it tells of life beyond the self. The coda, it is important to notice, is addressed to old and new friends alike. Lamb is no longer alone in being considered one of the elect. Wordsworth and Dorothy too, despite their non-Unitarian background, and even their semi-atheism, can be assumed to share his beliefs.

(ii) '*With Other Ministrations*'

For Wordsworth, the period July–November 1797 was mostly one for taking stock. Coleridge's conversation, according to Dorothy, 'teem[ed] with soul, mind, and spirit' (*EY*, 188). For Coleridge, on the other hand, it was a time of rapid and noticeable change. Not only did he write a good deal more than half of *Osorio* before October, when Wordsworth can at most have been revising *The Borderers*; he also began to write differently. Two passages, both composed for *Osorio* in the early autumn, both later excerpted for inclusion in *Lyrical Ballads*, demonstrate the change that is taking place, and pay tribute in their different ways to the new relationship. *The Dungeon* has been frequently discussed. It suggests that, under Wordsworth's influence, Coleridge has come not only to believe his own earlier theory—that by 'beholding constantly the Best possible we at last become ourselves the best possible' (Griggs, i. 154)—but also to write about Nature, with its 'healing', 'influencing' and 'harmonising' powers, as though he feels them himself. *The Foster Mother's Tale* is less well known,

---

[17] See *Lines Left Upon a Seat*, 4.

but more important. The first in a sequence of poems to do with childhood, it shows Coleridge thinking about the benefits of an instinctual education, and tacitly comparing Wordsworth's childhood experience with his own. It is one of the poems of this period most frequently drawn upon in later years. Already, by February 1798, Wordsworth is using it in his own account of early education, *The Pedlar*; by summer 1802 it is being applied by Coleridge to his son Hartley (Griggs, ii. 804) and in February–March 1804 it is in Wordsworth's mind as he describes Nature's 'foster child her Inmate man' (*Intimations*, 82).[18] The poem concerns the history of a foundling, who seems from the first to be one of the elect—discovered in a sacred place (l. 22) and cared for by Nature:

> wrapt in mosses, lined
> With thistle-beards, and such small locks of wool
> As hang on brambles.
>
> (ll. 24–6)

Birdlike already, in his nest, the child becomes associated with birds as he grows older—mocking their notes, and planting seeds of wild flowers on the stumps of trees (ll. 32–6). Life is entirely untouched by the restrictions of formal education. Book learning begins, not as an imperative, but as a pleasure (ll. 37–47) and leads on, because unguided, into unconventional ways of thought:

> But Oh! poor wretch!—he read, and read, and read,
> Till his brain turn'd—and ere his twentieth year,
> He had unlawful thoughts of many things . . .
>
> (ll. 42–4)

Heretical and lawless talk lands the youth in prison, where, cut off from books and Nature, he creates in his imagination a paradisal land (ll. 62–5). The poem ends, not with yearning and nostalgia, but with a realization of his desires. He escapes, leaves civilization behind, and wins through (ll. 78–81) to an existence more primitive than either his childhood or his dreams.

It is a very diverse poem. Coleridge has not yet formulated his ideal, but is seen playing with different ways of thinking about childhood, not all of them his own. In the background one is aware not just of Rousseau but of practical conversations between Wordsworth and Dorothy about how to

---

[18] See Chapter Two for a discussion of *The Pedlar*, and Chapter Six for Hartley Coleridge's failure to live up to the expectations of his father and Wordsworth.

bring up the five-year-old Basil Montagu.[19] 'We teach him nothing at present', Dorothy writes in March, 'but what he learns from the evidence of his senses':

> He knows his letters, but we have not attempted any further step in the path of *book learning*. Our grand study has been to make him *happy* in which we have not been altogether disappointed . . .

> (*EY*, 180)

Coleridge, influenced by the Wordsworths' stance against systems, has modelled the early childhood of the foundling partly on Basil, partly on Wordsworth himself. The mocking of birdsong could be a detail borrowed from Wordsworth's past,[20] but the process of naming is also symbolic. It gives the child affinities with Adam, and makes of childhood itself the paradise which for Coleridge it had never been.

The account given of the foster-child's booklearning, on the other hand (ll. 42–3), is based on Coleridge's idealized image of himself at the age of six, retreating from the unhappiness of the real world into a life of the mind:

> the School-boys drove me from play, & were always tormenting me—& hence I took no pleasure in boyish sports—but read incessantly. . . . At six years old I remember to have read Belisarius, Robinson Crusoe, & Philip Quarle [Quarll]—and then I found the Arabian Nights' entertainments . . .

> (Griggs, i. 347)

'Should children be permitted to read Romances & Relations of Giants & Magicians, & Genii? he asks, in a letter written within days of *The Foster Mother's Tale*, and answers without hesitation: 'I have formed my faith in the affirmative' (Griggs, i. 354).[21] The imaginative world of books, which gives the mind 'a love of "the Great" & "the Whole"', is a compensation for the Wordsworthian childhood he has not had. It is the mental equivalent of sublime landscape: a means of becoming 'habituated *to the Vast*' (ibid.).

If the first half of *The Foster Mother's Tale* is a composite of childhood

---

[19] For an account of the more ambitious educational scheme proposed by Tom Wedgwood, in 1797, and designed—with the help of Wordsworth and Coleridge—to speed up man's progress towards Godwinian perfection, see David V. Erdman, 'Coleridge, Wordsworth and the Wedgwood Fund: Part 1, Tom Wedgwood's "Master Stroke"' (*BNYPL*, 9, 10 September 1956), 425–43.

[20] See *There was a Boy*, 7–16.

[21] See Griggs, i. 347, for an account of how his father burnt the books Coleridge most enjoyed reading.

experiences, the second mythologizes Coleridge himself. In the behaviour of the youth—his isolation, his premature learning, his apparent madness—one can scarcely fail to see self-portraiture; while the 'unlawful thoughts' (l. 44) recall the 'shapings of the *unregenerate mind*' which had been Coleridge's two years before.[22] The longing 'to hunt for food, and be a naked man' (l. 64) is connected at some level with the abandoned pantisocratic scheme; while the final lines dramatize a personal yearning:

> [He] seiz'd a boat,
> And all alone, set sail by silent moonlight
> Up a great river, great as any sea,
> and ne'er was heard of more: but 'tis suppos'd,
> He liv'd and died among the savage men.

> (ll. 77–81)

There is no other Coleridge poem in which so final an assimilation takes place. Hartley, in *Frost at Midnight*, becomes half-absorbed as a child into the landscape and the godhead; but the foundling (despite the disadvantages of adulthood) is offered the grandest and most romantic of escapes. The poem, which began as an exploration of educational theory (borrowing memories from Wordsworth, as well as ideals) has ended, as wish-fulfilment, with Coleridgean myth.

(iii) *The Poetry of Companionship*

When in late January 1798 Wordsworth begins to write again, after six months of Coleridge's company, a change has come over him also. The major poems of this month are like nothing he has ever written before. *A Night Piece* is his first real landscape-poem since *An Evening Walk* and his first ever description of a visionary moment:

> At last a pleasant instantaneous light
> Startles the musing man whose eyes are bent
> To earth. He looks around, the clouds are split
> Asunder, and above his head he views
> The clear moon & the glory of the heavens.
> There in a black-blue vault she sails along
> Followed by multitudes of stars, that small,
> And bright, & sharp along the gloomy vault
> Drive as she drives.[23]

---

[22] See *The Eolian Harp*, 55, my italics.
[23] *BWS*, 431; ll. 6–14.

Behind this passage is not only the careful naturalism of Dorothy's Journal
entry (on which it is clearly based),[24] but the allegorical significance of
Religious Musings which is its less obvious Coleridgean source:

> As when a Shepherd on a vernal morn
> Thro' some thick fog creeps tim'rous with slow foot,
> Darkling he fixes on th'immediate road
> His downward eye: all else of fairest kind
> Hid or deform'd. But lo, the bursting Sun!
> Touched by th'enchantment of that sudden beam
> Strait the black vapor melteth, and in globes
> Of dewy glitter gems each plant and tree:
> On every leaf, on every blade it hangs!
> Dance glad the new-born intermingling rays,
> And wide around the landscape streams with glory!
>
> (ll. 103–13)

Wordsworth's writing is not didactic, but the shepherd's illumination
leads into his own imaginative claims. Eight months earlier, in *Lines Left
Upon a Seat*, he had echoed the same Coleridgean passage:

> And on these barren rocks, with juniper,
> And heath, and thistle, thinly sprinkled o'er,
> *Fixing his downward eye*, he many an hour
> A morbid pleasure nourished, tracing here
> An emblem of his own unfruitful life . . .
>
> (ll. 25–9; my italics)

Now, as though conscious of the reversal, he stresses release, not an
introverted state of mind:

> There in a black-blue vault she sails along
> Followed by multitudes of stars, that small,
> And bright, & sharp along the gloomy vault
> Drive as she drives. . . .
>   Still they roll along
> Immeasurably distant, and the vault
> Built round by those white clouds, enormous clouds,
> Still deepens its interminable depth.
>
> (ll. 11–14, 16–19)

The moving moon evokes aspiration,[25] and the gloomy vault creates an
impression of unending potential within the mind—as though mental

---

[24] See *DWJ*, 2.   [25] Compare *The Ancient Mariner*, 263–6.

space, like the heavens, 'still deepens its interminable depth' while the poet's vision is sustained.[26] Wordsworth has made no overt allusions, but his return to the passage in *Religious Musings*, via the *Lines Left upon a Seat*, gives a subtle sense of Coleridge's poetic presence. Vision, related not just to expanding mental landscape but to the 'One Life' itself,[27] has replaced a solipsistic view.

In *The Discharged Soldier*, written within days, the preoccupation with mental process continues. The poet's state of mind, not what he meets with on the road, is the centre of attention (ll. 11–20), and his quiescence allows him completely to withdraw from the external scene (ll. 24–7). In this embowered state, the mind takes on the depth of its lonely surroundings, and makes the solitude its own:

> What beauteous pictures now
> Rose in harmonious imagery—they rose
> As from some distant region of my soul
> And came along like dreams . . .
>
> (ll. 28–31)

In *The Borderers* it was suffering that 'had the nature of infinity'. Here it is pleasurable awareness which deepens the mind and reveals 'some distant region of [the] soul'.

Language, in *A Night Piece*, was privately echoic. Now it takes the reader back to Milton, whose presence will later become so dominant:

> While thus I wandered step by step led on,
> It chanced a sudden turning of the road
> Presented to my view an uncouth shape
> So near that, stepping back into the shade
> Of a thick hawthorn, I could mark him well,
> Myself unseen.
>
> (ll. 36–41)

The first line here recalls Christ, in *Paradise Regained*, as he goes into the desert to pray. 'Meanwhile the Son of God', Milton writes,

> One day forth walked alone, the spirit leading
> And his deep thoughts, the better to converse
> With solitude, till far from track of men,

[26] See Kenneth Johnston, 'The Idiom of Vision', *New Perspectives on Coleridge and Wordsworth*, ed. Geoffrey H. Hartman (New York and London, 1972), 1–39.

[27] The lines from *Religious Musings* on which the poem is based are immediately followed by one of Coleridge's central claims: 'There is one Mind, one Omnipresent Mind, |Omnific.' (ll. 114–15).

> *Thought following thought, and step by step led on,*
> He entered now the bordering desert wild,
> And with dark shades and rocks environed round,
> His holy meditations thus pursued.

(Paradise Regained, i. 189–95; my italics)

Coleridge said of *Paradise Lost* that its 'sublimest parts' were the 'revelations of Milton's own mind, producing itself and evolving its own greatness'.[28] In Milton's Christ, we see a forerunner of all those Romantic poet-heroes whose quests are internal. As his steps and his thoughts lead him on, he travels deeper into his solitude. The 'bordering desert wild' in which he finds himself is the landscape of his own mind. As if to confirm that the subject of the writing is subjectivity, Christ asks, in the opening lines of his prayer, some central Romantic questions:

> O what a multitude of thoughts at once
> Awakened in me swarm, while I consider
> What from within I feel myself, and hear
> What from without comes often to my ears . . .

(ll. 196–9)

Questions of this sort had been in Wordsworth's mind as he wrote of the 'beauteous pictures' which 'rose | As from some distant region of [his] soul | And came along like dreams' (ll. 28–31), and they are still important as he describes his dramatic encounter. It is a 'sudden turning of the road' (l. 37) which *presents* the soldier to his view, and he has no proof that what he sees is actually there. The man is a strange combination of private fantasy and literary myth. The second of two Miltonic allusions, present in the phrase 'an uncouth shape', turns him into Death—'The other shape, | If shape it might be called that shape had none' (*PL*, ii. 666–7)— and the poet himself into Satan at the gates of Hell. As Wordsworth proceeds with his interrogation, the echo becomes more appropriate. Milton's Death, like the ghost of Hamlet's father, is a 'questionable shape', and Satan is a questioner:

> Whence and what art thou, execrable shape,
> That darest, though grim and terrible, advance
> Thy miscreated front athwart my way
> To yonder gates?

(PL, II. 681–4)

---

[28] *Coleridge on the Seventeenth Century*, ed. Roberta Florence Brinkley (Durham, 1955), 518.

The literariness of Wordsworth's seeing both imaginatively enhances the poetry and presents imagination itself in a sceptical light. The poem reaches the man's actuality by exposing the poet's transformation of him. All the qualities with which he is initially invested (ghostliness, fixity, inhumanness) are presented as gothic distortions. Each of them must be stripped away, before his matter-of-factness can be revealed.[29] For Wordsworth, as for Lamb, the imagination thrives where 'the seeds of exaggeration' are 'busy . . . and vital';[30] but mistrust accompanies the admission of power.

The new elements in Wordsworth's writing (a concern with mental process, and the sudden prominence of Milton) are mutually enhancing. As the poet turns inward, to observe the workings of his mind, his writing becomes more self-aware: producing its own greatness by reference to other poems. *Kubla Khan*, written the previous November, had enacted the same dual process, but Coleridge's influence is not so specific that it can be pinned down. What matters in this case is not the chronology of change so much as the compatibility, despite difference, of the writers. Both poets are preoccupied with imagination, and both are using verbal reference in new ways.

[29] For a reversal of this process, in *The Leechgatherer*, see Chapter Five below.
[30] See *The Old Benchers of the Inner Temple* in *Elia and the Last Essays of Elia*, ed. E. V. Lucas (1912), 103.

2

Collaboration and Independence:
Alfoxden and the making of a Myth

Bringing *The Prelude* to its conclusion, in May 1805, Wordsworth recalls the year spent at Alfoxden, and, treating it as the source of his creative power, draws from its memory an assurance of Coleridge's continuing support:

> When thou dost to that summer turn thy thoughts,
> And hast before thee all which then we were,
> To thee, in memory of that happiness,
> It will be known—by thee at least, my friend,
> Felt—that the history of a poet's mind
> Is labour not unworthy of regard:
> To thee the work shall justify itself.

> (*1805*, xiii. 404–10)

Mythologized by the passage of time, and by Wordsworth's present sense of loss,[1] the countryside surrounding Alfoxden, with its 'grassy hills' and 'sylvan coombs', has come to seem a paradise.[2] The two poets—companions in their pre-lapsarian state—are permitted to 'range far', and seem unconscious of limits and restrictions. They speak to each other in a language that is joyful and untroubled:

> Thou in delicious words, with happy heart,
> Didst speak the vision of that ancient man,
> The bright-eyed Mariner, and rueful woes
> Didst utter of the Lady Christabel;
> And I, associate in such labour, walked
> Murmuring of him, who—joyous hap—was found,
> After the perils of his moonlight ride,
> Near the loud waterfall, or her who sate
> In misery near the miserable thorn . . .

> (ll. 395–403)

[1] Wordsworth's brother John had been tragically drowned three months before.

[2] The phrase 'sylvan coombs' (l. 394) may in fact echo 'A sylvan scene', used by Milton to describe Eden as it first appeared to Satan (*PL*, iv. 140).

In another context, each of the poems mentioned could be used to draw attention to striking differences, even divisions, between the two writers. Making his selection, Wordsworth must have been aware of painful associations that might be called to mind. *The Ancient Mariner*, insensitively criticized by him in his Note of 1800, and stripped of archaism at his bidding;[3] *Christabel*, excluded from the second volume of *Lyrical Ballads* on the grounds of incompleteness, and destined to remain a fragment forever; *The Thorn* and *The Idiot Boy*, both probably by 1805 rousing in Coleridge the criticisms later expressed in *Biographia*. Yet Wordsworth, grouping the four poems together, seems not to doubt that his friend will be happy with the memories they evoke.

Unmythologized, the Alfoxden period offers no actual collaborations. It was a time of sharing, but of a kind that nourished (and was itself nourished by) creative difference. The story of the two poets' formal attempts to co-operate, first on *The Wanderings of Cain*, then on *The Ancient Mariner*, is well known. According to Coleridge's affectionate account of 1828, the scheme for *The Wanderings of Cain* was abandoned almost at once because of Wordsworth's laughable inability to adapt himself.[4] And though his contributions to *The Ancient Mariner* were more positive, there is no reason to think of him as 'collaborating', in a formal sense, at all.

Writing joint poems could never have worked:[5] the style of the two poets, as Wordsworth himself later put it, '*would not assimilate*'.[6] *Lyrical Ballads*, which critic after critic has contrived to see as a planned and shared enterprise, is in reality a volume of heterogeneous poems which is most unlikely to have been thought out with any care.[7] Coleridge's famous

---

[3] In a letter to Cottle of 24 June 1799, Wordsworth had written, 'From what I can gather it seems that The Ancyent Mariner has upon the whole been an injury to the volume, I mean that the old words and the strangeness of it have deterred readers from going on.' (*EY*, 264.) Archaism is much reduced in 1800, though there is no evidence that Coleridge had thought it a deterrent.

[4] See the Prefatory Note to *The Wanderings of Cain*, *EHC*, i. 287.

[5] It is true that in November 1797 Coleridge had taken over a number of Wordsworth bits and pieces, polishing them up before sending them to the *Morning Post*. But this had been a matter of expediency rather than of shared endeavour. For a detailed account, see Robert Woof 'Wordsworth's Poetry and Stuart's Newspapers: 1797–1803' *SIB*, 15 (1962), 149–89. Parrish discusses *Lyrical Ballads* variants of *The Convict* not included by Woof.

[6] *The Poetical Works of Samuel Taylor Coleridge*, ed. J. D. Campbell (London, 1893), 594; my italics.

[7] To a small extent, the myth surrounding *Lyrical Ballads* was questioned by Mark Reed, in 'Wordsworth, Coleridge, and the "Plan" of the *Lyrical Ballads*' *UTQ*, 34 (April, 1965), 238–53; and by John E. Jordan, *Why the Lyrical Ballads?* (1976), 9–17. But Mary Jacobus, 1–7, seems happy to reinstate it.

account of the division of labour between the supernatural and the poetry of everyday[8] ignores the fact that *The Ancient Mariner* (which constitutes the only 'supernatural' poem in the volume) had long been composed, and was written with other intentions. It seems in fact to have been largely chance that Cottle accepted a volume of shorter poems rather than publishing either *The Borderers* with *Osorio* or *The Ruined Cottage* with *Salisbury Plain*.[9] By the time he chose to do so a large proportion of the ballads had been composed, and those added to the volume show no obvious sign of having been written for a specific purpose. *Tintern Abbey*, aside from *The Ancient Mariner* the greatest poem in the volume, seems to have been put in as an afterthought.

In so far as Wordsworth and Coleridge could ever have been 'joint labourers in the work . . . | Of [man's] redemption' (*1805*, xiii. 439–41) it was presumably on the larger (though at this time not vaguer) scheme of *The Recluse*.[10] But the more ordinary pleasures of walking together, discussing ideas, and making schemes for publication, were what gave the year its excitement. Never again would the two poets have the sort of compatibility which allowed for major differences of opinion, without creating unease.

It is in poems written alongside (and against) each other, not in so-called 'collaborative' schemes, that one finds a true language of allusion. *Frost at Midnight* and *The Pedlar*, written in late February to early March, are the works most referred to in future years. If one puts their famous passages side by side, it seems as though the poets have changed places, for each has adopted the other's voice:

> *thou*, my babe! Shalt wander, like a breeze,
> By lakes and sandy shores, beneath the crags
> Of ancient mountain, and beneath the clouds,
> Which image in their bulk both lakes and shores
> And mountain crags . . .

> (*Frost at Midnight*, 59–63)

---

[8] See *Biographia*, ii. 6–7.   [9] See Griggs, i. 399–400, 402–3.

[10] The scheme for *The Recluse* has as its basis a pantheism which it is possible with Jonathan Wordsworth to see in rather solemn terms as deriving from Coleridge's Unitarianism, and offering a vision of millenarian future happiness (*Borders of Vision*, 320–77). One may on the other hand wish to stress the more personal aspects of the 'One Life' which emerge in the lyricism of the spring:

> Love, now an universal birth,
> From heart to heart is stealing,
> From earth to man, from man to earth,
> —It is the hour of feeling.

> (*Lines written at a Small Distance*, 21–4)

> He had early learned
> To reverence the volume which displays
> The mystery, the life which cannot die,
> But in the mountains did he FEEL his faith,
> There did he see the writing.
>
> (*The Pedlar*, 119–23)

The previous summer, *This Lime Tree Bower* had echoed and built upon *Lines Left upon a Seat*, but now a more complicated merging takes place. Instead of the straightforwardly didactic tones with which Coleridge had introduced his friend to the 'One Life', there is now the confident language in which both poets make their most important claims. And where before the borrowings had been one-sided, expressing the priority and dominance of a single writer, they are now reciprocal—showing the extent to which indebtedness is accompanied (and qualified) by self-definition. There can be little doubt that discussions with Wordsworth, during the autumn and winter of 1797, had interested Coleridge, not just in education (as *The Foster Mother's Tale* has shown) but in the whole question of early childhood. Writing the central passage of *Frost at Midnight*, he reaches back into his past for the source of imaginative power. He sets out to provide, from his own experience (limited as it had been), a basis for Wordsworthian assumptions and ideals:

> and oft belike,
> With unclos'd lids, already had I dreamt
> Of my sweet birthplace, and the old church-tower,
> Whose bells, the poor man's only music, rang
> From morn to evening, all the hot fair-day,
> So sweetly, that they stirr'd and haunted me
> With a wild pleasure, falling on mine ear
> Most like articulate sounds of things to come!
>
> (ll. 26–33)

This is not a genuine 'spot of time', like the more disturbing and traumatic moments of the Goslar *Prelude*, but it is none the less Wordsworthian. Intense and pleasurable childhood experiences are far more common than 'spots' in all the poetry of recollection yet to come.[11] *Tintern Abbey* contains one in which the bells of *Frost at Midnight* are remembered: 'The sounding cataract | Haunted me like a passion' (ll. 76–8). And a line in

---

[11] I distinguish, here, between the 'spots' which genuinely centre on guilt, trauma, or death (*Boatstealing*, *The Drowned Man*, *The Woman on the Hill*, *The Waiting for Horses*) and those which deal with more ordinary pleasures and epiphanies.

1799 Part One modifies Coleridge's phrase 'all the hot Fair-day' in a nostalgic memory of the same kind:

> I, a four years' child . . .
> Made one long bathing of a summer's day,
> Basked in the sun, or plunged into thy streams,
> Alternate, all a summer's day . . .
>
> (l. 17; 19–21)

Both the church bells and fair day are also (subliminally) recalled in the quotation from *Frost at Midnight* with which *The Prelude* opens:

> For this didst thou,
> O Derwent, travelling over the green plains
> Near my 'sweet birthplace', didst thou, beauteous stream,
> Make ceaseless music through the night and day . . .
>
> (*1799*, i. 6–9)

It is perhaps significant, in *Tintern Abbey*, that as the metaphor of haunting moves from Coleridge to Wordsworth, the religious associations of church music are displaced. It is even more so, here, that the music which nourished Wordsworth's childhood could be heard all day long, but also throughout the night.

In a poem written to his brother George, nine months before *Frost at Midnight*, he had revealed the loss and exclusion felt on leaving Ottery as a child:

> To me the Eternal Wisdom hath dispens'd
> A different fortune and more different mind—
> Me from the spot where first I sprang to light
> Too soon transplanted, ere my soul had fix'd
> Its first domestic loves; and hence through life
> Chasing chance-started friendships . . .
>
> (*To the Rev. George Coleridge*, 15–20)

And in *Frost at Midnight* a similar contrast (this time with Wordsworth) is implied:

> For I was rear'd
> In the great city, pent mid cloisters dim,
> And saw nought lovely but the sky and stars.
>
> (ll. 56–8)

The 'hot fair-day' memory seems fragile (even fictional) when compared with Wordsworth's, not just because it is by inference single, rather than continuous, but because it is clouded by the sense of difference and inferiority Coleridge feels. The fluttering '*stranger*', imprisoned behind 'bars', is an image, in both its adult and childhood contexts, of entrapment and discontent. Coleridge arrives at release through recollection, but as in *This Lime Tree Bower*, it is a release that is artificially arranged. What one actually remembers about *Frost at Midnight* is its chinese box effect: an imprisoned man, recalling his imprisoned childhood, recalling another childhood in which he was free. The structure is itself a kind of trap: initially, for the reader, who believes that beyond the final imprisonment there is a primal freedom; permanently, for the poem, because the intensity of present exclusion is shown inevitably to qualify what is past. It is as though the prophetic music is invented, to prevent the infinite regression of imprisonments that might otherwise happen.

If Coleridge envied his brother, for being privileged to return to their 'sweet birthplace' from the 'turmoil of the world' (*To the Rev. G. Coleridge*, 3), he envies Wordsworth more. Rhythmically echoing this earlier poem ('To me the Eternal wisdom hath dispens'd | A different fortune, and more different mind') are the lines addressed to Hartley in which a need for compensation emerges:

> My babe so beautiful! it fills my heart
> With tender gladness, thus to look at thee,
> And think that thou shalt learn far other lore,
> And in far other scenes!
>
> (ll. 53–6)

The future wished on the child is a blending of Wordsworthian and Coleridgean elements. The landscape in which he will wander 'like a breeze' is based on nothing Coleridge himself has ever seen. Its 'lakes and sandy shores', its 'crags | Of ancient mountain' belong, not to Devonshire or Somerset, but to the Cumbrian scenery of Wordsworth's boyhood, recreated here as a sort of *capriccio* setting for the child. Into this landscape, which one day (though Coleridge cannot foresee it) will indeed be Hartley's, the poet introduces his Berkeleyan view of Nature as the symbolic language of God. It is a view which formed no part of Wordsworth's childhood experience, and was seldom invoked by him as an adult. Hartley will fulfil the expectations raised by Coleridge's theoretical claims. Subjected to 'The lovely shapes and sounds intelligible' (l. 64) of God's 'eternal language', he will read the symbols intuitively, no 'stern preceptor' forcing him to learn the alphabet:

> Great universal Teacher! he shall mould
> Thy spirit, and by giving make it ask.

(ll. 68–9)

Imaginative vision, in Coleridge's poetry, is always vicariously achieved. In *This Lime Tree Bower*, Lamb had seen God from his hilltop as the poet's proxy—but in a repetition of his personal experience (or so the poem later claims).[12] Hartley's absorption of the 'One Life' takes place in a future tense that is more obviously wishful. In both poems, a sense of insecurity underlies the claims being made; and in each case it arises from our awareness of a distance between the poet's chosen surrogate and himself. *Frost at Midnight* is vulnerable twice over. The personal memory it celebrates early on is itself isolated and fragile; and the future it arranges is a confession of need. The fictionality of Hartley's idyllic childhood seems almost to acknowledge that Coleridge's 'hot fair-day' was a dream. It is the poet's sense of envy, above all, which finally emerges.

The blessing on Hartley offers an ideal childhood in which Wordsworth's actual experience and Coleridge's theoretical beliefs are fused. *The Pedlar*, written in the same month, embodies the reverse. Personal recollections do not underlie and direct Wordsworth's account of the perfect education, so much as modify and offset its Coleridgean emphasis. Where Coleridge achieves a synthesis between his own theory and his friend's practice, Wordsworth grafts personal memories onto a dogma that is borrowed. The result is a much less unified poem than critics have made out: where Hartley's childhood is integrated, the Pedlar's is an amalgam of elements which do not work together. Coleridge's presence is everywhere to be felt, but Wordsworth tests his ideas, and pulls against them, in order to define his own.

On first reading, it is the wholly Coleridgean elements which stand out:

> His mind was a thanksgiving to the power
> That made him. It was blessedness and love.

(ll. 113–14)

Structure, language, tone, assumptions, are all of them borrowed. Even the balancing of phrases brings Coleridge to mind:

> No wish profan'd my overwhelméd heart
> Blest hour! It was a luxury,—to be!

(*Reflections*, 41–2)

---

[12] See ll. 37–9 of the text published in *The Annual Anthology*, 1800.

This unquestioning absorption of Coleridge's ideas seems most often to occur in visionary moments, where a language to describe what is taking place has already been used in allusive exchange. 'In all things | He saw one life', Wordsworth writes, in the most quoted lines of the poem, 'and felt that it was joy' (ll. 217–18). The familiar abstract noun takes one back to *This Lime Tree Bower*, as do the more detailed resonances which follow:

> One song they sang, and it was audible—
> Most audible then when the fleshly ear,
> O'ercome by grosser prelude of that strain
> Forgot its functions, and slept undisturbed.
>
> (ll. 219–22)

The words 'fleshly' and 'grosser' clearly echo an earlier phrase 'Less gross than bodily' (*This Lime Tree Bower*, 23) and the dimming of sensory experience recalls the 'swimming sense' which had accompanied Lamb's vision of God. Former patterns of epiphany are borrowed because they are part of a language for the 'One Life' which is easily shared.

On further acquaintance, however, the poem's more complicated structures of allusion are revealed. Wordsworth does not just defer to Coleridge, by imparting his doctrine, but supplants him while keeping the propaganda intact. In a radical rereading of *The Foster Mother's Tale*, from the previous autumn, he trumps Coleridge in Coleridgean terms. *This Lime Tree Bower* had corrected *Lines Left upon a Seat* by showing how not to be a selfish recluse. *The Pedlar* corrects *The Foster Mother's Tale* by offering an education that works, and a visionary figure who teaches the 'One Life' to others, instead of escaping to foreign lands.

It is a strategic process, worth detailed observation. We are shown, first, a resistance to formal education:

> Though he was untaught,
> In the dead lore of schools undisciplined,
> Why should he grieve? He was a chosen son.
>
> (ll. 324–6)

The 'pretty boy' of Coleridge's poem, though similarly 'most unteachable' (l. 29), had lived as one of the elect only till adolescence came, when he turned mad through excessive reading. The Pedlar's immunity is less short-lived. Geometry, which has for him an abstract fascination, is kept in its place by the grandeur of visible forms. He brings 'austere truth' alive by clothing it in the 'hues' of a familiar landscape (ll. 161–3). And he responds to the perfection of geometric shapes via the taste for grandeur which early life has ensured: 'His triangles they were the stars of heaven, | The silent stars' (ll. 166–7). Nothing can make him betray his primal bond with Nature: he remains unseduced by books, abstract thoughts, and education.

The foster child, 'ere his twentieth year', had read so much that 'his brain turn'd' and 'He had unlawful thoughts of many things' (ll. 43–4). The Pedlar undergoes a comparable breakdown, at the same age, but for different reasons:

> now, before his twentieth year was passed,
> Accumulated feelings pressed his heart
> With an encreasing weight; he was o'erpowered
> By Nature, and his spirit was on fire
> With restless thoughts.

(ll. 185–9)

He is at the same turning-point as the foster child, and in the same danger of becoming solipsistic (ll. 194–6; 201–3), but his madness, far from being crippling, is temporary and beneficial. 'Resolved' because of the excessive power of Nature, 'to quit his native hills' (l. 226), he leaves behind a landscape which for all its sublimity has become constricting. Love of Nature genuinely leads to love of Man: not only does he manage to keep his responsiveness (unusual for an adult);[13] he finds his early vision enlarged and revitalized by contacts outside the mind. Like Luke in *Michael*, he leaves home with his father's uneasy blessing.[14] Unlike him, he thrives on being subjected to the corruption of city life:

> He walked
> Among the impure haunts of vulgar men
> Unstained; the talisman of constant thought
> And kind sensations in a gentle heart
> Preserved him.

(ll. 249–53)

He goes beyond the privacy of his early relationship with God, into a context where his own education can be passed on. As an exemplar of Coleridge's central values, he offers a critique of the selfishness involved in escaping up rivers to live and die among savage men.[15] At the time of writing, *The Foster Mother's Tale* had offered a valid imaginative solution

---

[13] See Chapter Six, below.
[14] See *Michael*, 422–33.
[15] See *The Foster Mother's Tale*, 77–81.

to the problem of being a visionary outsider. Wordsworth shows that it is no longer valid; yet he does so in terms that are Coleridge's own.

Aside from its didactic purpose, *The Pedlar* is also intended to explain the 'special privilege' which Wordsworth's childhood has supposedly given him. In this respect, the poem is not just broadly 'un-Coleridgean', but private to Wordsworth himself, celebrating values which cannot be shared. The 'communion, not from terror free', and especially the detail of the hills growing larger in the darkness (ll. 19–25) take the reader straight to the Wordsworthian childhood of the Goslar *Prelude*, and show the poet questing for the secret origins of adult power. Associationism, too, despite its obvious Coleridgean relevance, becomes an idiosyncratic process. Where Coleridge responds to Hartley in theoretical terms, Wordsworth interprets his psychology as literal fact. Great objects, rather than merely their likenesses, are impressed directly onto the mind by the power of 'deep feelings' (ll. 30–1). They lie there—unmodified as yet by imagination—with all the weight, colour, and texture of material substances, and their presence 'haunts' the 'bodily sense' like an ache or passion (ll. 33–4).[16] It is only at a secondary stage, after the receiving process has taken place, that the mind plays a more active role, and gives to the impressions an independent mental life (ll. 34–43). Though he had not written about it before, there is every reason to suppose that the 'special gift' Wordsworth ascribes to the Pedlar—the gift of receiving, storing, 'fasten'ing' images (l. 40)—is something he himself had possessed as a boy. A letter of 1790, written before he encountered Hartley's ideas,[17] establishes that at least by that stage he is thinking in the Pedlar's associationist terms. 'Again and again', he writes to Dorothy from the Alps,

in quitting a fortunate station have I returned to it with the most eager avidity, with the hope of bearing away a more lively picture. At this moment when many of these landscapes are floating before my mind, I feel a high [enjoyment] in reflecting that perhaps scarce a day of my life will pass [in] which I shall not derive some happiness from these images.

(*EY*, 35–6)

16 Compare *Tintern Abbey*, 77–8.
17 Despite the views of Alan Grob, *The Philosophic Mind: A Study of Wordsworth's Poetry and Thought, 1795–1805* (Colombus, Ohio, 1973), there is no reason to think that Wordsworth was ever sharply aware of Locke. To judge from the 1794 revisions of *An Evening Walk*, he first encountered Hartleyan associationism in poetic form, in Rogers' *Pleasures of Memory* (1792). It plays no part in his own work between 1794 and *The Pedlar*, except for an isolated reference in *The Borderers* (IV. ii. 133–5) which could be a revision inspired by Coleridge.

The Pedlar had been prepared 'While yet a child and *long before his time*' (l. 28; my italics) to receive the lesson of universal love. Similarly, the 'intense conceptions' of Wordsworth's own childhood had made way for the Hartleyan lesson Coleridge would teach him. He was by nature an associationist thinker. The philosophical system he encountered in 1797–8 served merely as a framework for his own ideas.

Berkeley, on the other hand, offers a (to Wordsworth) rather alien way of seeing. Six years later, in *The Prelude*, this is tacitly acknowledged:

> Nature's secondary grace,
> That outward illustration which is hers,
> Hath hitherto been barely touched upon:
> The charm more superficial and yet sweet,
> Which from her works finds way, contemplated
> As they hold forth a genuine counterpart
> And softening mirror of the moral world.

> (*1805*, xiii. 282–7)

There could be no better illustration, either of the natural differences between Wordsworth and Coleridge, or of their continuing need to take each other into account. A lack of sympathy is apparent in Wordsworth's tone of voice; but obligation forces him into an uneasy reference to the once dominant Berkeleyan view. In *The Pedlar*, the same process is already at work, though less guilt is involved. One is aware that Wordsworth himself is no symbolist: he needs a 'centre palpable' for his thoughts to revolve around.[18] But Berkeleyan ways of thinking must be given prominence, if only for Coleridge's sake.

Where Berkeley is present, then, it is either in the form of direct borrowings from a Coleridgean source, or in passages that are openly analogous to his didactic assertions. As a rule, these passages are neither successfully integrated, nor turned by Wordsworth into something his own. But there is one exception. Taking an idea that is spelt out in *Destiny of Nations*—'all that meets the bodily sense I deem | Symbolical, one mighty alphabet | For infant minds' (ll. 18–20)—Wordsworth rewrites it in his own terms:

> Oh *then* how beautiful, how bright, appeared
> The written promise. He had early learned

---

[18] See Wordsworth's own contrast, in Book Eight of *The Prelude*, between Coleridge the city dweller, 'in endless dreams | Of sickness, disjoining, joining things, | Without the light of knowledge' (ll. 608–10), and himself: 'I had forms distinct | To steady me. These thoughts did oft revolve | About some centre palpable' (viii. 598–600).

> To reverence the volume which displays
> The mystery, the life which cannot die,
> But in the mountains did he FEEL his faith,
> There did he see the writing.

(ll. 118–23)

All the Coleridgean ingredients are there, but theory is subordinated to practice, seeing to feeling. After he has released the power of his own spontaneous affirmation, Wordsworth is obliged to add a balancing Coleridgean clause. Yet the effect is to make the first look like a genuine claim, the second a tame concession. It may be unconsciously achieved, but it is a striking example of revisionism.

Other examples, outside a specifically Berkeleyan context, are just as intriguing. When he writes 'Such hour by prayer or praise was unprofaned' (l. 111), Wordsworth has, as we know, a Coleridgean source in mind: 'No wish profan'd my overwhelméd heart. | Blest hour! It was a luxury—to be!' He is, on the surface, accepting his friend's valuation of unconscious response.[19] But the echo, instead of highlighting agreement, tacitly undermines what Coleridge is saying. It suggests that prayer and praise, like 'wish', are conscious activities which interfere with joy, whereas in Coleridge's terms they are nothing of the sort. 'Nor did he *believe*; he saw' (l. 128) is another case in point. 'Seeing' this time is not the reading of sign-language,[20] but mere sensuous apprehension, which traditionally is of no importance beside an act of faith. To Wordsworth, it seems, the opposite is true. Defining himself against Coleridge's theoretical position, he is asserting the value of spontaneous response, and literal reality, in their own terms.

But it is Wordsworth's preoccupation with mental process, valued for itself, not for its connections with the 'One Life', that most distinguishes him from his friend:

> in the after day
> Of boyhood, many an hour in caves forlorn
> And in the hollow depths of naked crags
> He sate, and even in their fixed lineaments,
> Or from the power of a peculiar eye,
> Or by creative feeling overborne,

---

[19] See the blessing of the watersnakes in *The Ancient Mariner*: 'A spring of love gusht from my heart, | And I bless'd them unaware' (ll. 276–7), and the definition in *Biographia Literaria* of the secondary imagination as 'co-existing with the conscious will' (*Biographia*, i. 304).

[20] Contrast *The Pedlar*, 123.

> Or by predominance of thought oppressed,
> Even in their fixed and steady lineaments
> He traced an ebbing and a flowing mind,
> Expression ever varying.
>
> (ll. 48–57)

If it were Coleridge's poem one would expect the ebbing and flowing mind to belong to God. Wordsworth's language, in its hesitant ambiguity, tempts one with the suggestion that it could be his own. A few months away, in *Tintern Abbey*, is the celebration of 'the mighty world | Of eye and ear, both what they half-create, | And what perceive' (ll. 106–8). And in the 'Climbing of Snowdon' (February 1804) Wordsworth is to describe imagination as 'the sense of God, or whatso'er is dim | Or vast in its own being' (*1805*, xiii. 72–3). The greatest of his claims for the mind are characterized by indeterminacy—by a hedging of bets, in which the godhead and human potential are given equal weight. It is not always an equality that can be preserved (usurpation, either divine or human, tends naturally to take place) but it is one he aims for. The two poets, in this as in other important respects, are fundamentally different. Wordsworth, a 'semi-atheist' (for all the apparent absorption of his friend's views) can readily accept the imaginative challenge of displacing God. Coleridge, always and inescapably theocentric, can not. The temptation to do so is undeniable, but a cutting-off point always comes. Either the voice of orthodoxy intrudes, to rebuke such 'shapings of the unregenerate mind' (*The Eolian Harp*, 55), or vision occurs vicariously, at a distance that is safe.

It is one of *The Pedlar*'s striking features that it offers, alongside each other, the great didactic assertions of Coleridge and the very different (imaginative and personal) claims of Wordsworth himself. It is not a unified poem, because it is in effect written by two people—sustained, that is, by impulses which move naturally in different directions, though for the moment they are uneasily poised. At no other time in Wordsworth's career will such a balance be possible. In later years, the Coleridgean element in his poetry takes second place, as he becomes more dominant in the relationship itself, and more confident in his own right. But in February 1798, when his deference is at its height, a kind of strained equality is maintained. *The Pedlar* succeeds in at once celebrating the 'One Life' and offering a critique of Coleridge's ways of thinking.

The 'golden age' at Alfoxden had begun in July 1797 with a relationship in which Coleridge, though hero-worshipping Wordsworth, was unquestionably the more dominant of the two. It ends, a year later,[21] with the roles largely reversed. This about-turn is anticipated in *The Pedlar*'s challenging of Coleridgean abstraction, but not properly under way until two months later. Three poems written in April—*The Nightingale*, *Fears in Solitude*, and *Peter Bell*—establish the relationship on its new footing. *Tintern Abbey*, composed in July, offers a kind of postscript to the Alfoxden era.

The Nightingale, written after nine months of companionship and creative interchange, recalls and renews the values of *This Lime Tree Bower*. On this occasion, though, Coleridge is not correcting William and Dorothy in their ways of seeing, but using the language of allusion to express views they share. The nightingale's song, breaking the evening's stillness, is like the '*stranger*' in *Frost at Midnight*: it both mirrors and focuses meditation, ordering the associations and allusions through which the poem moves. As this connective sequence unfolds, the reader listens in, as it were, on an increasingly confidential discussion. The 'poor wretch' who 'fill[s] all things with himself' (l. 19) is a composite figure. He recalls the solitary of *Lines Left upon a Seat*, 'fixing his downward eye' on the rocks, and 'tracing here | An emblem of his own unfruitful life' (*Lines Left upon a Seat*, 28–9). He also (less saliently) reminds one of Coleridge himself, creating his own mental prison in *This Lime Tree Bower*. At once calling up, and disowning, his resemblance to this solipsistic man, Coleridge goes on to contrast the artificial poet (a city-dweller, who constructs poems about birds he never hears) with the genuine visionary, 'surrendering his whole spirit' to Nature's language (ll. 23–39). The latter is of course an embodiment of Wordsworthian ideals, resembling not only the 'dreaming man' of *The Ruined Cottage*—who 'on the soft cool moss | Extends his limbs', half-listening to a nearby wren (ll. 10–18)—but also the Pedlar himself, drinking the spectacle of joy, and allowing 'Sensation, soul, and form' to melt into him (ll. 103–4). The city bard, on the other hand, represents Coleridge's former self—the poet who, in 1795, had written a love-poem entitled *To the Nightingale*, conceitedly echoing Milton's conceit (l. 17) and using the phrase 'pity-pleading strains' (l. 11) in all seriousness.

Usually, in Wordsworth's and Coleridge's writing, the contrast between city and country draws attention to unchangeable differences between the two friends. On this occasion Coleridge at least *asks* it to do the reverse. Parodying his own earlier assumptions, he grants himself temporary membership of the Wordsworthian elect. 'My Friend', he

---

[21] Effectively in late June, when the lease on Alfoxden House runs out.

writes, turning from the 'youths and maidens most poetical' to his companion on the mossy bridge,

> My Friend, and thou, our Sister! we have learnt
> A different lore: we may not thus profane
> Nature's sweet voices, always full of love
> And joyance!
>
> (ll. 40–3)

The reference to *Frost at Midnight*, in 'we have learnt | A different lore', accentuates change. Two months ago, it had seemed possible for Coleridge to receive a Wordsworthian education only through his son Hartley. Now (or so the echoic language seems to claim) fulfilment is vicarious no longer. Retrospectively, and by implication through Wordsworth's companionship, he has been given the 'special privilege' he had earlier wished on his son.

The central passage of the poem (ll. 69–86) is an allusive portrait, designed for a private audience as a tribute not just to Dorothy herself but to the values she, Wordsworth, and Coleridge have shared. Her Journal is a focal point for the poetry of this period, and she is given, here, the status of poet herself. Not only does she, like the foster-child, know 'all the notes' of birds (l. 74); she is also the witness, in 'a pause of silence' (l. 77) which anticipates *There was a Boy*,[22] to a universal awakening. The climax of the poem (when the moon emerges from the clouds) is based on *A Night Piece*, itself drawn from one of her journal entries. Early Coleridge, too, is present. The elation described as 'choral minstrelsy' has its origins in *Reflections on Having Left a Place of Retirement*,[23] and is also consciously associated in Wordsworth's mind with the climax of *The Eolian Harp*.[24] This figure, then, like that of the reclining poet earlier on, provides a focus for Coleridgean ideals which have been modified, and given immediacy, by contact with Wordsworth.

The episode involving the child Hartley (which was presumably the poem's starting point) is given pride of place at the end, as though deliberately remembering *Frost at Midnight*. Coleridge introduces it by setting up Hartley as a young prophet—incapable of 'articulate sound', but with much precocious wisdom to offer:

> How he would place his hand beside his ear,
> His little hand, the small forefinger up,
> And bid us listen!
>
> (ll. 94–6)

---

[22] See l. 17.   [23] See the 'Unearthly minstrelsy' of l. 24.   [24] See ll. 44–8.

In his affinity with the moon, Hartley shows a responsiveness that is like the nightingales' joy:

> I hurried with him to our orchard-plot,
> And he beheld the moon, and, hushed at once,
> Suspends his sobs, and laughs most silently,
> While his fair eyes, that swam with undropped tears,
> Did glitter in the yellow moon-beam!

(ll. 101–5)

The glittering eyes recall not just the nightingales within the same poem (ll. 66–7), but the prophetic and experienced gaze of the Ancient Mariner. Like the bird-child of *The Foster Mother's Tale*, Hartley exists between two worlds. He carries about with him, in his human existence, an uncanny awareness of 'something more than Nature'.

It is, as the poem itself admits, 'a father's tale'. But despite the indulgence, it has an important didactic purpose. Coleridge is reaffirming, here, the Hartleyan philosophy which gave the child his name, and which (as *The Pedlar* has shown) is so important to Wordsworth:

> But if that Heaven
> Should give me life, his childhood shall grow up
> Familiar with these songs, that with the night
> He may associate joy.

(ll. 106–9)

The future Coleridge had wished (or foisted) on his son in *Frost at Midnight* is seen by him to be coming true. Living as a child of nature, and possessing an uncommon spiritual aptitude for perceiving joy, the child is the embodiment of shared ideals. He perpetuates Wordsworth's own childhood; he also validates the theories his father has evolved. His responsiveness, at the end of *The Nightingale*, is a guarantee of continued sharing: an insurance against inevitable change.[25] If life passes into fiction, then fiction in its turn can be used to impose patterns on life.

There is a tendency to stereotype the Coleridge of Alfoxden. Either he is the poet of *Kubla Khan*, *The Ancient Mariner*, and *Christabel* Part One, or he is the writer of 'Conversation Poems'. But there is another Coleridge, whose implications for the relationship with Wordsworth are equally important: the author of *France: an Ode*, *Recantation* and *Fears in*

---

[25] For an examination of the ways in which Hartley's symbolic value is undermined by the passage of time and by changes taking place in Wordsworth's and Coleridge's relationship, see Chapter Six, below.

Solitude. The last of these especially is a reminder of the extraordinary seriousness with which he took his own prophetic role:

> We have offended, O my countrymen!
> We have offended very grievously . . .
>
> (ll. 42–3)

Nothing could be more different, either from the personal, meditative tones of *The Nightingale* itself, or from the affectionate whimsicality of its companion-piece:

> In stale blank-verse a subject stale
> I send *per post* my *Nightingale*
> And like an honest bard, dear Wordsworth
> You'll tell me what you think, my Bird's worth.

It is no accident that the style and mood of *Fears in Solitude* go back to the period of *The Watchman* and the final apocalyptic sections of *Religious Musings*. The threat of French invasion in April 1798 turns Coleridge's mind once again to asking questions about his favoured and contemplative way of life. Now, however, the situation is importantly different from that in *Reflections on Having Left a Place of Retirement.* In place of the self-accusation of February 1796—'Was it right | While my unnumber'd brethren toil'd and bled, | That I should dream away the entrusted hours . . .' (ll. 44–6)—there is a sympathetic and confident portrayal of the meditative life that has to be interrupted:

> My God! it is a melancholy thing
> For such a man, who would full fain preserve
> His soul in calmness, yet perforce must feel
> For all his human brethren—O my God,
> It is indeed a melancholy thing,
> And weighs upon the heart, that he must think
> What uproar and what strife may now be stirring
> This way or that way o'er these silent hills . . .
>
> (*Fears in Solitude*, 29–36)

In his poem, Coleridge accepts a call to take up arms, but he does so without undermining the significance of the reclusive way of life.

It is Wordsworth's presence, of course, that explains this crucial change. As *The Nightingale* has shown, the values of solitude are now shared, and as *The Pedlar* had demonstrated, they are capable of wider implications. More than that, they are to be the subject of a redemptive work, showing what truly 'fraternizes' man. The Watchman, though he seemed at the time to have '*watched in vain!*',[26] turns out to have been cast in the role of John the Baptist: *Fears in Solitude*, written six weeks after Wordsworth's first announcement of *The Recluse*,[27] is a sort of trailer for the major work.

We begin, as in *The Ruined Cottage*, with a study of the man who has known 'meditative joy', and is capable of reading Nature as a religious text: a study of Coleridge at his most Wordsworthian, or of Wordsworth in the Pedlar's guise:

> Here he might lie on fern or wither'd heath,
> While from the singing lark (that sings unseen
> The minstrelsy which solitude loves best)
> And from the sun, and from the breezy air,
> Sweet influences trembled o'er his frame;
> And he with many feelings, many thoughts,
> Made up a meditative joy, and found
> Religious meanings in the forms of nature!
>
> (ll. 17–24)

But this time the poetry moves out into the world of war-wounds and slavery. The poem contains a magnificent indictment not just of governments, but of the whole 'Benefit-Club for mutual flattery' that society has become. The Blake of *Songs of Experience* could not better Coleridge's account of war reports and 'dainty terms for fratricide'—

> Terms which we trundle smoothly o'er our tongues
> Like mere abstractions, empty sounds to which
> We join no feeling and attach no form,
> As if the soldier died without a wound;
> As if the fibres of this godlike frame
> Were gor'd without a pang: as if the wretch,
> Who fell in battle doing bloody deeds,
> Passed off to heaven, *translated* and not kill'd;
> As tho' he had no wife to pine for him,
> No God to judge him!
>
> (ll. 111–20)

This is satire of a passionate kind—sharper, more articulate than *Salisbury Plain*, and not afraid of its implications: 'Therefore evil

---

[26] See the last words of Coleridge's *Address to the Readers of The Watchman* (May 1796), *CC*, ii. 375.

[27] 'My object is to give pictures of Nature, Man, and Society', Wordsworth writes to Tobin on 6 March 1798. 'Indeed', he continues, 'I know not any thing which will not come within the scope of my plan.' (*EY*, 212)

days | Are coming on us, O my countrymen!' (ll. 120–1) But how, one wonders, did Wordsworth respond? The poem returns to values, and a life, that are very much his own,[28] but not before it has offered a completely daunting view of the role of *The Recluse*. Wordsworth was ready to accept that the 'One Life' should have a social message, as *The Pedlar* had shown; and he had seen it at that time in Coleridge's messianic terms. But was he still, two months later, so committed? Did he feel he had the qualifications for the task he had been set?

The poetry he does write in April 1798 could scarcely be more different from Coleridge's ambitions for him. *Peter Bell*, begun by coincidence on the same day as *Fears in Solitude*,[29] shows him cheerfully unaware of his duty to *The Recluse*, and responsive instead to the more immediate claims of his imagination:

> There's something in a flying horse,
> There's something in a huge balloon,
> But through the clouds I'll never float
> Untill I have a little boat
> In shape just like the crescent moon.
>
> (ll. 1–5)[30]

It is poetry inspired by *The Ancient Mariner*—

> The moving Moon went up the sky
> And nowhere did abide:
> Softly she was going up
> And a star or two beside—
>
> (ll. 255–9)

—but poetry in which Coleridge's yearning aspiration has been playfully transformed. No devaluation has taken place: the symbols of moon and sea-voyage are just as Romantic as in their original context. But their conflation has its whimsical side, and this adds to the Wordsworthian 'glee' on which (as if by an act of faith) the poem is carried along.

It has been the custom to read *Peter Bell* in terms of the opposition between the supernatural and the everyday which Wordsworth himself sets up:

---

[28] The 'lakes and mountain-hills', the 'clouds' and 'quiet dales' (ll. 181–2) belong to a Cumbrian landscape, and Coleridge's reference to drinking 'all his intellectual life' recalls *The Pedlar*: 'his spirit drank | The spectacle.' (ll. 102–3)

[29] See Dorothy's Journal entry for 20 April (*DWJ*, 14).

[30] Text from *Peter Bell MS 2*. See Jordan, 44.

'Long have I lov'd what I behold,
The night that calms, the day that cheers;
The common growth of mother earth
Suffices me—her tears, her mirth,
Her humblest mirth and tears.

'The dragon's wing, the magic ring,
I shall not covet for my dower,
If I along that lowly way
With sympathetic heart may stray
And with a soul of power.

'These given, what more need I desire,
To stir—to soothe—or elevate?
What nobler marvels than the mind
May in life's daily prospect find,
May find or there create? . . .'

(*Prologue*, 136–50)[31]

But these famous and quotable lines were not written until 1806, and the
pattern they impose is tidier than the facts.[32] Like Coleridge's account of
the making of *Lyrical Ballads*, they suggest a division of labour which is a
rationalization (not a reconstruction) of different ways of seeing. The
contrast is easily grasped; but its convenience is an evasion of the more
subtle ways in which divergence happens.

If *Peter Bell* challenges Coleridge, it is not on theoretical grounds. The
narrative itself has affinities with *The Ancient Mariner*, and Mary Jacobus
is right in directing our attention also to important contrasts: 'Where
Coleridge's Ancient Mariner is alienated from the spiritual world, Peter is
alienated from the world of human feeling; shooting the albatross does
violence to a cosmic harmony, but beating the ass does violence to human
values (love, fidelity, and tenderness).' (Jacobus, 265) In terms of the
'Prologue', however, this opposition does not apply. The poetry has a
playfulness that offsets solemnity, and a concern with mental process that
makes none of the grander claims:

Away we go and what care we
For treasons, tumults, and for wars;
We are as calm in our delight
As is the crescent moon so bright
Among the scattered stars.

(ll. 26–30)

[31] Jordan, 55 (Not in MS 2).
[32] John E. Jordan, 'The Hewing of *Peter Bell*', *SEL*, 7, no. 4 (autumn 1967), 568, argues
that the lines probably date from after 1812, and characterize a later Wordsworth.

If the 'Prologue' is a manifesto,[33] then it is one that exalts enjoyment, pleasure, and fanciful response. The words 'I feel I am a man' do not amount to a solemn poetic credo but draw attention to the delight that emotion (of an unsophisticated kind) can give.[34] As in *The Idiot Boy*, this delight goes side by side with a deflation not just of the poet himself, but of the values his writing sustains. 'Oh! my poor heart's commotion!' (l. 50) for instance, recalls the first of the Higginbottom Sonnets, 'Ah! my *poor heart's* INEXPLICABLE SWELL!' (l. 14) Wordsworth, alongside Coleridge, is exciting 'a good-natured laugh at the spirit of *doleful egotism*',[35] but in a context where the 'heart's commotion' is highly prized. The comedy of the poem works constantly to undercut the serious readings one might impose upon it, and at the same time enhances what one should value most.

A Coleridgean belief in the 'One Life' must of course be implicit in the moral of *Peter Bell*; and Wordsworth does incorporate into *The Ruined Cottage*, at around this time, a reference to *The Ancient Mariner* which shows him adopting its didactic framework almost wholesale.[36] But outside a strictly moral context, his friend's influence is barely perceptible in the latter part of the spring. Two months before, when writing *The Pedlar*, he had begun the process of defining himself against Coleridge in Coleridgean terms. Now, having found a style and mood that are his own, he goes further. He does not reject the values which lie behind *The Recluse*, but his writing suggests an avoidance of the task he has been set, and an insistence on *not* taking Coleridge's views into account. Independence, from now on, will be more significant than collaboration.

Tintern Abbey is the last and greatest poem of the Alfoxden period. Written in July 1798, it comes between the Wordsworths' departure from Alfoxden House and their delivery to Cottle in Bristol of the manuscript of *Lyrical Ballads*: both symbolic events, marking the completion of a creative partnership and the ending of an era. It is the first poem in which the year shared with Coleridge is treated as a 'golden age', and in it one sees the origin of a private myth.

[33] Jacobus, 262–72.
[34] The 'Prologue' can be seen in many ways as an anticipation of the fanciful lyric writing of spring 1802. See Chapter Four, below.
[35] See *Biographia*, i. 27.
[36]   'I turned to the old man, & said my friend
                       Your words have consecrated many things
                       And for the tale which you have told I think
                       I am a better and a wiser man

                                    (Cancelled passage from *MS B*; Butler, 259).

Loss, on several different levels—sometimes distinct, more often seemingly confused—is the poem's real subject. On the surface, it explores change after a period of five years. On closer inspection, it involves many kinds and stages of looking back. Wordsworth uses the religious language of *The Pedlar* and *This Lime Tree Bower* to celebrate moments when 'we are laid asleep | In body, and become a living soul' (ll. 46–7). Such moments are based on a faith in the Coleridgean 'One Life' which, five months before, Wordsworth had partially held. Now, however, he feels doubts, which the language of allusion is there to hold at bay:

> If this
> Be but a vain belief, yet, oh! how oft,
> In darkness, and amid the many shapes
> Of joyless day-light; when the fretful stir
> Unprofitable, and the fever of the world,
> Have hung upon the beatings of my heart,
> How oft, in spirit, have I turned to thee
> O sylvan Wye! Thou wanderer through the woods,
> How often has my spirit turned to thee!
>
> (ll. 50–8)

Frost at Midnight is remembered, not just in the yearning nostalgic tone, but in the words themselves:

> How often in my early school-boy days,
> With most believing superstitious wish
> Presageful have I gaz'd upon the bars,
> To watch the *stranger* there!
>
> (ll. 28–31)

In Coleridge's isolation, the grate had seemed a kind of prison. He had 'gaz'd upon the bars' and longed for liberation from himself. Wordsworth, similarly trapped, turns to the Wye for release through recollection.[37] As he borrows the language of Coleridge's most private and personal writing to date, he draws not only on his wishfulness,[38] but on the commitment to shared ideals which retrospectively seems to typify the Alfoxden relationship. It is the first example of a nostalgic echo, and it comes at a

---

[37] At a later stage, when Coleridge comes to revise *Frost at Midnight*, he presumably remembers *Tintern Abbey*, for the line 'How often in my early school-boy days' is altered to read 'But O! how oft, | How oft, at school, with most believing mind . . .' (ll. 23–4).

[38] In *Frost at Midnight* it had been the 'most believing superstitious wish' of childhood that allowed the adult Coleridge to escape from himself.

moment when faith begins to weaken. A significant pattern, for it shows that allusion is essentially strategic: a means of recovering strength and revisiting sources of power.

As *Tintern Abbey* continues, further layers of past experience are uncovered. Reaching back beyond the Alfoxden relationship, Wordsworth recalls the period immediately preceding Coleridge's influence upon him:

> And so I dare to hope
> Though changed, no doubt, from what I was, when first
> I came among these hills; when like a roe
> I bounded o'er the mountains, by the sides
> Of the deep rivers, and the lonely streams,
> Wherever nature led; more like a man
> Flying from something that he dreads, than one
> Who sought the thing he loved.
>
> (ll. 66–73)

He is careful to distinguish between the spontaneity of his response five years before and the exuberance of childhood itself—

> For nature then
> (The coarser pleasures of my boyish days,
> And their glad animal movements all gone by,)
> To me was all in all.
>
> (ll. 73–6)

But already the reference to bounding like a roe has broken down such distinctions. As the passage gathers momentum, Wordsworth's remembrance of an early response to Nature becomes increasingly confused with his first visit to the Wye:

> —I cannot paint
> What then I was. The sounding cataract
> Haunted me like a passion . . .
>
> (ll. 76–8)

So dramatically has the relationship with Coleridge altered his responses that the different stages of Wordsworth's development (up till about 1795) become conflated as he looks back. All time, before Coleridge's influence, is one time. The 'tall rock, | The mountain, and the deep and gloomy wood' (ll. 78–9) take on the significance of archetypes, and their power over the poet's imagination seems to go back to the beginning of his life. The insistent repetitions—'For nature *then* . . . To me was all in all'; 'I

cannot paint | What *then* I was'; 'Their colours and their forms were *then*
to me | An appetite'—serve to emphasize both the singleness of past time
and the absoluteness of its loss.

The verse moves onward, without faltering, towards the climax
determined for it, but the emotions pull against the claims:

> That time is past,
> And all its aching joys are now no more,
> And all its dizzy raptures. Not for this
> Faint I, nor mourn nor murmur: other gifts
> Have followed, for such loss, I would believe,
> Abundant recompence.

> (ll. 84–9)

The structure of Wordsworth's sentence, 'Not for *this* | Faint I, nor
mourn nor murmur', suggests a comparison being made, and a clause yet
to come.[39] But our expectations are disappointed. The sentence, left
hanging in mid-air, draws attention to itself, and to the emotions it is
seeking to deny. For this loss the poet does indeed mourn and murmur;
for this loss no recompense can be found.[40]

The second pantheist climax in the poem (ll. 94–103) attempts to
redress the balance, but is so evidently Coleridgean in its emphasis that
Wordsworth has problems tying it in with the more personal aspects of his
poem.[41] In the weak connection that follows, 'Therefore am I still | A lover
of the meadows and the woods' (ll. 103–4), one sees his last attempt to do
so. His definition, at ll. 105–7 of 'the mighty world | Of eye and ear, both
what they half-create, | And what perceive', is entirely un-Coleridgean.
Its juxtaposition with ll. 94–103 produces one of those odd moments of
blending between Wordsworthian and Coleridgean elements which in
The Pedlar had been frequent and which (in the Goslar *Prelude*, also) tend
to register unease.

---

[39] 'Not for *these*' he writes, in *Intimations*,

> *Not for these* I raise
> The song of thanks and praise
> *But for* those blank misgivings . . .

> (ll. 140–2; my italics)

[40] The unconfidence of certain passages in *Tintern Abbey* has been noticed by Onorato,
34, and by Baker, 58–9. More recently, David Pirie, *William Wordsworth: The Poetry of
Grandeur and of Tenderness* (1982), 269–78, has examined in detail the hesitancy and doubt of
Wordsworth's rhetoric.

[41] Compare ll. 102–3 with *Religious Musings*, 420–5.

The transition into the next verse paragraph takes one into a different kind of poetry:

> Nor, perchance,
> If I were not thus taught, should I the more
> Suffer my genial spirits to decay:
> For thou art with me, here, upon the banks
> Of this fair river; thou, my dearest Friend,
> My dear, dear Friend . . .

(ll. 112–17)

The 'One Life' and all it represents are put firmly to one side as Wordsworth reaches back to a pre-Coleridgean era and to the bond with his sister that can never be replaced (ll. 117–22). It is Dorothy, not Coleridge, who holds the key to Wordsworth's past: through her that 'the language of [his] former heart' can be preserved. The 'shooting lights | Of [her] wild eyes' take the poet back, not just to the time of his first visit to the Wye, but to the 'glad animal movements' of childhood. In these 'gleams of past existence' Wordsworth finds the abundant recompense he seeks. The poem ends in a blessing that recalls *Frost at Midnight*:

> Therefore let the moon
> Shine on thee in thy solitary walk;
> And let the misty mountain winds be free
> To blow against thee . . .

(ll. 135–8)

But Dorothy's future, in contrast to Hartley's, is imagined outside the framework of the 'One Life'. As is so often the case, when hearing verbal echoes, one becomes aware of difference even while responding to what remains unchanged. Wordsworth uses Coleridgean language, but as personal association supplants religious dogma, Coleridge is himself displaced.

Part Two

The Myth of Loss

3

'The Language of my Former Heart': Coleridge's Letter to Sara Hutchinson, April 1802

On 25 March 1801, Coleridge wrote to Godwin, complaining that the poet in him was 'dead'. His letter is poised between the serious and the whimsical—lament and affirmation:

You would not know me—! all sounds of similitude keep at such a distance from each other in my mind, that I have *forgotten* how to make a rhyme—I look at the Mountains (that visible God Almighty that looks in at all my windows) I look at the Mountains only for the Curves of their outlines; the Stars, as I behold them, form themselves into Triangles . . .

'The Poet is dead in me', he continues:

—my imagination (or rather the Somewhat that had been imaginative) lies, like a Cold Snuff on the circular Rim of a Brass Candle-stick, without even a stink of Tallow to remind you that it was once cloathed & mitred with Flame. That is past by!—I was once a Volume of Gold Leaf, rising & riding on every breath of Fancy—but I have beaten myself back into weight & density, & now I sink in quick-silver, yea, remain squat and square on the earth amid the hurricane, that makes Oaks and Straws join in one Dance, fifty yards high in the Element.

(Griggs, ii. 714)

Like much Romantic writing, the passage contains a version of the fall; or rather, several versions—serious, bathetic, self-parodic, fanciful—of a single myth of loss. First, there is the fall from plenitude into the ordinary, evoked in the 'Cold Snuff' metaphor; then of spirit into matter, figured in the hammering of 'Gold Leaf' into 'weight & density'; finally, there is a sequence of allusions to earlier poetry, which recreate (or nostalgically attempt to do so) distant and better times. The phrase 'sounds of similitude' recalls a moment in Wordsworth's *Two Part Prelude*, when the poet notes in passing 'That sense of dim similitude which links | Our moral feelings with external forms' (*1799*, ii. 164–5). Coleridge's sounds, the echo would suggest, are not just like each other; they evoke a sense of analogy between feelings and things, or create links between poetry and God. What has been 'lost' is not the capacity for making poems, but an assumption about how perception works, and how writing is related to it: 'I look at the Mountains only for the Curves of their outlines . . .' This time, Coleridge recalls a fragment (describing the Pedlar of *The Ruined Cottage*) written by Wordsworth in February 1798:

> To his mind
> The mountain's outline and its steady form
> Gave simple grandeur, and its presence shaped
> The measure and the prospect of his soul
> To majesty . . .[1]

Consciously measuring the present against the past, and his own responses against those of his friend, Coleridge's language draws attention to loss. Wordsworth had seen in the mountain's 'steady form' a grand, shaping power. He sees only its outline. The external scene had been for Wordsworth a 'prospect in [the] mind'. For Coleridge it is a 'soulless image on the eye'.[2] 'The Stars', he writes, 'as I behold them, form themselves into Triangles'. It is *The Pedlar* he has in mind, and in his reversal of Wordsworth's lines—'His triangles they were the stars of heaven, | The silent stars' (ll. 166–7)—he records the undermining of assumptions supposedly shared at Alfoxden by them both. Instead of turning the aridness of geometry into something exalted and mysterious (making triangles into patterns of stars) he is reducing beauty to barren formulas.[3] The allusiveness of his language acknowledges, focuses, intensifies the sense of reversal he feels; but it points also, beyond this, to an underlying awareness of the difference between Wordsworth and himself.[4]

The private, inward-turning poetry of Coleridge's *Letter to Sara*

---

[1] *In storm and tempest*, 23–7; by 1801 the bulk of the fragment had already been incorporated in *The Prelude* as *1799*, ii. 351–71. The lines that Coleridge has in mind were inserted in 1804, as *1805*, vii. 722–6.

[2] See *1805*, ii. 371; vi. 454.

[3] 'Was it ever meant', Wordsworth asks, in a draft conclusion for *The Ruined Cottage* (March, 1798), which seems to anticipate Coleridge's questions of 1801–2: 'That this majestic imagery the clouds, | The ocean & the firmament of heaven | Should lie a barren picture on the mind . . .' (Butler, 269). Wordsworth's phrase 'a soulless image on the eye' (*1805*, vi. 454) seems to be a recollection.

[4] Coleridge's metaphor of the hurricane, 'that makes Oaks and Straws join in one Dance, fifty yards high in the Element', probably contains an allusion to Wordsworth's *A Whirl Blast* (spring 1798) written as a celebration of joy. For Wordsworth's memories of the poem as they emerge in *The Barberry Tree* (spring 1802), also reflecting a sense of loss, see Chapter Four below.

Hutchinson, composed a year later (April 1802), has much in common with
this letter to Godwin. Written in a densely allusive idiom, it offers a
personal version of the fall, in which the year at Alfoxden stands for
paradise, and everything after it fragmentation. The letter is addressed to
Sara, but is seldom straightforward love-poetry. Brooding, instead, over
its own relationship with earlier poems, it turns and returns to the loss
which is its real subject. The poet's past and present selves are invoked,
contrasted, used to pinpoint change; while the continuity of
Wordsworth's life, and the stability of his creative power, amount to a
fiction of success against which Coleridge himself is measured. In this
chapter, I shall examine the complex framework of echoes, allusions and
cross-references that holds the poem together,[5] seeming at one and the
same time to assert a connection with the past and to suggest that this has
been dissolved. Though offering a close reading, and mainly following the
poem's own structure, I shall pursue associations where they lead, in the
hope of understanding what Coleridge called 'that subtle Vulcanian
Spider-web Net of Steel—strong as Steel yet subtle as the Ether . . . in
which my soul flutters inclosed with the Idea of [Sara's]'.[6] And not only
with Sara's: Wordsworth, too, is caught in this strong entanglement.

Even the poetry of the *Letter* that directly concerns Sara, or Coleridge's
marriage, or his children, has if one looks closely at its allusive patterns a
bearing on his two central relationships—with Wordsworth, and with his
former self. In his reworking of the poem during the summer Coleridge of
course retains the most densely allusive philosophical sequences (those
that deal with imagination), and his cutting has the effect of packing them
together. The result is a poem that centres, both more consciously and
more evidently, on the contrast between Wordsworth and himself. But not
one that has new things to say about the major relationships. The revisions
have been made to displace Sara, create an acceptable poem, not to
enhance Wordsworth's importance. Even the fact that the *Ode* is
addressed to him, though making it in an obvious sense more his poem,
distracts attention from his pervasive and complex presence in Coleridge's
mind. Envy, resentment, anxiety, love—all of them bound up in the
untidy early poem—give way, in the *Ode*, to tact, compliment, public

---

[5] I shall be dealing exclusively with the *Letter* in its original form, not with *Dejection: an
Ode* as first published in *The Morning Post* on Wordsworth's wedding day, and addressed to
him under the pseudonym Edmund. A full account of the different stages and versions of the
Letter to Sara is given by David Pirie in his essay 'A Letter to [Asra]', *BWS*, 294–339. I am
indebted to it throughout this chapter.
[6] *Notebooks*, iii. 3708.

recognition, praise. The *Letter* was Coleridge's immediate response to the first four stanzas of *Intimations*.[7] The *Ode* represents a more distant and formal profession of esteem.

The *Letter* opens (as it intends to go on) with self-echo:

> WELL! if the Bard was weatherwise, who made
> The grand old Ballad of Sir Patrick Spence,
> This Night, so tranquil now, will not go hence
> Unrous'd by winds . . .

(ll. 1–4)

The word 'WELL!' calls up the opening of *This Lime Tree Bower*: a poem Coleridge associates with the beginnings of his closeness to Wordsworth, and the origin of his poetic power. The mood of exclusion in which it was written had been controlled by playfulness and dispelled by imagination. Coleridge, in the *Letter*, desires the power to move out from the self. But his allusions, meant as a device for bringing release, inevitably heighten contrasts between the present and the past:

> This Night, so tranquil now, will not go hence
> Unrous'd by winds, that ply a busier trade
> Than that, which moulds yon clouds in lazy flakes,
> Or the dull sobbing Draft, that drones & rakes
> Upon the Strings of this Eolian Lute,
>   Which better far were mute.

(ll. 3–8)

The tranquillity of the night is a version of the silence in *Frost at Midnight*, though it lacks the numinous, mysterious quality; and the phrase 'Unrous'd by winds' recalls the frost itself, which had performed its ministry 'unhelp'd by any wind' (l. 2). In the early context, this quality had been something Coleridge envied. It showed the frost to be independent: a secret, creative force that needed no stimulus from outside. Here, the night is resented for reflecting the poet's lethargy—for being 'unrous'd', as he is himself. The wind now seems a parody of the creative process, moulding the clouds in a desultory way, but only to create fleeting shapes which ('*stranger*'-like) reflect the mind's own laziness.[8] Lines 6–8 recall the rhythms and phrasing of *The Eolian Harp*:

---

[7] Read aloud to him by Dorothy on 4 April. See *DWJ*, 113. For a discussion of Dorothy's response on hearing the *Letter*, see Chapter Five, below.

[8] For Coleridge's use of the word 'mould' in a creative context, see *Frost at Midnight*, 'Great Universal Teacher! he shall mould | Thy spirit, and by giving make it ask.' (ll. 68–9)

> Full many a thought uncall'd and undetain'd,
> And many idle flitting phantasies,
> Traverse my indolent and passive brain
> As wild and various, as *the random gales*
> *That swell or flutter on this subject Lute!*
>
> (ll. 39–43)

Where the 'gales' had been exuberant, working harmoniously on the whole instrument to produce organized sound, the draught is a denial of life. It makes its own persistent, complaining noise, and plays on the individual strings, not the lute as a whole. It is a mockery of the 'One Life', like the 'hollow Sound' in *Lines written in the Album at Elbingerode*.[9] Coleridge no longer thinks of the creative breeze as the breath of God. The original sense of analogy has been dissolved, and he is left playing associative games that strive to bring it back, while at the same time acknowledging its loss. The writing is elegiac, but its power lies also in a series of ironies: in the exaggerated self-pity of the 'dull sobbing Draft' (which is separate and inferior to the external 'winds'); in the comic reversal implied by the verbs 'drone' and 'rake'; and in the peevishness of that final dismissive comment, 'which better far were mute'. At the centre of these layers of irony is the harp itself, representing a way of seeing which, because it has been lost, it is safer to think of as anachronistic.[10] Contrived at the best of times, the metaphor comes to stand for an outmoded sensibility, a highly refined egotism, that seeks in everything an 'echo or mirror' for its own pathos.

The first seven lines of *A Letter* explore the loss of symbolic vision, and ask how far analogy will take one, if the faith that accompanies it has gone. (Of what use is the storm, if there is no longer a union between the outer and inner?) The next eight lines offer a response, carefully structured in terms of earlier poems:

> For, lo! the New Moon, winter-bright!
> And overspread with phantom Light,
> (With swimming phantom Light o'erspread
> But rimm'd & circled with a silver Thread)

[9] The sweet Bird's song became an hollow Sound;
And the Gale murmuring indivisibly
Preserv'd it's solemn murmur most distinct
From many a Note of many a Waterbreak,
And the Brook's *Chatter* . . .

(ll. 8–12; Griggs, i. 504)

[10] Dekker, 112, claims that *Dejection* 'can be read as a sad repudiation of some of the most cherished portions of Coleridge's literary inheritance'. 'But', he adds, 'a repulse is also an implicit acknowledgment of attractive force . . .' For his analysis of the Eolian Harp metaphor, see 112–36.

> I see the Old Moon in her Lap, foretelling
> The coming-on of Rain & squally Blast—
> O! Sara! that the Gust ev'n now were swelling,
> And the slant Night-shower driving loud & fast!

(ll. 9–16)

Coleridge associates the word 'swimming' with usurpation: the subjugating of normal sense perceptions to the power of 'Joy'.[11] He suggests this first in *Religious Musings*: 'His countenance settles: a soft solemn bliss | Swims in his eye: his swimming eye uprais'd' (ll. 79–80), and then again in the revised climax of *This Lime Tree Bower*.[12] The 'swimming phantom Light' is a quality of vision that seems to emanate from the moon, but is really projected onto it: an ambiguity suggested primarily by the verb 'o'erspread', but also by the subtle implication that the moon is the eye itself (an 'echo or mirror' of the poet's eye). Later in the poem, Coleridge will be more explicit: the 'swimming phantom Light' will become the 'luminous Cloud' of joy that the human mind first creates and then perceives. Projection will become creative, but for the moment potential is withheld.

As Coleridge turns to address Sara, a note of urgency enters the poem: the words 'swelling' and 'driving' are full of energy, and almost convince one the external world will come alive.[13] But the tone implores too much. Like Wordsworth's Pedlar, who 'wished the winds might rage | When they were silent' (ll. 190–1), Coleridge longs to be reassured that Nature has not betrayed him, that something exists outside his own mood. Reassurance not being provided, the self shrinks back:

> A Grief without a pang, void, dark, & drear,
> A stifling, drowsy, unimpassion'd Grief
> That finds no natural Outlet, no Relief
> > In word, or sigh, or tear . . .

(ll. 17–20)[14]

[11] Wordsworth's eye in *Tintern Abbey* is similarly 'made quiet' by joy. See ll. 48–9.

[12] Lamb stands on the hilltop 'Silent with swimming sense' (*Annual Anthology*, l. 39). See also *The Nightingale* 102–5, where Hartley's 'undropped tears' indicate his receptiveness to the moon.

[13] Called up by Coleridge's language are lines 40–3 of *The Eolian Harp* (quoted above) asserting an intimate connection between the beginnings of an associative process and the external wind.

[14] The language is close to *The Pains of Sleep*; but here the hell that Coleridge evokes is created by apathy or indifference, and its horrors are internalized, psychological versions of the ones described in *The Dungeon*:

> Each pore and natural outlet shrivell'd up
> By Ignorance and parching Poverty,
> His energies roll back upon his heart,
> And stagnate and corrupt . . .

(ll. 6–9)

Indifference, Coleridge believes, has supplanted his earlier symbolic vision. He can make the expected observations, but only mechanically, following patterns of private and literary association that have become traps:

> In this heartless Mood,
> To other thoughts by yonder Throstle woo'd,
> That pipes within the Larch tree, not unseen,
> (The Larch, which pushes out in tassels green
> It's bundled Leafits) woo'd to mild Delights
> By all the tender Sounds & gentle Sights
> Of this sweet Primrose-month—& *vainly* woo'd . . .
>
> (ll. 23–9)

A lyric of Wordsworth's, addressed to Dorothy in the spring of 1798, had used both larch and bird to evoke joyous renewal:

> It is the first mild day of March;
> Each minute sweeter than before,
> The red-breast sings from the tall larch
> That stands beside our door.
>
> (*Lines written at a small distance from my House*, 1–4)

But more relevant to Coleridge in his present mood is the memory of a stanza from *Tis said, that some have died for love* (1800), Wordsworth's study of solipsism and madness:

> O! what a weight is in these shades! Ye leaves,
> When will that dying murmur be suppress'd?
> Your sound my heart of peace bereaves,
> It robs my heart of rest.
> Thou Thrush, that singest loud and loud and free,
> Into yon row of willows flit,
> Upon that alder sit;
> Or sing another song, or chuse another tree.
>
> (ll. 21–8)

The first part of the *Letter* comes to its climax in a moving evocation of beauty, which the poet himself is unable to feel:

> O dearest Sara! In this heartless Mood
> All this long Eve, so balmy & serene,
> Have I been gazing on the Western Sky
> And it's peculiar Tint of Yellow Green—
> And still I gaze—& with how blank an eye!

And those thin Clouds above, in flakes & bars,
That give away their Motion to the Stars;
Those Stars, that glide behind them, or between,
Now sparkling, now bedimm'd, but always seen;
Yon crescent Moon, as fix'd as if it grew
In it's own cloudless, starless Lake of Blue—
A boat becalm'd! dear William's Sky Canoe!
—I see them all, so excellently fair!
I see, not feel, how beautiful they are.

(ll. 30–43)

Every word has its symbolic significance; every detail of the landscape contains a private reference suggesting loss.[15] The atmosphere of the evening recalls a 'balmy night' in April four years ago:

No cloud, no relique of the sunken day
Distinguishes the West, no long thin slip
Of sullen light, no obscure trembling hues.

(*The Nightingale*, 1–3)

But subtle reversals are also implied. There is something unnerving in the quality of the light and the presence of clouds. They are 'reliques of the sunken day' and they mirror the poet's own sense of prolonged dying. The 'peculiar Tint of Yellow Green' lingers on as a reminder of supernatural moments of vision in the earlier poetry.[16] The motion of the clouds, like that of the fluttering '*stranger*' in *Frost at Midnight*, is feeble and random—all that remains of an activity now suspended. The 'flakes and bars', representing a sort of death-in-life, connect not just with the dying embers and grate in *Frost at Midnight*, but with the spectre-ship in *The Ancient Mariner*:

And strait the Sun was *fleck'd with bars*
(Heaven's mother send us grace)
As if thro' a dungeon-grate he peer'd
With broad and burning face.

(ll. 169–72; my italics)

[15] Coleridge takes his description of the larch with its 'bundled leafits' and 'tassels green' from a Notebook Entry for March 1802, when he was visiting Sara at Gallow Hill. See *Notebooks*, i. 1142.

[16] McFarland draws attention to a possible recollection of the phrase 'green radiance' from *Lines written at Shurton Bars* (1795)—a phrase which had of course very strong associations with the earliest stages of Coleridge's relationship with Wordsworth. See McFarland, 76–7 and Chapter One, above. For another resonance, see *Fears in Solitude*: 'When thro' its half-transparent stalks, at eve, | The level sunshine glimmers with green light' (ll. 10–11).

Coleridge is himself suspended in Death-in-Life, or Life-in-Death. Traces of former vision remind him of his potential; but he cannot synthesize (and thereby feel) what he perceives as dissociated impressions. In *This Lime Tree Bower*, intense concentration had subdued the tyranny of the eye:

> gazing round
> On the wide view, may gaze till all doth seem
> Less gross than bodily . . .

> (ll. 21–3)

but this can no longer work. The effort and concentration are there ('All this long eve . . . have I been gazing . . . and still I gaze'),[17] yet inward vision is not experienced, and the poetry collapses into monosyllables that express despair:

> And still I gaze—& with how blank an eye![18]

As Coleridge shifts the focus away from himself,

> And those thin Clouds above, in flakes & bars,
> That *give away their Motion to the Stars*

> (ll. 35–6; my italics)

one is momentarily aware of the Wordsworth who had written, in *Skating*, of receptive and passionate embraces, 'When we had *given our bodies to the wind*, | And all the shadowy banks on either side | Came sweeping through the darkness' (*1799*, i. 175–7; my italics). This Wordsworthian presence is confirmed by the reference to *Peter Bell* (ll. 39–41) which on one level is tender and affectionate (like its parallel in *The Soliloquy of the Full Moon*)[19] but on another can be read as the resentful acknowledgement of difference. Wordsworth's euphoric questing ('Away we go, my Boat and

---

17 The construction 'gaze . . . gaze . . . till . . .' is used very frequently by Wordsworth and Coleridge to indicate a sublime moment of perception. See *The Foster Mother's Tale*, 14–16; *Lines Left upon a Seat*, 30–4; and *Frost at Midnight*, 30; 39.

18 The rhythms of this line appropriately echo Sidney, 'With how sad steps, oh moon, thou climbst the skies, | *How silently and with how wan a face*' (*Astrophel and Stella* xxxi, 1–2; my italics).

19
> A Night or two after a worse Rogue there came,
> The head of the Gang, one Wordsworth by name—
> 'Ho! What's in the Wind?' 'Tis the voice of a Wizzard!
> I saw him look at me most terribly blue!
> He was hunting for witch-rhymes from great A to Izzard,
> And soon as he'd found them made no more ado
> But chang'd me at once to a little Canoe . . .'

> (ll. 26–32)

I, | Sure never man had such another')[20] is tacitly contrasted with
Coleridge's own mood of torpor. The moon, one observes, is not moving
rapidly behind and between the clouds. Nor is it given the gentle
ascending motion that is associated with imaginative yearning: 'Softly she
was going up | And a star or two beside'.[21] Instead, it is standing still,
deprived of the companionship and humanness originally implied by the
stars: 'as fix'd as if it grew | In it's own cloudless, starless Lake of Blue'
(ll. 39–40). Though the rhythms are compelling, the analogy itself is one
of stultification:

> Day after day, day after day,
>   We stuck, ne breath ne motion,
> As idle as a painted Ship
> Upon a painted Ocean.

(ll. 111–14)

Wordsworth, in the 'Prologue' to *Peter Bell*, had turned the solemnity of
Romantic aspiration into the self-delight of Fancy. Coleridge, in a
counter-move, fixes Wordsworth's sky-boat in a starless lake—turns
Fancy into something static. Each poet, in revising the other, defines
himself: Wordsworth, actively and positively, Coleridge in a kind of
negation.

The contrast is even sharper in their habits of Miltonic allusion.
Coleridge's famous reference to *Samson Agonistes*, at ll. 44–6,[22] suggests
the complexity of his sense of failure. It is (publicly) an appropriate
literary quotation, drawing an obvious parallel between 'the blind, lonely
hero mourning a gift he had lost through an imprudent marriage',[23] and
Coleridge himself. But its more private (and potent) meaning comes to us,
filtered, as it were, through Wordsworthian echo:

> Nor, perchance
> If I were not thus taught, should I the more
> Suffer my genial spirits to decay . . .

(*Tintern Abbey*, 112–14)

The doubleness of Coleridge's reference has been noted before, but not

---

[20] See the 'Prologue' to *Peter Bell*, 21–2, and my discussion in Chapter Two above.
[21] See *The Ancient Mariner*, 255–6.
[22] Compare *Samson Agonistes*, 594–6:

> So much I feel my genial spirits droop,
> My hopes all flat, nature within me seems
> In all her functions weary of herself . . .

[23] See David Pirie, *BWS*, 309.

the heaviness of the irony implied. Wordsworth's response to landscape, because it is shared by Dorothy, will live on through change and decay. (Samson's despair is left behind.) Coleridge's feelings for Sara cannot enhance his imagination. (Despair returns.) Verbal echo suggests a parallel between Coleridge and Wordsworth, which the facts work against. Miltonic allusion becomes a shared habit, a token of exchange; but also a signal of divergence and a self-directed weapon. In a letter of December 1800, Coleridge had quoted from *Tintern Abbey* with the same envy for Wordsworth's apparent confidence, and the same awareness of a discrepancy between them:

Amid all these changes & humiliations & fears, the sense of the Eternal abides in me, and preserves unsubdued

> My chearful Faith that all which I endure
> Is full of Blessings!

> (Griggs, i. 649)

George Dekker observes that the quotation helps us 'to understand how Wordsworth's precepts and example both sustained and intimidated his friend' (40). What he fails to point out is the bitter implication of '*endure*', insidiously displacing Wordsworth's '*behold*'.

Alongside the *Samson* reference, with its public and private meanings, is a sequence of unconscious associations:

> My genial Spirits fail—
> And what can these avail
> To lift the smoth'ring Weight from off my Breast?

> I spake with rash Despair,
> And ere I was aware,
> The weight was somewhat lifted from my Breast!

> (ll. 44–6, 76–9)

One would expect the 'smoth'ring Weight' simply to stand for Coleridge's unhappy marriage, but reference is again double. Leaving aside the possible Freudian slip ('this mothering weight') there is the muddling fact that Coleridge had used the image both of his wife and of Sara Hutchinson. Of the first, he had written, in a poem perhaps begun in Germany,[24] but completed in spring 1802:

[24] The poem is subtitled 'From an Emigrant to his Absent Wife' and contains reminiscences of Nether Stowey, as well as verbal echoes from *The Complaint of the Forsaken Indian Woman*. Only the final lines, with their reference to Hartley as an active child, seem clearly of the later period.

> Across my chest there lay a weight, so warm!
>   As if some bird had taken shelter there;
>   And lo! I seemed to see a woman's form—
>   Thine, Sara, thine? O joy, if thine it were!

                              (*The Day-Dream*, 19–22)[25]

Of the second, just before composing the *Letter* itself:

>   O ever—ever be thou blest!
>   For dearly, Asra! love I thee!
>   This brooding warmth across my breast,
>   This depth of tranquil bliss—ah, me!

                              (*A Day-Dream*, 19–22)

Images which in the daydreams are comforting and tender, take on a threatening quality as they move into the longer poem. Love itself, in this confused and heartless mood, seems a 'smoth'ring weight'.

Despite the Miltonic echo with which it opens, literary allusions, in the long central section of the *Letter* (ll. 47–183), are few and far between. A private reference to *Frost at Midnight* implies the simple and familiar contrast on which both poets—attempting to rationalize more complex differences—so often depend:

>   At eve, sky-gazing in 'ecstatic fit'
>   (Alas, for cloister'd in a city School
>   The Sky was all, I knew, of Beautiful)
>   At the barr'd window often did I sit,
>   And oft upon the leaded School-roof lay . . .

                              (ll. 62–6)

And the first in a sequence of echoes from *Intimations* gives us a Coleridge who hides bitterness, envy and resentment behind affectionate self-deprecation:

>   When thou, & with thee those, whom thou lov'st best,
>   Shall dwell together in one happy Home,
>   One House, the dear *abiding* Home of All,
>   I too will crown me with a Coronal . . .

                              (ll. 133–6)

---

[25] Given the coincidence of Christian names (soon to be further confused by a daughter, Sara, begotten in March or April) the final quoted line of the first Day-Dream is deeply ambiguous. It could indeed have been written about one woman in 1799 then mentally transferred to another in 1802.

The exuberance of the early stanzas of *Intimations* is at best wishful, at worst fake:

> My heart is at your festival
> My head hath your coronal
> Even yet more gladness I can hold it all . . .
>
> (ll. 38–40)[26]

But joy and jollity are equally valued by those who are excluded from both, and for Coleridge any coronal would do.[27] It is the sense of being shut off from Wordsworthian values (at one time shared) which dominates the verse:

> While *ye* are *well* & *happy*, 'twould but wrong you
> If I should fondly yearn to be among you—
> Wherefore, O wherefore! should I wish to be
> A wither'd branch upon a blossoming Tree?
>
> (ll. 165–8)

The storm-sequence, which occupies a climactic position in the *Letter*, is a kind of associative game, played by the poet as a way of ordering his experience:

> Nay, wherefore did I let it haunt my Mind
>   The dark distressful Dream!
> I turn from it, & listen to the Wind
> Which long has rav'd unnotic'd! What a Scream
> Of agony by Torture lengthen'd out
> That Lute sent forth!
>
> (ll. 184–9)

The passage is powerful in its complications. Taken literally, it suggests Coleridge's hope that he will arrest his own solipsism. (This corresponds

---

[26] A pastoral, *The Idle Shepherd Boys*, written by Wordsworth in 1800, provides the mood, and some of the imagery, behind *Intimations* I–IV:

> A thousand lambs are on the rocks,
> All newly-born! both earth and sky
> Keep jubilee, and more than all,
> Those Boys with their green Coronal,
> They never hear the cry . . .
>
> (ll. 27–31)

The last quoted line, here, might serve as an ironic comment on *Intimations*. Jollity is used to keep loss at bay.

[27] The distinction is made by Jonathan Wordsworth in his chapter on the poetry of spring 1802. See *Borders of Vision*.

to Wordsworth's need for reassurance from tangible objects, or his craving for powerful stimuli.)[28] Taken metaphorically, it suggests the hope that symbolic vision will return: that the power to project will lead ultimately to the power of blessing. Self-consciousness, present in the rhapsodic passage that follows, is there to control the randomness of associationism, and lead into symbolic vision:

> O thou wild Storm without!
> Jagg'd Rock, or mountain Pond, or blasted Tree,
> Or Pine-Grove, whither Woodman never clomb,
> Or lonely House, long held the Witches' Home,
> Methinks were fitter Instruments for Thee,
> Mad Lutanist! that in this month of Showers,
> Of dark brown Gardens, & of peeping Flowers,
> Mak'st Devil's Yule, with worse than wintry Song
> The Blossoms, Buds, and timorous Leaves among!
>
> (ll. 189–97)

It would be wrong to dismiss the earlier images in this passage as bad poetry, and to ignore the awareness they imply.[29] The list of gothic settings is mechanical, exaggerated, superstitious—and pervaded, furthermore, by self-echo:

> Ye woods, that listen to the night-bird's singing,
> Midway the smooth and perilous steep reclin'd;
> Save when your own imperious branches swinging
> Have made a solemn music of the wind!
> Where, like a man belov'd of God,
> Thro' glooms, which never woodman trod,
> How oft, pursuing fancies holy,
> My moonlight way o'er flow'ring weeds I wound,
> Inspir'd beyond the guess of folly,
> By each rude shape, and wild unconquerable sound!
>
> (France: an Ode, 5–14)

Coleridge is not writing badly, but observing patterns of association that automatically come to him. He slides into anachronism to show the insidiousness of literary expectation. To ignore the humour is to miss the parodic control. It is not, however, a control that can be maintained.

---

[28] See the Fenwick Note to *Intimations*: 'Many times while going to school have I grasped at a wall or tree to recall myself from [the] abyss of idealism to the reality.' (*PW*, iv. 463)

[29] Dekker, 240, writes 'If "Hence viper thoughts" annoys us, how shall we pass by "whither Woodman never clomb" or "e'en to Frenzy bold" without a tasteful shudder?'

'Thou Actor, perfect in all tragic Sounds!' Coleridge writes—addressing the wind in a language he will later, in Wordsworth, describe as bombast:[30]

> Thou mighty Poet, even to frenzy bold!
> What tell'st thou now about?
>
> (ll. 198–200)

Coleridge's tone is indulgent. Knowing he should disapprove, he none the less allows associationism to lead him on:

> 'Tis of the Rushing of an Host in Rout—
> And many Groans from men with smarting Wounds—
> At once they groan with smart, and shudder with the Cold!
> 'Tis hush'd! There is a Trance of deepest Silence,
> Again! but all that Sound, as of a rushing Crowd,
> And Groans & tremulous Shudderings, all are over—
> And it has other Sounds, and all less deep, less loud!
>   A Tale of less Affright,
>   And temper'd with Delight,
> As William's Self had made the tender Lay—
>   'Tis of a little Child
>   Upon a heathy Wild,
> Not far from home—but it has lost it's way—
> And now moans low in utter grief & fear—
> And now screams loud, & hopes to make it's Mother hear!
>
> (ll. 201–15)

The lost child is Lucy Gray, but she is transformed almost beyond recognition. For Wordsworth, her death had not been a finality, or a cause of grief. She had been assimilated into the harmony from which she came—a portion of the eternal:

> Yet some maintain that to this day
> She is a living Child,
> That you may see sweet Lucy Gray
> Upon the lonesome Wild.
>
> O'er rough and smooth she trips along,
> And never looks behind;
> And sings a solitary song
> That whistles in the wind.
>
> (ll. 57–64)

---

[30] See *Biographia*, ii. 136 for a definition of 'mental bombast', and *Biographia*, ii. 138 for its application to *Intimations*.

For Coleridge, she has a quite different, much more personal, significance.[31] The storm sequence ends, not on a note of reconciliation or control, but in a climax of desolation: 'And now moans low in utter grief & fear— | And now screams loud, & hopes to make it's Mother hear!' We are back with the 'Scream | Of agony' sent forth by the lute. Any hope Coleridge has had of subduing the power of association has been abandoned—for the moment at least.

The next part of the *Letter* begins like a new poem:

> 'Tis Midnight! and small Thoughts have I of Sleep!
> Full seldom may my Friend such Vigils keep—
> O breathe She softly in her gentle Sleep!
> Cover her, gentle Sleep! with wings of Healing.
> And be this Tempest but a Mountain Birth!
> May all the Stars hang bright about her Dwelling,
> Silent, as tho' they *watch'd* the sleeping Earth!
> Healthful & light, my Darling! may'st thou rise
>   With clear & chearful Eyes—
> And of the same good Tidings to me send!
>
>   (ll. 216–25)

This prayer recalls and relives Wordsworth's blessing on Dorothy in *Tintern Abbey*, not just in the rhythms, which are cumulative, passionate, psalm-like, but in the language itself, which reveals a deep sense of Wordsworth's poetic presence. Coleridge protects Sara from the violence implied in the storm—'And be this Tempest but a Mountain Birth'—but he also wishes vitality on her, as Wordsworth had his sister with the 'misty mountain winds' (*Tintern Abbey*, 137). The moon which shone on Dorothy, and guided her 'solitary walk' (ll. 135–6) has been replaced by the stars which 'hang bright about [Sara's] Dwelling'. Again, one is conscious in the echo of both adjustment and retention. Dorothy had moved through danger and loneliness, protected by her memory, which provided a 'mansion' or 'dwelling place' for forms, sounds, and harmonies, but also by implication for herself. Sara, by contrast, remains in one place, protected by the guardian stars, safe in a dwelling that is at once actual (her home in Sockburn) and metaphor: the dwelling-place of the mind, which 'keeps its own | Inviolate retirement'.[32] Giving the passage a deeper resonance are a number of cadences and words that recall

---

[31] In February 1801, writing to Thomas Poole, Coleridge had described the 'Night Wind that pipes it's thin doleful climbing sinking Notes like a child that has lost it's way and is crying aloud, half in grief and half in the hope to be heard by it's Mother' (Griggs, ii. 669).

[32] 'Prospectus' to *The Recluse* (1800), 11–12 (Darlington, 100).

the blessing on Hartley in *Frost at Midnight*. The verb 'hang', for instance—used in one context for icicles,[33] in the other for distant stars—evokes in each case a sense of being watched over as one of the 'elect'. And the wish that Sara should 'breathe . . . softly in her gentle Sleep', recalls the 'gentle breathings' of Hartley, 'heard in [the] dead calm' (l. 50) of an earlier midnight scene.

The blending of *Tintern Abbey* and *Frost at Midnight* in the background of Coleridge's prayer gives it allusive richness on a private level. But there is, in addition, a more public relationship going on. In the joyous lyricism of his final wish—'Healthful & light, my Darling! may'st thou rise | With clear & chearful Eyes' (ll. 223–4)—and in the tender, solicitous details, one hears echoes from a much earlier, more hopeful, love poem—Spenser's *Epithalamion*:

> Now welcome night, thou night so long expected,
> That long daies labour doest at last defray,
> And all my cares, which cruell loue collected,
> Hast sumd in one, and cancelled for aye:
> Spread thy broad wing ouer my loue and me,
> That no man may vs see,
> And in thy sable mantle vs enwrap,
> From feare of perill and foule horror free.
> Let no false treason seeke vs to entrap,
> Nor any dread disquiet once annoy
> The safety of our ioy:
> But let the night be calme and quietsome,
> Without tempestuous storms or sad afray . . .
> Let no lamenting cryes, nor dolefull teares
> Be heard all night within nor yet without:
> Ne let false whispers breeding hidden feares,
> Breake gentle sleepe with misconceiued dout.
>
> (ll. 315–27; 334–7)[34]

Verbally, the prayers have much in common. Spenser's night, stretching its protective wings over the sleeping couple (ll. 324–6) becomes Coleridge's bird, covering Sara with wings of healing; while his wish to fend off the 'tempestuous storms' (l. 327) is mirrored, by Coleridge, in 'be this Tempest but a Mountain Birth!' (l. 220). Beyond the verbal echoes, a

---

[33] See *Frost at Midnight*; 77–9: 'Or whether the secret ministery of cold | Shall hang them up in silent icicles, | Quietly shining to the quiet moon . . .'

[34] See *The Works of Edmund Spenser, A variorum edition*, ed. E. Greenlaw *et al.*, 11 vols., Baltimore 1932–57, *The Minor Poems*, vol. ii (1947).

deeper affinity emerges, which can partly be ascribed to rhythm, but is more to do with tone, feeling, mood. Coleridge has absorbed *Epithalamion* at a deep level, making connections with it in the *Letter* which, given the complexity of his own marital problems, and his envy for Wordsworth's more hopeful domestic life,[35] have their ironies.

Alternation between public and private reference is a constant feature in the language of allusion. The link with Spenser gives way to arcane self-reference and personal Wordsworthian echo:

> For, oh! beloved Friend!
> I am not the buoyant Thing, I was of yore—
> When, like an own Child, I to JOY belong'd;
> For others mourning oft, myself oft surely wrong'd,
> Yet bearing all things then, as if I nothing bore!
>
> Yes, dearest Sara! Yes!
> There *was* a time when tho' my path was rough,
> The Joy within me dallied with Distress;
> And all Misfortunes were but as the Stuff
> Whence Fancy made me Dreams of Happiness:
> For Hope grew round me, like the climbing Vine,
> And Leaves & Fruitage, not my own, seem'd mine!
> But now Ill Tidings bow me down to earth—
> Nor care I, that they rob me of my Mirth—
>   But oh! each Visitation
> Suspends what Nature gave me at my Birth,
>   My shaping Spirit of Imagination!
>
>   (ll. 226–42)

Loss, in Wordsworth's poetry, is so prevalent a mood that it takes on the status of myth. For Coleridge, on the other hand, it is always tied down by circumstance and the personal self. When he alludes to *Intimations*, one has a sense of unease: as though something disproportionate has entered the poetry, or the wrong comparisons are being implied. Take, for instance, the words 'I am not the buoyant Thing, I was of yore' (l. 227). The extra syllable in Coleridge's line adds a clumsiness that is almost comical. The power that should emerge in Wordsworth's vagueness is forfeited in a sense of tampering. The next deliberate reference—'There

---

[35] Alluding of course to 'It is not now as it hath been of yore' (*Intimations*, 6). Coleridge's phrase 'the buoyant Thing' is recalled years later in his unfinished poem *The Blossoming of the Solidary Date Tree*: 'The buoyant child surviving in the man' (l. 53). The idea of buoyancy had occurred earlier, in Coleridge's letter to Godwin (March, 1801), quoted at the beginning of this chapter.

was a time when tho' my path was rough, | The Joy within me dallied with Distress' (ll. 232–3)—is equally uncomfortable. Where Wordsworth mourns the passing of 'a glory from the earth'—a glory that seems inherent, even if it is projected—Coleridge writes about a crippling sense of personal change. He uses Wordsworthian myth to suggest a potential for joy which has disappeared; but the shift of emphasis ('There *was* a time') and the hackneyed metaphor ('my path was rough') make his quotation incongruous. Instead of the intended sympathy, one feels how limited his self-scrutiny appears beside Wordsworth's grand elegiac vision.

Other energies at work in this passage can (at least partially) be understood in Bloomian terms. A poet's relationship with his peer (or, indeed, his former self) can play just as anxious a part in his writing as the struggle with his 'father' or precursor. And in a poem that so consistently explores literary relationship, one can hardly ignore ambiguity in the words, 'Leaves & Fruitage, not my own, seem'd mine!' The metaphor can be followed on two related levels. In terms of conscious allegorization, it is the vine of Hope that grows around the poet, producing fruit that could not be there if hope were not. On an unconscious level, the vine is not 'Hope' at all, but Wordsworth; which makes the 'Leaves & Fruitage' Wordsworth's poems, or Coleridge's poems inspired by Wordsworth, or even, as one critic has suggested, Wordsworth's poems inspired by Coleridge.[36] If the metaphor as a whole evokes 'the completely balanced interdependence of 1798',[37] it does so in a special way. The poet, passing a fiction upon himself, recreates the past in terms of present needs. The Alfoxden era represents a time when, even if he felt his poems were written by someone else, it did not matter: the sharing of creativity was an end in itself. Instead of accepting the nostalgia on its own terms, one should find out what it shows about Coleridge's needs and fears.

It reveals, first of all, that the need for a myth of loss, in personal

---

[36] See Pirie, *BWS*, 317. There is a Miltonic source for Coleridge's leaves and fruitage metaphor which has not been pointed out. Adam and Eve, in Book Five of *Paradise Lost*, reunite after Eve's dream, and the wedding of elm and vine allegorically enacts their union:

> they led the vine
> To wed her elm; she spoused about him twines
> Her marriageable arms, and with her brings
> Her dower the adopted clusters, to adorn
> His barren leaves.
>
> (*PL*, v. 215–19)

[37] Pirie, *BWS*, 317.

relationships, as well as in imaginative creeds, is strong. And it tells one, secondly, that Coleridge's anxiety about Wordsworth pervades everything, including the imagery used to describe his marriage. It is a language that persistently returns to metaphors of borrowing and stealing. Coleridge has already written of the ill tidings that 'rob' him of his mirth, and the process continues with the terrible claim that his marriage has known 'No hopes of its own Vintage' (l. 262). Two separate readings are possible: 'no hopes that the marriage will produce a vintage', and 'no hopes produced as the vintage of marriage'. But beyond this ambiguity, there is a further strangeness. For a moment Coleridge is returning to the vine image used in the earlier passage, and the implication of this self-echo is clear: the only hope he has felt is a hope for others ('Leaves & Fruitage, not my own'), and the only happiness he has achieved is vicarious. He has no store of emotions on which to draw: 'None, O! none— | Whence when I mourn'd for you, *my Heart might borrow | Fair forms & living Motions for it's Sorrow*' (my italics).[38] The imagery reaches its climax in Coleridge's metaphor of the mind stealing its own energy and perverting it— destroying the creative impulse by 'infecting' it with the aridness of 'abstruse research':

> For not to think of what I needs must feel,
> But to be still & patient all I can;
> And haply by abstruse Research to steal
> From my own Nature all the Natural Man—
> This was my sole Resource, my wisest plan!
> And that, which suits a part, infects the whole,
> And now is almost grown the Temper of my Soul.

> (ll. 265–71)

Coleridge makes a concession, here, to what remains in him of the 'Natural Man'; but the movement of the whole passage convinces one that he feels his identity has been completely, not 'almost', taken over. The 'Temper of [his] Soul' is not something that changes; it is a habit that settles into a disposition and then hardens into permanence.[39]

Quoting Wordsworth, but writing at two removes from his emotions, Coleridge creates the impression of a hopelessly mechanical response:

[38] To complicate matters still further, the phrase 'Fair forms & living Motions' seems itself to be a borrowing from that most Wordsworthian of Coleridge's early poems, *The Dungeon*: 'Thou pourest on him thy soft influences, | Thy sunny hues, *fair forms*, and breathing sweets' (ll. 22–3; my italics).

[39] In the final version of the poem, *Dejection: an Ode*, Coleridge writes, 'Till that which suits a part infects the whole, | And now is almost grown the *habit* of my soul.' (ll. 92–3; my italics) He is playing, very possibly, on the subdued clothing metaphor in 'suits'.

These Mountains too, these Vales, these Woods, these Lakes,
Scenes full of Beauty & of Loftiness
Where all my Life I fondly hop'd to live—
I were sunk low indeed, did they *no* solace give;
But oft I seem to feel, & evermore I fear,
They are not to me now the Things, which once they were.

(ll. 290–5)

In the background, once again, is the lamenting voice of *Intimations*. It is
there in the list of nouns (Mountains, Vales, Woods, Lakes)[40] and again in
the dreary repetitions echoing the Ode's first stanza:

Turn whereso'er I may
By night or day
The things which I have seen I see them now no more

(ll. 7–9)

Every word in the passage—from the ambiguity of 'I seem to feel' down to
the clumsy, unmemorable rhythm of 'They are not to me now . . .'—
shows Coleridge deliberately playing down the power of his own poetry,
in order to defer to that of *Intimations*. The passage reads like a lesson he
has learnt by rote: it deliberately fails to call up an intensity of feeling.[41]
One need not assume that, because he exploits the tricks of Wordsworth's
style, Coleridge is attempting to surpass the early stanzas of the Ode.[42] He
acknowledges their separateness, and relies on their power. What is finally
both strange and moving is his awareness that *Intimations* evokes no
corresponding intensity in himself. There is nothing in the *Letter* that
mirrors its grandeur of loss.

The last part of the poem, though less densely allusive, is more
complex. Not because it explores difficult philosophical issues, but
because it offers a resolution to the poem's central problem in terms that
seem directly to argue with the poet's emotional claims. Out of the mood
of the moment comes an acknowledgement of solipsism and a recapitulation of loss. But from older patterns of thinking there emerges a more
reassuring theory, that unites perception with creativity, and both with
God. Coming in quick succession, the two ways of seeing offer more than a

[40] Coleridge is echoing, of course, Wordsworth's catalogue of daily sights—'meadow
grove and stream | The earth and every common sight' (*Intimations*, 1–2)—which itself
recalls Milton: 'O woods, O fountains, hillocks, dales and bowers, | With other echo late I
taught your shades | To answer, and resound for other song.' (*PL*, x. 860–2)
[41] Compare Wordsworth's line 'The pansy at my feet | Doth the same tale repeat'
(*Intimations*, 54–5).
[42] Here I take issue with David Pirie (*BWS*, 321).

puzzling contrast. They draw attention to deeper conflicts, which are a permanent feature of Coleridge's imagination:

> O Sara! we receive but what we give,
> And in *our* Life alone does Nature live.
> Our's is her Wedding Garment, our's her Shroud—
> And would we aught behold of higher Worth
> Than that inanimate cold World allow'd
> To the poor loveless ever-anxious Crowd,
> Ah! from the Soul itself must issue forth
> A Light, a Glory, and a luminous Cloud
>   Enveloping the Earth!
> And from the Soul itself must there be sent
> A sweet & potent Voice, of it's own Birth,
> Of all sweet Sounds the Life & Element.

(ll. 296–307)

In the first couplet, Coleridge denies the whole basis of his earlier faith, using the words 'give' and 'receive' to recall the shared assumptions of 1797–8. It had seemed, then, that through the 'shapes and sounds' of Nature, God moulded the human spirit, 'and by giving ma[de] it ask' (*Frost at Midnight*, 69); that the mind of man could *receive* impressions, but also had an 'active power' to transform them by creative brooding (*The Pedlar*, 41–2); and that the senses could at once 'perceive' and 'half-create' the 'mighty world' (*Tintern Abbey*, 107–8). Coleridge's language re-evokes all this, with a sharp awareness of betrayal. According to these famous, elegiac lines, Nature can give only what it receives from the human mind. It cannot give freely of itself, nor does it enhance what it gives back. All beauty or meaning is projected. There is extreme power in this persuasion, as the metaphor of the wedding garment, with all its associations, suggests.[43] But there is also vulnerability: an awareness that sorrow, or even deadness, can cover nature like a shroud. The two extremes of human ceremony—wedding and funeral—suggest that the imagination, being capable of so much, is both a privilege and a burden.

The climax of *This Lime Tree Bower* also has, at its centre, the metaphor of clothing—

---

[43] Coleridge could not, of course, make use of the wedding garment metaphor without a sharp sense of the ambiguities it contained. When first writing the poem in April, it must have been his own failed marriage that was uppermost in his mind—giving a sardonic twist to what should be a positive moment in the poetry. When the first printed version of *Dejection, an Ode* appeared in the *Morning Post* on October 4—Wordsworth's wedding day, as well as his own—the ambiguities had deepened.

> gazing round
> On the wide view, may gaze till all doth seem
> Less gross than bodily, a living Thing
> That acts upon the mind, and with such hues
> As cloathe the almighty Spirit, when he makes
> Spirits perceive His presence!

(ll. 21–6)

And the passages are different, in obvious ways. As David Pirie puts it, 'Natural objects which in the *Lime Tree Bower* had been the garments of [God] . . . are now visible only through the clothing of man's emotions.' (*BWS*, 302) One could claim, therefore, that a straightforward process of reversal was taking place, and that Coleridge was using earlier metaphor to display loss. But there is in all echoic language a balance of adjustment and retention. Nostalgic self-echoes imply the sense of alteration; they also bring with them into the present something of the past. The underlying implication, then, is that imagination has its God-like potential. It invests Nature with meaning, and the veil it gives to finite forms is one that reveals the imaginative truth which is incarnate within it.[44] By what seems almost a trick of private associationism, Coleridge can transform what is negative (limited, projectionist) into something that will lead him back to God:

> And would we aught behold of higher Worth
> Than that inanimate cold World allow'd
> To the poor loveless ever-anxious Crowd,
> Ah! from the Soul itself must issue forth
> A Light, a Glory, and a luminous Cloud
> Enveloping the Earth!
> And from the Soul itself must there be sent
> A sweet & potent Voice, of it's own Birth,
> Of all sweet Sounds the Life & Element.

(ll. 299–307)

Nothing, in the language or the rhythms, suggests he is still lamenting. The 'Soul' is active and positive—not projecting a mood or emotion, but

[44] According to numerous Old Testament passages, a direct apprehension of God is inconceivable except for the chosen few. God must be veiled because his light is blinding, and Moses, descending from Mount Sinai after seeing Him, must wear a veil to protect his followers from the light reflected in his face (Exodus 34:33–5). For an impression of the extent to which this veiling imagery was a part of Coleridge's thinking over many years, see *The Destiny of Nations*, 15–17; *On a Cataract* (1799), 10–11; and *The Veil of Light* (1806), 1–4. A veil that both conceals and reveals can be found in this fragment of ?1810: 'The body | Eternal Shadow of the finite Soul, | The Soul's self-symbol | its image of itself, | Its own yet not itself' (Beer, 304).

transforming the external world. The 'luminous Cloud' is like the veil that covers God but does not hide Him; the 'Light' and 'Glory'—normally divine attributes—are clearly identified as belonging to the human soul; and the 'Voice', though self-generated, is the 'Life & Element' of all other sounds. Like Wordsworth, at the end of *Tintern Abbey*, Coleridge is asking that a depth of shared emotion should provide recompense for all that has been lost. The urgency of personal need seems in its momentum to generate larger and still larger claims. 'Joy' is not simply exuberance, but a return to direct apprehensions of the 'One Life' that in 1798 had (supposedly) been Wordsworth's too:

> Joy, innocent Sara! Joy, that ne'er was given
> Save to the Pure, & in their purest Hour,
> JOY, Sara! is the Spirit & the Power,
> That wedding Nature to us gives in Dower
>   A new Earth & new Heaven
> Undreamt of by the Sensual & the Proud!

>   (ll. 313–8)

Public allusion and private reference are seen to merge, as Coleridge prepares the way for his blessing on Sara. The wedding and dowry imagery, present throughout the poem, is brought to a suitably hopeful climax (l. 316). The allusion to Revelation (l. 316) contains a submerged parallel between Sara and 'the holy city, new Jerusalem coming down from God out of heaven, prepared as a bride adorned for her husband'.[45] And the phrase 'Undreamt of by the Sensual & the Proud' is a self-echo, from *France: an Ode*, which clearly distinguishes the Coleridgean elect from those who are 'Slaves by their own compulsion'.[46] Associative language, instead of trapping the poet within his 'personal self', is being deliberately used by him as a means of release.

As one might expect, it is an increasingly religious language which does the trick. The blessing on Sara is full of biblical resonance:

> Sister & Friend of my devoutest Choice!
> Thou being innocent & full of love,
> And nested with the Darlings of thy love,
> And feeling in thy Soul, Heart, Lips, & Arms
> Even what the conjugal & mother Dove
> That borrows genial Warmth from those, she warms,
> Feels in her thrill'd wings, blessedly outspread . . .

>   (ll. 324–30)

[45] In Revelation 21: 1–2, the description of 'a new heaven and a new earth' is immediately followed by that of the 'holy city, new Jerusalem'.

[46] See ll. 85–6: 'The sensual and the dark rebel in vain, | Slaves by their own compulsion!'

Coleridge, who has just addressed Sara as 'pure of Heart!' is clearly recalling Milton's invocation to the Spirit that prefers 'Before all temples the upright heart and pure':

> thou from the first
> Wast present, and with mighty wings outspread
> Dove-like sat'st brooding on the vast abyss
> And madest it pregnant: what in me is dark
> Illumine, what is low raise and support . . .
>
> (*PL*, i. 18–23)

In *Paradise Lost*, the dove is performing the original creative act; in the *Letter* she is protecting her young. Coleridge has replaced the apocalyptic with homeliness; he has also moved the brooding process on a stage. Both poets imagine the dove, its wings 'blessedly outspread' in a gesture of love. But Sara also receives back genial warmth from her nestlings. Giving and receiving, in her case, seem scarcely distinguishable.[47]

The transition from private association into a language of religious symbolism is accompanied by a complete retraction from the elegiac tone of 'we receive but what we give', and an emotional recapitulation of earlier, more optimistic beliefs. At this final stage in the poem, every word is a reminder of imaginative patterns which go back, beyond the Alfoxden relationship, to the Unitarian early Coleridge. 'To thee would all things live', he writes, addressing Sara in her role as Holy Spirit:

> To thee would all things live from Pole to Pole,
> Their Life the Eddying of thy Living Soul.
>
> (ll. 335–6)

---

[47] In a draft conclusion to *The Ruined Cottage*, Wordsworth had used the same image of brooding to suggest the autonomy of mind:

> He had discoursed
> Like one who in the slow & silent works
> The manifold conclusions of his thought
> Had brooded till Imaginations power
> Condensed them to a passion whence she drew
> Herself, new energies, resistless force . . .
>
> (Butler, 275)

The line 'That borrows genial Warmth from those, she warms' (*Letter*, 329) offers much the same idea. When Wordsworth uses the dove image again, in Book Five of *The Prelude*, it is in a more homely context. With Milton, Coleridge and his former self in mind, he transforms the dove into a farmyard hen, moving with her brood 'in tenderness and love, | A centre of the circle which they make' (*1805*, v. 251–2). Coleridge's description (*Letter*, 327–9) is by comparison grand, sensual, passionate.

The image is of concentric circles, spreading outward to include first the earth, then God.[48] One is reminded of three early passages, the first from Coleridge's *Lectures on Revealed Religion*, the other two from *Religious Musings*:

> Jesus knew our nature—and that expands like the circles of a Lake—the Love of our Friends, parents and neighbours lead[s] us to the love of our Country to the love of all Mankind. The intensity of private attachment encourages, not prevents, universal philanthropy . . .

(C.C., i. 163)

> From HOPE and stronger FAITH to perfect LOVE
> Attracted and absorbed: and center'd there
> GOD only to behold, and know, and feel,
> Till by exclusive Consciousness of GOD
> All self-annihilated it shall make
> GOD it's Identity: God all in all!
> We and our Father ONE!

(ll. 45–51)

> Mid countless brethren with a lonely heart
> Thro' courts and cities the smooth Savage roams
> Feeling himself, his own low Self the whole,
> When he by sacred sympathy might make
> The whole ONE SELF! SELF, that no alien knows!
> SELF, far diffus'd as Fancy's wing can travel!
> SELF, spreading still! Oblivious of it's own,
> Yet all of all possessing!

(ll. 164–71)

Coleridge has used the structure of former epiphanies to stand for a 'symbolical language within [him]' which 'already and forever exists'.[49] Biblical resonance, Miltonic allusion, and his own earlier poems, all combine to rescue him from the dangers of the projectionist self.

They are dangers which by now have become familiar, and which seem always, in Coleridge's poetry, to emerge in the same way. The expansion

---

[48] A Notebook entry of March–April 1802 connects 'eddying' with God: 'Quiet stream, with all its eddies, & the moonlight playing on them, quiet as if they were Ideas in the divine mind anterior to the Creation' (*Notebooks*, i. 1154).

[49] 'In looking at objects of Nature', Coleridge writes in a famous *Notebook* entry of 1805, 'I seem rather to be seeking, as it were *asking*, a symbolical language for something within me that already and forever exists, than observing any thing new. Even when that latter is the case, yet still I have always an obscurecure feeling as if that new phaenomenon were the dim Awakening of a forgotten or hidden Truth of my inner Nature | It is still interesting as a Word, a Symbol! It is λoyos, the Creator! ⟨and the Evolver!⟩' (*Notebooks*, ii. 2546)

of the human ego leads ultimately (and logically) to the displacement of God. But for Coleridge, such displacement is unthinkable:

> O Wedding Guest! this soul hath been
> Alone on a wide wide sea
> So lonely 'twas that God himself
> Scarce seemed there to be.

(*The Ancient Mariner*, 630–3)

If the mind is to be thought of as having God-like powers, they must be kept in their place, not allowed to take over. Likeness only, not equality or sameness, can be admitted. The self, expanded to its utmost capacity, must at that point retract, allowing God's 'Identity' to become all in all: 'We begin with the I KNOW MYSELF, in order to end with the absolute I AM. We proceed from the SELF, in order to lose and find all self in GOD.'[50] Coleridge defines the limitations of imaginative potential in the act of making for it the greatest possible claims. Imagination is the living power and prime agent of all human perception. But it is also a *'repetition in the finite mind'* of God's eternal act of creation.[51] One might be tempted, from an atheistical (or ahistorical) perspective, to see the 'infinite I AM' as the human imagination, usurping God. But Coleridge will not allow either the reader, or himself, to indulge in such misreading. The deference to an absolute, outside the self, is an absolute precondition of the self's power. Finiteness is reassuring: it means that imagination can be contained.

In Coleridge's poetry, then, God and imagination are engaged in a struggle for power. The climax of the *Letter to Sara* (like the *Biographia* definition) offers a merging of human and divine identities, where no such merging can in fact take place. As Coleridge moves from a solipsism which is both elegiac and triumphant—'In our life alone does Nature live'—into an essentially theocentric affirmation (ll. 324–40), one becomes aware of conflicting interests, which the poetry itself seeks to deny. The rift between one kind of statement and the other is slurred over, by a language that is emotionally imprecise, and charged with religious significance. As Sara becomes the Holy Spirit, Coleridge regains—or seems, by a trick of language, to regain—symbolic vision. The soul no longer forms 'narrower and narrower circles till . . . its wings beat against the *personal self*',[52] but is released into 'λογος, the Creator! ⟨and the Evolver⟩'.[53] The

---

[50] *Biographia*, i. 283.
[51] *Biographia*, i. 304; my italics.
[52] *Notebooks*, ii. 2531.
[53] *Notebooks*, ii. 2546.

achievement is made to seem more vulnerable and fictional, not less so, by Coleridge's strategic exploitation of a proxy to do his seeing for him. Despite the boldness of his affirmation—'We, we ourselves rejoice' (l. 320)—joy is not something he can feel himself. The present tense suggests potential not experience, and the same goes for the plural pronoun.[54] Imaginative vision, as always in his poetry, is vicariously achieved. The distancing device ensures the withdrawal of his own ego, which is necessary if divine power is to get the upper hand. It also allows for a reduction of guilt, if by any chance usurpation should go the other way. Coleridge is to be seen playing an elaborate game of brinkmanship, of which he is himself no doubt partly aware. The *status* of imaginative release, in these circumstances, inevitably seems questionable. The power of the writing, on the other hand, does not. If the mind 'knowingly passes a fiction on itself', at the end of the *Letter*, it is a magnificent fiction:

> Total grandeur of a total edifice,
> Chosen by an inquisitor of structures
> For himself. He stops upon this threshold,
> As if the design of all his words takes form
> And frame from thinking and is realized.[55]

[54] Coleridge's hopes for a personal redemption are best typified by the wistful conditional tense in *Kubla Khan*: 'Could I revive within me | Her symphony and song . . .' (ll. 42–3). But Lamb in *This Lime Tree Bower*, Hartley in *Frost at Midnight*, Sara in the *Letter* and Wordsworth in '*To William Wordsworth*', all offer him vicarious fulfilment.

[55] Wallace Stevens, *To an Old Philosopher in Rome*, 76–80.

4

'Radical Difference':
Wordsworth and Coleridge in 1802

(i) *Theory or Practice?*

Coleridge's growing sense of distance from Wordsworth was not entirely emotional. It was accentuated, not caused, by his 'own peculiar lot' in 1802; and did not always produce the envy and exclusion so clearly present in the *Letter to Sara Hutchinson*. The two men were in fact moving, intellectually and creatively, in opposite directions. Wordsworth at times seemed oblivious of change, and wrote as though the closeness of their earlier relationship still existed. But Coleridge became increasingly aware of ways in which they differed. In a series of justly famous letters, written during this year, one sees him not merely acknowledging divergence, but also (with a sort of doggedness) tracking down its causes. 'I rather suspect', he writes to Robert Southey, in July:

that some where or other there is a radical Difference in our theoretical opinions respecting Poetry— | this I shall endeavour to go to the Bottom of—and acting the arbitrator between the old School & the New School hope to lay down some plain, & perspicuous, tho' not superficial, Canons of Criticism respecting Poetry.

(Griggs, ii. 830)

This is the germ of *Biographia Literaria*. 'Radical Difference' is something Coleridge believes to have grown from his increasing dissatisfaction with the 1800 Preface. Wordsworth's claim there, that the language of ordinary life is appropriate for poetry, seems questionable to him, though he cannot yet say why. Two weeks earlier, he had written to Sotheby:

In my opinion, Poetry justifies, as *Poetry* independent of any other Passion, some new combinations of language, & *commands* the omission of many others allowable in other compositions | Now Wordsworth, me saltem judice, has in his system not sufficiently admitted the former, & in his practice has too frequently sinned against the latter.

(Griggs, ii. 812)

This seems clear enough: poetry must be granted a degree of autonomy, and should in some cases have an obligation to be selective in what it takes from ordinary life. Wordsworth, by implication, is too wholesale in his use of everyday language, and follows too rigidly the theory of the 1800 Preface. In October, however, writing to Thomas Wedgwood, Coleridge seems less sure: 'in point of poetic Diction I am not so well s[atisf]ied that you do not require a certain *Aloofness* from [the la]nguage of real life, which I think deadly to Poetry.' (Griggs, ii. 877) George Watson, misinterpreting the comment, writes that Coleridge 'has moved so far from the Preface that he feels poetic diction to "require a certain *aloofness* from [the la]nguage of real Life"'.[1] In fact, he means precisely the reverse. The 'you' of 'you do not require' does not mean 'one'; it refers directly to Thomas Wedgwood, who has just criticized some of Coleridge's poems for their 'feeble expressions & unpolished Lines' (Griggs, ii. 876). 'I sometimes suspect', he goes on to explain,

that my foul Copy would often appear to general Readers more polished, than my fair Copy—many of the feeble & colloquial Expressions have been industriously substituted for others, which struck me as artificial, & not standing the test—as being neither the language of passion nor distinct Conceptions.

(Griggs, ii. 877)

Here, then, one sees Coleridge returning to the values of the 1800 Preface. He is expressing his own preference for a colloquial 'language of passion', as opposed to the 'polished' and 'artificial' diction admired by his readers. And he is doing so in terms that seem entirely to contradict his statement of three months before. It is important, first, that he makes these comments about his own poetic practice, and is not likely, therefore, to be bluffing; second, that he is seriously implying criticism of a man he would normally flatter.[2] One can hardly doubt that he is expressing a genuine opinion, yet the change of mind, within three months, seems perverse. An explanation for the discrepancy is needed.

Coleridge's statement to Sotheby in July, 'Poetry justifies, as *Poetry* independent of any other Passion, some new combinations of Language', does not deny the connection between poetry and passion; it requires that the language of real life should be refined to give poetry its intenseness. There is nothing inconsistent here with the thinking that lies behind the

---

[1] *Biographia Literaria*, ed. George Watson (Everyman, 1975), p. xi.
[2] 'You are a perfect electrometer in these things' he confides to Wedgwood earlier in the same letter (Griggs, ii. 877)—reusing a phrase he had once applied to Dorothy Wordsworth (Griggs, i. 331).

1800 Preface—'the Reader cannot be too often reminded that Poetry is passion: it is the history or science of feelings'[3]—and it is important that Coleridge remains faithful to this belief right through the period of his rethinking, and on into *Biographia* itself.[4] Taking 'passion' as a central criterion, he first states carefully in Chapter Seventeen that 'the property of passion is not to *create*; but to set in increased activity.' (*Biographia*, ii. 57), then makes a distinction between the poetic and undiscriminating use of ordinary language:

It is indeed very possible to adopt in a poem the unmeaning repetitions, habitual phrases, and other blank counters, which an unfurnished or confused understanding interposes at short intervals, in order to keep hold of his subject which is still slipping from him, and to give him time for recollection . . . . But what assistance to the poet, or ornament to the poem, these can supply, I am at a loss to conjecture.

'Nothing', he continues, making clear his distinctions,

assuredly can differ either in origin or in mode more widely from the *apparent* tautologies of intense and turbulent feeling, in which the passion is greater and of longer endurance, than to be exhausted or satisfied by a single representation of the image or incident exciting it.[5]

Reading between the lines, one suspects that Coleridge sees in Wordsworth an inability to distinguish between these two kinds of language. It is not clear, however, whether he thinks this lack of discrimination a feature of Wordsworth's theory, or merely an occasional failure in his poetry. In the letter to Sotheby he puts forward both possibilities, but conducts his argument on a largely theoretical basis. In *Biographia* (where his main aim is to prove a disparity between the claims of the 1800 Preface and the poetry itself) he argues, again, in terms of the theory. But what, in both cases, is the real source of his unease?

To return to the letter Coleridge writes to Southey in July:

altho' Wordsworth's Preface is half a child of my own Brain |& so arose out of Conversations, so frequent, that with few exceptions we could scarcely either of us perhaps positively say, which first started any particular Thought . . . yet I am far from going all lengths with Wordsworth | He has written lately a number of Poems (32 in all) some of them of considerable Length (the longest 160 Lines) the greater

---

[3] See the Note to *The Thorn* in *Lyrical Ballads*, 1800 (Brett and Jones, 289).

[4] See, particularly, *Biographia*, ii. 41. That Wordsworth too maintains the belief can be seen in his letter to Thelwall of January 1804, where he speaks of 'the passion of the subject', 'the passion of the metre', 'the Passion of the sense', and adds that he can scarcely 'admit any limits to the dislocation of the verse . . . that may not be justified by some passion or other' (*EY*, 434–5).

[5] *Biographia*, ii. 57. Coleridge goes on to quote from the Song of Deborah, 'as illustrated by Wordsworth himself'.

number of these to my feelings very excellent Compositions | but here & there a daring Humbleness of Language & Versification, and a strict adherence to matter of fact, even to prolixity, that startled me | his alterations likewise in Ruth perplexed me | and I have thought & thought again | & have not had my doubts solved by Wordsworth . . .

(Griggs, ii. 830)

The criticisms seem to be levelled at individual poems, but it is not easy to say which. If one takes it that Coleridge has the language of real life in mind, only a small group out of the 32 lyrics is eligible. *The Leechgatherer* in its early form is presumably the poem estimated at '160 lines'; there is a scattering of 'lyrical ballads' like *The Sailor's Mother*, *Alice Fell*, *Beggars* (and possibly, *The Affliction of Margaret*); and Coleridge might also include such playful, garrulous poems as *The Tinker*, *To a Skylark* and *The Barberry Tree*. In each case, his criticism would have a good deal of justice. *The Leechgatherer*, before Wordsworth revises it, might easily be condemned for its 'strict adherence to matter of fact, even to prolixity'. (Sara Hutchinson's comment that it is 'tedious' amounts to the same thing.)[6] Equally, the ballads of 1802 are a disappointment after their earlier counterparts. They slip into banality, and often seem too close to the events that inspired them. Of *Beggars*, for instance, Dorothy writes in her Journal for 13 March: 'After tea I read to William that account of the little Boys belonging to the tall woman and *an unlucky thing it was for he could not escape from those very words*, and so he could not write the poem. He left it unfinished and went tired to Bed.' (*DWJ*, 101; my italics) As for poems like *The Tinker* and *The Skylark*, there cannot be much doubt as to their 'daring Humbleness of Language & Versification':

> Right before the Farmer's door
> Down he sits his brows he knits:
> Then his hammer he rouzes
>   Batter, batter, batter
>   He begins to clatter
> And while the work is going on
> Right good ale he bouzes

(The Tinker, 9–15)

---

[6] 'You speak of [the Leechgatherer's] speech as tedious', Wordsworth writes to Sara in June, outraged by her recent letter: 'everything is tedious when one does not read with the feelings of the Author—'The Thorn' is tedious to hundreds; and so is the 'Idiot Boy' to hundreds. It is in the character of the old man to tell his story in a manner which an *impatient* reader must necessarily feel as tedious.' (*EY*, 367) The extreme defensiveness is typical of Wordsworth's state of mind in 1802, but the revisions made to *The Leechgatherer*, as a direct consequence of Sara's criticisms, show his absorption of her point of view. For a discussion of the revisions and their implications for the relationship with Coleridge, see Chapter Five, below.

But even having acknowledged the appropriateness of Coleridge's remarks (and they are largely, it seems, value-judgements) one has not arrived at the centre of his critical position. Something in his reaction against Wordsworth's lyrics goes deeper than his specific objections might suggest, causing him first to make vague approving comments he cannot support ('the greater number of these to my feelings very excellent Compositions'), then to search for labels like 'daring Humbleness' or 'strict adherence to matter of fact' to explain his unease. The labels are not arbitrary, but they apply to so small a proportion of the lyrics that one senses deeper underlying reservations which Coleridge is not choosing to acknowledge.

Other letters, written during 1802, tell one a good deal more. The famous one to Sotheby, written on 10 September, contains a reaffirmation of values supposedly shared by Wordsworth in 1798:

> Nature has her proper interest; & he will know what it is, who believes & feels, that every Thing has a Life of it's own, & that we are all *one Life*. A Poet's *Heart & Intellect* should be *combined, intimately* combined & *unified*, with the great appearances in Nature—& not merely held in solution & loose mixture with them, in the shape of formal Similies. I do not mean to *exclude* these formal Similies— there are moods of mind, in which they are natural—pleasing moods of mind, & such as a Poet will often have, & sometimes express; but they are not his highest, & most appropriate moods.
>
> (Griggs, ii. 864)

The poet Coleridge has in mind is Bowles, whose 'perpetual trick of *moralizing* every thing' (Griggs, ii. 864) goes against his own most basic requirement, that 'every phrase, every metaphor, every personification, should have it's justifying cause in some *passion* either of the Poet's mind, or of the Characters described by the poet' (Griggs, ii. 812). Judged by this criterion, Bowles is bound to fail. His poetry, at one time greatly admired and imitated by Coleridge, now seems to deny the values of the 'One Life'.

Coleridge would not have intended it to do so, but his critique of Bowles applies equally well to the Wordsworth of 1802. When he makes the concession—'I do not mean to *exclude* these formal Similies—there are moods of mind, in which they are natural—pleasing moods of mind . . .' he might very easily be thinking of *To a Butterfly*, or *To A Daisy*. It is interesting, in this connection, to notice that a number of Wordsworth's lyrics are grouped in 1807 under the heading 'Moods of my own Mind'. There is an acceptance of limitation in the slightness of the label, as though Wordsworth were himself conceding that 'they are not his highest, & most appropriate moods'. If one takes the analogy further, Coleridge's phrase 'merely held in solution & loose mixture' exactly describes the quality of Wordsworth's response in spring 1802:

> Oft do I sit by thee at ease,
> And weave a web of similies,
> Loose types of Things through all degrees,
>   Thoughts of thy raising;
> And many a fond and idle name
> I give to thee, for praise or blame,
> As is the humour of the game,
>   While I am gazing.

(To the Daisy [2], 9–16)

Here, as in many of the 1802 lyrics, Wordsworth is writing about the workings of fancy, and is intrigued by the possibilities it opens up. Fancy is a sort of loose associationism. It does not bind thoughts and images tightly together, but allows them to proliferate, as though they had a will of their own: 'Loose types of Things through all degrees, | *Thoughts of thy raising*'. By implication, the process is rapid and aimless. It involves the thinker, not in a full engagement with the natural object, but in a sequence of namings and re-namings, which certainly do not seem to have their 'justifying cause in some *passion* . . . of the poet's mind'. Wordsworth is not making claims for fancy as more than a 'game'; in fact, he stresses its 'ease', 'fond'-ness, 'idle'-ness, and 'humour'. Yet there is something magical in 'weav[ing] a web of similies' which gives the process a creative status. Later, in his Preface to *Poems*, 1815, Wordsworth writes, 'Fancy depends upon the rapidity and profusion with which she scatters her thoughts and images . . . or she prides herself upon the curious subtilty and the successful elaboration with which she can detect their lurking affinities.' (*Prose Works*, iii. 36) This is by no means a limited claim: fancy is capable of 'insinuating herself into the heart of objects with creative activity.' (ibid., 30) The language Wordsworth uses—'curious subtilty', 'detect', 'lurking', and 'insinuating'—gives her an unpredictable, almost insidious, power. One recalls that in *Prelude* Book Eight, the '*wilfulness* of fancy and conceit', intruding into human relationships, gives 'them new importance to the mind' (*1805*, viii. 520–2; my italics). It is in this context that Wordsworth first defines the relation between fancy and passion:

>   My present theme
> Is to retrace the way that led me on
> Through Nature to the love of human-kind;

> Nor could I with such object overlook
> The influence of this power which turned itself
> Instinctively to human passions . . .
>
> (*1805*, viii. 586–91)

Fancy may be capricious, but it is redeemed by its connection with human feelings. They allow it to find its way 'into the heart of objects'—to merge, in other words, with the creative imagination.

For the Coleridge of 1798, such merging had been a possibility. *Frost at Midnight*—in so far as poetry of this kind *can* offer definitions—had done so in Wordsworthian terms. Fancy (emblematized in the fluttering movement of the '*stranger*') had seemed at first to be a form of entrapment: evidence of the 'self-watching subtilizing mind' (l. 27). But through a sequence of associations, activated and validated by emotion, it had led to the memory within a memory of church bells, which were 'most like articulate sounds of things to come' (l. 38). The 'most believing superstitious wish' of childhood (l. 29)—as opposed, by implication, to the introversion of the adult—was thus able to guide Coleridge from pure associationism into imagination. Fancy, in the process, had been exonerated. All quotations, here, refer to the text of *Frost at Midnight* published in the Quarto volume of 1798. When he came to revise the poem for publication in *Sibylline Leaves*, Coleridge made alterations that were in keeping with the disparagement of fancy that one sees in *Biographia*. Completely missing from the best-known published text are lines in which he had carefully juxtaposed the seriousness and frivolity of fancy's workings, seeing creative potential alongside idleness:

> But still the living spirit in our frame,
> That loves not to behold a lifeless thing,
> Transfuses into all it's own delights
> Its own volition, sometimes with deep faith,
> And sometimes with fantastic playfulness
>
> (ll. 21–5)

In their place one finds the famous and much quoted lines about solipsism, in which—with a tone almost of contempt—Coleridge describes the fluttering '*stranger*',

> Whose puny flaps and freaks the idling Spirit
> By its own moods interprets, every where
> Echo or mirror seeking of itself,
> And makes a toy of Thought.
>
> (ll. 20–3)

Damage is done, in the process of revision, to the logic of the poem: for how, if the workings of fancy are so narcissistic, can release from the self be achieved? But in its own right, the alteration is fascinating, as a record of the major change that Coleridge's thinking has undergone.

All the evidence suggests that it is already an articulated change by 1802. The merging of fancy and imagination, possible for Wordsworth not only in the *Prelude* lines already quoted (which belong to October 1804), but right through into the Preface of 1815, is already by 1802 a closed option for Coleridge. *Biographia*—implicitly refuting the 1815 Preface—tells one very briefly what the division between these two faculties is, but the letter to Sotheby, written fifteen years earlier, gives a clearer idea of why it should exist:

It must occur to every Reader that the Greeks in their religious poems address always the Numina Loci, the Genii, the Dryads, the Naiads, &c &c—All natural Objects were *dead*—mere hollow Statues—but there was a godkin or Goddessling *included* in each—In the Hebrew Poetry you find nothing of this poor Stuff—as poor in genuine Imagination, as it is mean in Intellect— | At best, it is but Fancy, or the aggregating Faculty of the mind—not *Imagination*, or the *modifying*, and *co-adunating* Faculty. This the Hebrew Poets appear to me to have possessed beyond all others—& next to them the English. In the Hebrew Poets each Thing has a Life of it's own, & yet they are all one Life.

(Griggs, ii. 865–6)

The connection between this and Coleridge's criticism of Bowles must be apparent. Greek poetry deals with natural objects as though they were 'dead'—'mere hollow Statues'. Any life they might seem to have is conferred on them, or 'included' in them, by an essentially limited faculty of the mind. This faculty interprets things not as parts or symbols of a whole, but as separate, fixed entities—each with its own diminutive property of conferred life. To put it in the terms applied to Bowles: imagination causes the '*Heart & Intellect*' to be '*combined, intimately* combined & *unified*, with the great appearances in Nature'; fancy holds the mind and natural objects 'in solution & loose mixture . . . in the shape of formal Similies.' (Griggs, ii. 864) Coleridge makes no allowance, as Wordsworth does, for the connection between fancy and human emotion. 'Godkins and Goddesslings' do not have their 'justifying cause in some *passion* . . . of the Poet's mind', but are merely a decoration or afterthought. As he puts it, dismissively, in *Biographia*:

FANCY . . . has no other counters to play with, but fixities and definites. The Fancy is indeed no other than a mode of Memory emancipated from the order of time and space; and blended with, and modified by that empirical phenomenon of the will, which we express by the word CHOICE. But equally with the ordinary memory it must receive all its materials ready made from the law of association.[7]

If fancy really is no more than 'a mode of Memory emancipated from the order of time and space', it is both limited and dangerous—limited, because it can play only with 'fixities and definites' (the ready made materials of 'the law of association'); dangerous, because it has the capacity to run riot, destroying true poetry. In this respect it resembles the 'false diction' referred to by Wordsworth as 'the gaudiness and inane phraseology of many modern writers' in the Advertisement to *Lyrical Ballads*, 1798 (*Prose Works*, i. 116), and later defined more fully in the 1800 Preface:

Poets . . . think that they are conferring honour upon themselves and their art in proportion as they separate themselves from the sympathies of men, and indulge in *arbitrary and capricious habits of expression* in order to furnish food for fickle tastes and fickle appetites of their own creation.

(*Prose Works*, i. 124; my italics)

There is no obvious connection between fancy and the language of ordinary life. But for Coleridge in 1802 they are felt to have an affinity. Just as fancy can be 'insinuating' in the *wrong* sense (like false diction, not like a 'creative activity'), so too can the 'daring Humbleness' of Wordsworth's language. To return, for a moment, to *Biographia*, and the end of Chapter Seventeen:

It is indeed very possible to adopt in a poem the unmeaning repetitions, habitual phrases, and other blank counters, which an unfurnished or confused understanding interposes at short intervals, in order to keep hold of his subject, which is still slipping from him, and to give him time for recollection; or in mere aid of vacancy, as in the scanty companies of a country stage the same player pops backwards and forwards, in order to prevent the appearance of empty spaces . . .

(*Biographia*, ii. 57)

The phrase 'blank counters' and the stress on automatic movement—'the same player pops backwards and forwards'—convey Coleridge's horror of anything that breaks down the poet's control of his own words, destroying the connection between language and emotion.[8] False diction, fancy, and 'daring Humbleness' have it in common that they are anarchic. They

---

[7] *Biographia*, i. 305.

[8] Coleridge is not far, here, from Wordsworth's fear of anarchic language, described in the second of his *Essays on Epitaphs* as 'a counter-spirit, unremittingly and noiselessly at work to derange, to subvert, to lay waste, to vitiate, and to dissolve.' (*Prose Works*, ii. 85)

threaten the sanctity of poetic language, which should be (as Milton puts it) 'simple, sensuous, passionate'.

When Coleridge quotes this phrase, in his letter to Southey of July (Griggs, ii. 830), it is in the context of his dissatisfaction with Wordsworth. One feels that he turns to Milton in reaction against Wordsworth, because Milton allows him to think in his customary symbolic terms. Two months later, in the letter to Sotheby, he gives a long and detailed analysis of the famous passage in *Comus* about 'Haemony'. It is here that one sees him most carefully defining his own ideals:

all the puzzle [amongst Milton's commentators] is to find out what Plant Haemony is—which they discover to be the English Spleenwort—& decked out, as a mere play & licence of poetic Fancy, with all the strange properties suited to the purpose of the Drama—They thought little of Milton's platonizing Spirit—who wrote nothing without an interior meaning. 'Where more is meant, than meets the ear' is true of himself beyond all writers. He was so great a Man, that he seems to have considered Fiction as profane, unless where it is consecrated by being emblematic of some Truth . . . Do look at the passage—apply it as an Allegory of Christianity, or to speak more precisely of the Redemption by the Cross—every syllable is full of Light!

(Griggs, ii. 866–7)

Coleridge preserves, here, an implicit distinction between the Bowlesian 'trick of *moralizing* everything', and the power Milton has to perceive and create through symbols. His interpretation of the passage from *Comus* seems far-fetched, and tells one little about Milton; but it does show how strongly Coleridge believes that poetry is 'consecrated by being emblematic of some Truth'. And it reveals, moreover, what sort of 'Truth' he has in mind:

Now what is Haemony? Aἷμα-oἶνoς—Blood-wine.—And he took the wine & blessed it, & said—This is my Blood— | the great Symbol of the Death on the Cross.—There is a general Ridicule cast on all allegorizers of Poets—read Milton's prose works, & observe whether he was one of those who joined in this Ridicule.

(Griggs, ii. 867)

Coleridge values symbolic vision, in this sacramental sense, more highly than any other mode of perception or creation.[9] Hebrew poetry comes

---

[9] For comparable definitions of the sacramental, see *The Destiny of Nations*, 18–20, *The Statesman's Manual* (*CC*, vi. 29–30), and *Notebooks*, ii. 2546. Robert Barth, S. J., in *The Symbolic Imagination, Coleridge and the Romantic Tradition* (Princeton, 1977), examines this aspect of Coleridge's thought in detail.

nearest to embodying it, because 'In the Hebrew poets each Thing has a Life of it's own, & yet they are all one Life.' Bowles and the Greek poets are farthest from it, because according to them 'All natural objects [are] *dead*'. Neither words nor things point beyond themselves, or carry religious implications.

Coleridge is, in fact, with extraordinary consistency, restating beliefs which go as far back as 1796. 'Is not Milton a *sublimer* poet than Homer or Virgil?' he had asked Thelwall, in a letter written in December of that year:

Are not his Personages more sublimely cloathed? And do you not know, that there is not perhaps *one* page in Milton's Paradise Lost, in which he has not borrowed his imagery from the *Scriptures*? I allow, and rejoice that *Christ* appealed only to the understanding & the affections; but I affirm that, after reading Isaiah, or St Paul's Epistle to the Hebrews, Homer & Virgil are disgustingly *tame* to me, & Milton himself barely tolerable.

(Griggs, i. 281)

Measured according to Coleridge's standards, which have remained the same in kind (if not in degree) since 1795, Wordsworth fails absolutely. By rights, he should be in the company of the 'Hebrew' poets: that, Coleridge feels, is the status he deserves for his earlier writing. But the lyrics of 1802 are slight, limited, and lacking in symbolic potential. They reveal, by implication, a new poet: one who is content, like the bad commentators on Milton, that things should be 'decked out, as a mere play & license of poetic Fancy' (Griggs, ii. 866)—one who has more affinities with Bowles, the discarded hero, than with the great precursors in a symbolic tradition.

This lowering of Wordsworth's status is confirmed for Coleridge by his neglect of *The Recluse*, which in its original conception had been designed to celebrate the 'One Life', and which he himself goes on thinking of in such terms.[10] Writing to Poole in October 1803, when he briefly thinks Wordsworth has gone back to working on it, Coleridge stresses the waste that is implied by the shorter lyrics: 'The habit . . . of writing such a multitude of small Poems was . . . hurtful to him . . . I really consider it as a misfortune, that [he] ever deserted his former mountain Track to wander in Lanes & allies' (Griggs, ii. 1013). In returning to *The Recluse*, Wordsworth is re-entering his 'natural Element'. He is confirming the values originally given him by Coleridge, in 1798, and writing a 'great

---

[10] See the letter to Wordsworth of *c*. 10 September 1799, which clearly connects the idea of *The Recluse* with 'hopes of the amelioration of mankind' (Griggs, i. 527), and that of May 1815, in which the same idealistic aims are still preserved (Griggs, iv. 574–5).

work necessarily comprehending his attention & Feelings within the circle of great objects & elevated Conceptions' (ibid.)—a work, in other words, which has real affinities with Milton or 'Hebrew' poetry.[11]

Coleridge seems as a rule to have found it nearly impossible to make ordinary evaluative criticisms of his friend's writing. For an accurate, and in some ways moving, picture of his confusion at having to criticize the friend, 'to whom for the more substantial Third of a Life [he has] been habituated to look up', and for whom 'Love . . . begun and throve and knit it's joints in the perception of his Superiority', one has only to look at the letter written in May 1815, hesitantly explaining his reservations about *The Excursion* (Griggs, iv. 571–3), but never once openly confronting the depth of disappointment he feels. By comparison, the letter to Poole of 1803, quoted above, is unusually honest, since the emotional basis for the criticism it offers is tacitly acknowledged. It is a letter that should put Coleridge's exploratory criticisms of 1802 in perspective. Phrases like 'daring Humbleness of Language & Versification' or 'strict adherence to matter of fact, even to prolixity' (Griggs, ii. 830) stand out as over-specific labels which are used to rationalize, even to explain away, the sense of disillusionment Coleridge actually feels. One could argue that this is simply a matter of articulation: that he is still wondering, in 1802, what is the cause of the unease, and that by 1803 he has things clearer in his own mind. It seems more likely, however, that 1802 is a time when he makes intuitive value-judgements, then blocks them on an intellectual level. This is partly because the reverence for his friend is a habit that sticks, whatever else is changed, partly because he is surprised that Wordsworth, of all people, should be content with so little.

Coleridge's thinking about fancy and imagination, cryptically summarized in *Biographia*, has a private history (part emotional, part intellectual) which I have tried to unfold. It goes back to the period in these poets' relationship when two separate things were happening: Wordsworth was composing his most overtly fanciful poetry, and Coleridge was downgrading fancy to the merely mechanical. A causal connection between the two cannot absolutely be proven, but Coleridge's disappointment and betrayal—even when disguised—speak for themselves. As is so often the case with these two writers, the causes of fundamental difference are not acknowledged. It is the disparity between, on the one hand, Coleridge's increasingly confirmed symbolic thinking,

---

[11] It was presumably Coleridge's admiration for 'Hebrew' poetry that made him write his *Hymn before Sunrise in the Vale of Chamouny* (September, 1802), which strains after religious sublimity in a sequence of sub-Miltonic exclamations.

and, on the other, Wordsworth's entrenched literal-mindedness, that explains the growing divergence in 1802. Not, as Coleridge would have it, a disagreement about poetic diction. 'Radical Difference', then, is a more appropriate phrase than either poet perhaps realized: Coleridge's famous distinction between fancy and imagination rests on a profound, though unvoiced, criticism of his friend.

(ii) *Weaving a Web of Similies: The Lyrics of 1802*

Wordsworth was less alert to change than Coleridge, or perhaps less honest with himself about it. The great opening stanzas of *Intimations* are, admittedly, a confrontation of loss. They show the poet mourning a change which is absolute, and mourning on a level that Coleridge never matches:

> But there's a tree of many one
> A single field which I have look'd upon
> Both of them speak of something that is gone . . .
> Whither is fled the visionary gleam
> Where is it gone the glory and the dream . . .[12]

But the questions are rhetorical, and not for two years does he concern himself with the possibility that they might be answered.[13] Nothing Wordsworth writes in 1802 shows a need to enquire about the causes of loss, and nowhere does he reveal the sort of probing curiosity that is Coleridge's at this time. His poetry is full of what Alan Grob has called 'a mood of passionate nostalgia for the heightened sensibility of childhood'.[14] It is also—at a level he never acknowledges—full of nostalgia for the year at Alfoxden. Revising the first volume of *Lyrical Ballads* for its third edition, and doing a great deal of work on *The Pedlar*, Wordsworth must have been reminded at this period of the exuberance he had felt, with Coleridge and Dorothy, only four years before:

> One moment now may give us more
> Than fifty years of reason;
> Our minds shall drink at every pore
> The spirit of the season.

[12] *Intimations*, 51–3; 56–7. All references are to the text as it stands in MSM (Curtis, 164–70).
[13] See Chapter Six, below.
[14] 'Wordsworth's *Immortality Ode* and the Search for Identity', *ELH*, 32, no. 1 (March, 1965), 35.

> Some silent laws our hearts may make,
> Which they shall long obey;
> We for the year to come may take
> Our temper from to-day.
>
> (*Lines Written at a small distance
> from my House*, 25–32)

Looking back on this joy, he attempts to retrieve his former self, not in the voice of religious or philosophical commitment, but in the lyric voice of personal response. The collapse of *Home at Grasmere* had perhaps, by this time, been recognized as a failure to sustain the early Coleridgean dedication to the 'One Life'.[15] At least a more personal faith might survive.

A small group of 'lyrical ballads'—*Alice Fell, Beggars, The Emigrant Mother, The Forsaken*, with two or three others—seem to have been written with the responses of 1798 in mind, and intended to recapture a former intensity. With few exceptions, they fail to live up to their earlier counterparts. *Alice Fell* attempts, like *Simon Lee*, to turn a minor episode into something more significant, but the poet's message intrudes from the start. Alice is preoccupied with her tattered cloak, instead of with the destitution it stands for (ll. 25–8). She is to be pitied for her state, but admired for her peculiar stoicism, which fixes on material detail instead of brooding over real loss. One could forgive the poem its neatness if it ended well, but by comparison with *Simon Lee* it does not:

> Up to the Tavern-door we post,
> Of Alice and her grief I told
> And I gave money to the host
> To buy a new cloak for the old.
>
> "And let it be of duffel grey
> As warm a cloak as man can sell"
> Proud Creature was she the next day
> The little orphan Alice Fell.—
>
> (ll. 53–60)

The child's delight in her new coat stands for two things: Wordsworth's self-pleasure at being the coat-provider, and his sentimentality at achieving something so touchingly small. It is as though the purchasing of a duffel-coat is enough, so long as it fends off the need to ask larger questions.

[15] See Jonathan Wordsworth, 'On Man, on Nature and on Human Life', *RES* New Series, 31, 121 (February, 1980), 17–29; and *Borders of Vision*, 132–48; 357–61.

Imitating an earlier style, and straining to re-establish the assumptions that went with it, Wordsworth writes poetry that is self-conscious, uneasy, even dull. There is evidence of a lack of humour here, which clearly separates the writing of 1802 from its earlier counterpart in 1798. *We are Seven* and *Anecdote for Fathers* had moved towards their deeper truths through ambiguity; but four years later, the poet seems unwilling to deflate his own role. *The Leechgatherer* is an outstanding exception, as I shall argue at a later stage;[16] yet Lewis Carroll's parody, in general terms, strikes one as cruelly right:

> I met an aged, aged man
>   Upon the lonely moor:
> I knew I was a gentleman,
>   And he was but a boor.
>
> So I stopped and roughly questioned him,
>   "Come tell me how you live!"
> But his words impressed my ear no more
>   Than if it were a sieve.

(Upon the Lonely Moor, 1–8)

It is not Wordsworth's cross-questioning one objects to, so much as the posturing it implies. His interest in beggars, emigrants, orphans, seems at this period in his life to be little more than a self-conscious gesture towards the subject of human pain. The sharpness of his earlier perception of injustice has disappeared, and with it the intuition of mental suffering as 'permanent, obscure and dark' (*Borderers*, III. v. 64). Lacking his earlier awareness, Wordsworth turns to suffering in a literary search for disquietude. He is worried by the parochialism of his life in Grasmere—'With little here to do or see | Of things that in the great world be'[17]—and is anxious, above all, about the irresponsibility that his retreat implies:

> My whole life I have liv'd in pleasant thought
> As if life's business were a summer mood:
> Who will not wade to seek a bridge or boat
> How can he ever hope to cross the flood?
> How can he e'er expect that others should
> Build for him, sow for him, and at his call
> Love him who for himself will take no heed at all?

(The Leechgatherer, 36–42)[18]

16 See Chapter Five, below.

17 See *To the Daisy* [2], 1–2.

18 I quote from the early version (3–9 May 1802), transcribed by Curtis, 186 ff. The lines are usually interpreted as referring to Coleridge. See Chapter Five, below, for a more detailed discussion.

Like Cowper before him, he feels the need to justify (as well as to celebrate) his retirement from the world. Writing about beggars is a sobering reminder of different ways of life. It keeps up the semblance of responsibility, and, though carrying little genuine commitment, provides an outlet for personal guilt.

Occasionally, the poetry rises above these considerations. *The Emigrant Mother*, for instance, has lines of tenderness that recall *The Forsaken Indian Woman*:

> Dear Babe! thou daughter of another
> One moment let me be thy mother!
> An infant's face and looks are thine,
> And sure a mother's heart is mine.
>
> (*The Emigrant Mother*, 1–4)[19]

While in *The Forsaken*, Wordsworth thinks himself back, not just into the story of *The Ruined Cottage*, but into its emotional intensity as well:

> Ofttimes it seems that silent years
> Bring an unquestionable tale
> And yet they leave it short, & fears
> And hopes are strong & will prevail
> My calmest faith escapes not pain
> And feeling that the hope is vain
> I think that he will come again.
>
> (ll. 8–14)[20]

Moments like these are rare, however. For the most part, Wordsworth's attention to suffering is little more than formal. When it gathers emotional implications, they are personal, and centre on the need for continuity with the past.

Outside the group of 'lyrical ballads' this same need persists, but under complex and variable conditions. There are the more honest, thoughtful moments—

> Joy will be gone in its mortality,
> Something must stay to tell us of the rest . . .
>
> (*A Farewell*, 51–2)

—but on the whole Wordsworth is resolute in asserting that he can and will go on responding as he did, that no change has taken place:

[19] See particularly *The Forsaken Indian Woman*, 1–10.
[20] Of equal power are ll. 64–70 in *The Affliction of Mary — of —*.

My heart leaps up when I behold
A Rainbow in the sky:
So was it when my life began;
So is it, now I am a man,
So be it, when I shall grow old
Or let me die!
The Child is Father of the man;
And I should wish that all my days may be
Bound each to each by natural Piety.

Even without knowing that *Intimations* was begun the next day, one would read this as a defence against loss. The pathos lies not so much in the apparent self-deception as in the weightiness of rhetoric, which is disproportionate to the claim that is made. Wordsworth is assuring himself that his responsiveness continues; but the type of response he describes is limited and easy—something everyone can feel, not something reserved for the genius or the child. However hard one tries to give the poem a symbolic value, and to read 'my heart leaps up' as an assertion of primal sympathy, one still feels its limitations.[21] Wordsworth's unconfidence emerges, not elegiacally (as in the Ode) but in the cheerfulness with which he retreats into values that lack all courage and grandeur.

The best lyrics of the period are those which set out to make no claims:

The cock is crowing,
The stream is flowing,
The small birds twitter,
The Lake doth glitter,
The green field sleeps in the sun;
The Horse and his Marrow
Drag the plow and the harrow,
The cattle are grazing,
Their heads never raising,
There are forty feeding like one.[22]

---

[21] In *Frost at Midnight*, where the phrase first appears, it is equally wishful:

I snatch'd
A hasty glance, and still my heart leapt up,
For still I hop'd to see the *stranger's* face . . .

(ll. 44–6)

[22] 'The cock is crowing', 1–10.

Remaining as close as he dares to Dorothy's prose (*DWJ*, 111), and never
pausing to describe response, Wordsworth creates a sense of a distanced
vitality. The effect of a list is maintained, not just to heighten objectivity
(this is a minimal *recording* of sights and sounds), but to intensify each of
the components in a total mood. The relaxed, iterative rhythm seems to be
promising climax, but at every fifth line holds still in a restful pause. Any
pleasure one might feel from a sense of progression, or from a disclosure of
the poet's feelings, is withheld. In its place is the more subtle pleasure of
receiving distinct images, through which private emotion is conveyed.
Wordsworth draws his reader, as by a spell, into a 'mood of [his] own
mind'. And having done so, he can break through from passive
observation into excited involvement:

> The Plough-boy is whooping—anon—anon;
> There's joy in the mountains,
> There's life in the fountains,
> Small clouds are sailing,
> Blue sky prevailing;
> The rain is over and gone.—
>
>   (ll. 15–20)

For all its apparent simplicity, the poem has a persuasive rhetoric. It
guides one through a sequence of passive, literal observations into
subjective response.[23] Similar qualities are to be found in a short poem
composed two months later:

> The Sun has long been set
> The stars are out by twos and threes
> The little birds are piping yet
> Among the bushes and the trees.
> —There's the Cuckoo and one or two thrushes
> And a noise of wind that rushes
> With a noise of water that gushes:
> And the cuckoo's sovereign cry
> Fills all the hollow of the sky.
>
>   (*The Sun has long been set*, 1–9)

A transition from the actual to the numinous is effected, almost
imperceptibly, by repetition: 'a noise of wind that rushes | With a noise of
water that gushes (ll. 6–7). No claims are openly made, but the words
suggest more than a literal wind or a particular stream. The cuckoo's voice
completes the spell. It resounds, not through a 'heaven' containing the

---

[23] 'The rain is over and gone' is a quotation from The Song of Solomon, 2:2.

certainty of God's presence, but through 'the *hollow* of the sky'. Its
sovereignty displaces God's, standing rather for the poet's lonely
imagination.[24] But if Wordsworth can move from the palpable to the
numinous, he can also return to a slighter tone:

> Who would go parading
> In London, and masquerading,
> On such a night of June
> With that beautiful soft half-moon;
> And all those innocent blisses
> On such a night as this is!—

> (ll. 10–15)

There are unmistakeable touches of humour here: the final rhyme,
Byronically far-fetched; and the playful sideways-reference to Lamb's
London.[25] As on so many occasions in 1802, the poet withdraws from the
full possibilities suggested by his imagination and returns instead to the
safe, the whimsical, the palpable.

Joy, at this period, is for Wordsworth a dwindling power. It lacks the
religious possibilities it once implied, and never rises to the intensity of
The Pedlar:

> Wonder not
> If such his transports were; for in all things
> He saw one life, and felt that it was joy.

> (ll. 216–18)

In place of 'bliss ineffable' (*Pedlar*, 207), there is the more circumscribed
sense of appreciable happiness:

> When stately passions in me burn
> If some chance look to thee should turn

---

[24] Compare *To A Cuckoo* 13–16:

> Thrice welcome, darling of the spring!
> Ev'n yet thou art to me
> No Bird, but an invisible thing,
> A voice, a mystery . . .

The poem was composed in March (see Curtis, 161), and Wordsworth clearly has it in mind
in June.

[25] 'London itself, a pantomime and a masquerade', writes Lamb to Wordsworth in
January 1801 (Marrs, i. 267). For a discussion of Lamb's anti-Wordsworthian view of
London life, see my '"In City Pent": Echo and Allusion in Wordsworth, Coleridge and
Lamb, 1797–1801', *RES* New Series, 32, 128. And for a more detailed context in which to see
the conflict between them, see my 'Lamb, Lloyd, London: A perspective on Book Seven of
"The Prelude"', *The Charles Lamb Bulletin* (Special Sesquicentennial Number) New Series,
nos 47–8, 169–87.

> I drink out of an humbler urn
>   A lowlier pleasure
> A homely sympathy that heeds
> The common life our nature breeds
> A wisdom fitted to the needs
>   Of hearts at leisure . . .

(*To the Daisy* [1], 57–64)

It is not clear what 'stately passions' might be, but the tone suggests a slightly dismissive attitude towards earlier raptures. And though he writes of turning a '*chance* look' to the daisy, there is a sense of purpose in his appreciation of the 'lowlier pleasure' it affords. He is not just accepting new limitations, he is rejoicing in his capacity to see their value. Hence the self-congratulation, and hence also the unease.

The tones may be unacceptable, but the intention is genuine enough. What Wordsworth needs is a range of feelings that can be valued for themselves, not for their further implications:

> A thousand times in rock or bower
> Ere thus I have lain couch'd an hour
> Have I deriv'd from thy sweet power
>   Some apprehension
> Some steady love some chance delight
> Some memory that had taken flight
> Some chime of fancy wrong or right
>   Or stray invention . . .

(*To the Daisy* [1], 49–56)

The writing is casual, almost slapdash, as though there is no discrimination involved. Each type of response is given an equal weight ('some chance delight' is valued as highly as 'some steady love'), and the chiming of fancy need not be morally or aesthetically approved to be enjoyed. Wordsworth is holding off from the creed of 1798 ('One impulse from a vernal wood | May teach you more of man . . .'), and is choosing, instead, to value all that is non-instructive, non-formative, in Nature:

> An instinct, call it a blind sense,
> A happy genial influence,
> Coming one knows not how nor whence,
> Nor whither going.

(*To the Daisy* [1], 69–71)[26]

---

[26] James Scoggins writes that 'Fancy's less ambitious aims and its ability to turn any materials to its task protect it from the constant threat of failure that challenges the imagination.' See *Imagination and Fancy: Complementary Modes in the Poetry of Wordsworth* (University of Nebraska Press, 1966), 83.

The most striking demonstration, in 1802, of Alfoxden's vanishment is to be found in the ludic poetry of *The Barberry Tree*, which is also, paradoxically, the most exuberant outpouring of the spring. It is a poem that borrows earlier language in its quest for creative power, seeming, in the frankness with which it does so, to declare its own inadequate supply of responses. *A Whirl Blast from behind the Hill* (composed in spring 1798) is the poem's source.[27] In the relationship between them, we see not only the habit of self-reference which is central to a poetry of loss, but the emerging pattern of contrast and change which is both its outward manifestation and its inner meaning. Joy, in *A Whirl Blast*, had worked secretly, mysteriously, and unhelped by any wind:

> There's not a breeze—no breath of air—
> Yet here, and there, and every where
> Along the floor, beneath the shade
> By those embowering hollies made,
> The leaves in myriads jump and spring,
> As if with pipes and music rare
> Some Robin Good-fellow were there,
> And all those leaves, that jump and spring,
> Were each a joyous, living thing.
>
> (*A Whirl Blast*, 15–23)

Robin Goodfellow may be seen as Pan (a whimsical personification of the motion and spirit that impels all living things); but he could equally well be a fanciful representation of the poet himself. The pleasure of the writing lies in Wordsworth's refusal to trace the source of joy. It might reside in Nature; it might also be projected onto Nature by imagination.[28] In *The Barberry Tree*, on the other hand, there are certain conditions under which the external world will not come alive, however strong the observer's capacity for joy:

> If Jacob Jones you have at heart
>   To hear this sound and see this sight:
> [Then this] advice I do impart,
>   [That] Jacob you don't go by night;
> [For then 'tis] possible the shrub so green
> [To toss and b]low may not well be seen:

---

[27] To a limited extent, the relationship between these two poems has been explored by Heath, 57–8.

[28] See my discussion of *The Pedlar* (Chapter Two, above) for Wordsworth's equivocating language.

> [Nor Jaco]b would I have you go
> When the blithe winds forbear to blow;
> I think it may be safely then averr'd
> The piping leaves will not be heard.[29]

In relation to its source, this passage cannot but seem an involuntary expression of loss.

A Whirl Blast, anticipating *The Rainbow*, had ended in prayer:

> Oh! grant me Heaven a heart at ease
> That I may never cease to find,
> Even in appearances like these
> Enough to nourish and to stir my mind!

> (ll. 24–7)

—to which *The Barberry Tree* is at one level an answer. Wordsworth sets out to record the experience of joy which the dancing tree has given him (ll. 1–12), and he stays resolutely on this level, as though the 'appearance' is really 'enough to nourish and to stir [his] mind', and as though the questions his mind asks are irrelevant to the experience:

> But whether it be thus or no;
> That while they danc'd upon the wind
> They felt a joy like humankind . . .
> And whether, as I said before,
>   These golden blossoms dancing high,
>   These breezes piping thro' the sky
> Have in themselves of joy a store . . .
> If living sympathy be theirs
>   And leaves and airs,
> The piping breeze and dancing tree
> Are all alive and glad as we;
> Whether it be truth or no
> I cannot tell, I do not know . . .

> (ll. 16–18; 25–8; 37–42)

In *The Borders of Vision*, Jonathan Wordsworth has argued that the bantering humour is to be read as a teasing and affronting response to the Coleridgean belief that 'we receive but what we give'.[30] One can go further, though, and see this affected indifference as a defence against what Coleridge is saying. Evasions are carefully handled to deflate

---

[29] Italicized words in square brackets are supplied in *Borders of Vision*, 151.
[30] *Borders of Vision*, 166.

philosophical enquiry, and strong echoes from *The Thorn*[31] suggest that the poet prefers to align himself with a tiresomely loquacious narrator rather than with a serious philosopher. Garrulity helps to build up a kind of mock suspense, which increases the bathos of his final assertion:

> But this I know, and will declare,
>   Rightly and surely *this* I know;
> That never here, that never there,
>   Around me, aloft, or alow;
> Nor here nor there, nor anywhere
> Saw I a scene so very fair.
>
> (ll. 45–50)

The solipsism of the *Letter to Sara* offers a powerful threat to Wordsworth's security, and to the trust in things palpable on which his own theories of imagination habitually rest. He chooses to make the least courageous of claims, not just so as to affront Coleridge, but so as to be safe.

(iii) *Change and Interchange: self-portraiture in 1802*

Wordsworth would not himself have admitted to the dwindling of conviction that *The Barberry Tree* implies. Again and again during 1802 one sees him writing as though neither his response, nor the conditions which sustain it (most importantly, of course, the relationship with Coleridge) have altered. The tendency is particularly marked in a poem composed in May: the *Stanzas written in My Pocket Copy of the Castle of Indolence*. Here, using Canto I, verses lvii–lx of Thomson's poem, not just as a stylistic model, but as a framework for subtle allusions of a rather complicated kind, Wordsworth offers two portraits, one of himself, one of Coleridge.[32] Matthew Arnold confused them, but he was imaginatively right to do so.[33] They are neither true to life when correctly identified, nor separable in the first instance. A merging of personalities takes place in the

---

[31] 'I cannot tell; I wish I could | For the true reasons no one knows' (*The Thorn*, 90–1). See also ll. 104–5; 155–6; 214; 243–4.

[32] I have confined myself, here, to a discussion of the poem in terms of its portraiture. For the relationship with Thomson that is implied, see my article, 'Wordsworth, Coleridge, and "The Castle of Indolence" Stanzas' *WC*, 12, 2 (Spring, 1981), 106–13.

[33] De Selincourt writes 'Matthew Arnold, in his Selection of the Poems published in the *Golden Treasury Series*, was responsible for circulating the error, which he afterwards admitted, that the first 4 stanzas referred to C. and the next three to W. But the evidence is overwhelming that the reverse is the case.' (*PW*, ii. 470)

poetry which can be interpreted as wish-fulfilment: it implies the need for
similar mergings to happen in real life.

The process is worth observing in detail, since the kinds of distortion
which occur tell us not only about Wordsworth's ideals at this time, but
about the extent to which he was aware of their distance from the facts. As
the poem unfolds, the authenticity of individual portraiture gives way to
the impressionism of overall effect. Recognizable features are subsumed
by myth. The completeness of the take-over, as well as the gradualness
with which it occurs, suggest a poet who knows what he is doing: who is
aware of the strains involved in difference, and wishes to keep them under
control.

We begin with a self-portrait that is recognizable, if one is looking for
something that reflects the moods and preoccupations of Wordsworth's
writing in 1802:

> never sun on living creature shone
> Who more devout enjoyment with us took.
> Here on his hours he hung as on a book;
> On his own time he here would float away;
> As doth a fly upon a summer brook . . .

(ll. 3–7)

But it is soon complicated by hints of Coleridge's behaviour during this
period, which imply one has made the wrong identification:

> Ah! piteous sight it was to see this Man,
> When he came back to us a wither'd flower;
> Or like a sinful creature pale & wan . . .

(ll. 19–21)[34]

Arnold, for precisely this reason, swapped the identity of the two portraits
round, and as one moves on into the stanzas about Coleridge, one becomes
increasingly attracted by his misreading.

Again, we are at first disarmed by a description which rings true:

> With him there often walked in friendly wise,
> Or lay upon the moss, by brook or tree,

---

[34] 'We were rouzed by Coleridge's voice below' writes Dorothy, on 12 May 1802 '—he
had walked, looked palish but was not much tired.' (*DWJ*, 124) 'We went with him after tea'
(13 May) '. . . he did not look very well when we parted from him.' (*DWJ*, 124) 'We had a
melancholy letter from Coleridge just at Bed-time.' (15 May) 'It distressed me very much.'
(*DWJ*, 126)

> A noticeable Man, with large dark eyes
> And a pale face, that seem'd undoubtedly
> As if a *blooming* face it *ought* to be:
> Heavy his low-hung lip did oft appear,
> A face divine of heaven-born ideotcy!
> Profound his forehead was, though not severe;
> Yet some did think that he had little business here.
>
> (ll. 37–45)[35]

But this gives way, in the next verse, to an ideal portrait, which is at once wish-fulfilment and advice:

> Ah! God forfend! his was a lawful right.
> Noisy he was, and gamesome as a boy:
> His limbs would toss about him with delight,
> Like branches when strong winds the trees annoy.
> He lack'd not implement, device, or toy,
> To cheat away the hours that silent were:
> He would have taught you how you might employ
> Yourself; & many did to him repair,
> And, certes, not in vain;—he had inventions rare.
>
> (ll. 46–54)

It would be wrong to suppose that this ideal is based on anything either observed in Coleridge's behaviour, or hidden in his nature.[36] It is a projection of Wordsworth's preoccupations and achievements in 1802: an ideal conceived resolutely in his own terms.[37] Coleridge's boyish joy, for instance, is compared with the tossing of branches 'when strong winds the trees annoy': an allusion to *The Barberry Tree* that is unmistakeable; while the natural world he is in touch with is one of objects minutely observed:

[35] The line 'A face divine of heaven-born ideotcy' seems particularly accurate. Coleridge himself had referred to his face as expressing 'great Sloth, & great, indeed almost ideotic, good nature.' (Griggs, i. 259)

[36] *A Character, in the antithetical manner* gives a description that is much closer to the Coleridge one knows:

> I marvel how Nature could ever find space
> For the weight and the levity seen in his face:
> There's thought and no thought, and there's paleness and bloom,
> And bustle and sluggishness, pleasure and gloom.
>
> (ll. 1–4)

According to the Fenwick Note, *A Character* describes Robert Jones. But Coleridge regarded the lines as being about him (Griggs, ii. 784). Compare the conflation of Ellen Cruikshank and Dorothy in *The Nightingale*.

[37] Hodgson, 84, argues that the portrait of Coleridge is 'deliberately superficial, knowingly misleading', but offers no reasons for Wordsworth's distortions.

> Instruments had he, playthings for the ear,
> Long blades of grass pluck'd round him as he lay;
> These serv'd to catch the wind as it came near
> Glasses he had with many colours gay;
> Others that did all little things display;
> The beetle with his radiance manifold,
> A mailed angel on a battle day,
> And leaves & flowers, & herbage green & gold
> And all the glorious sights which fairies do behold.

(ll. 55–63)

This is the world greeted by Wordsworth as his 'Paradise' in the opening sequence of *Home at Grasmere*: a world

> Of Sunbeams, Shadows, Butterflies, and Birds,
> Angels, and winged Creatures that are Lords
> Without restraint of all which they behold.[38]

It is also the world he reveals in his 1802 lyrics—varied, colourful, full of joyous vitality, but essentially of the fancy rather than the imagination. Presumably Coleridge would not have been solemn enough to read the phrase 'little things' as an oblique criticism of his way of seeing;[39] but he might easily have been offended that Wordsworth should choose to foist on him his own rather limited values at this time. It is one thing to be admired for remaining fully oneself despite unfavourable circumstances; quite another to be praised for showing qualities one neither has nor wishes to have.

Wordsworth even goes so far as to imply that his companion is more productive and creative than he is himself:

> He would entice that other man to hear
> His music & to view his imagery:
> And sooth, these two did love each other dear,
> As far as love in such a place could be . . .

(ll. 64–7)

Coleridge, who by this stage regarded himself as a metaphysician, not a poet,[40] is here transformed into a figure of capable imagination. So

---

[38] *Home at Grasmere* MS B, 31–3 (Darlington, 40).

[39] Coincidentally, Wordsworth recalls a disparaging phrase of Coleridge's own, used in his famous early letter to Thelwall: 'the universe itself—what but an immense heap of *little things*?' (Griggs, i. 349)

[40] As is habitually the case, Coleridge's observation is sharpened and embittered by envy: 'He is a great, a true Poet', he had written of Wordsworth, as early as 1800: 'I am only a kind of a Meta-physician.' (Griggs, i. 658) The claim had been repeated, of course, and many times over, in the *Letter to Sara*.

capable, in fact, that he has music and imagery to share with his friend. By most standards, there would seem to be an element of aggression (however unconscious) in the reversal.[41] But there is a constructive purpose behind it, too. Milton Teichman has suggested that 'Wordsworth asks Coleridge to remember . . . the happiness to be derived from their relationship and from their shared delights . . .'.[42] But his intention is not just corrective, in the sense that it offers personal advice; it is self-sustaining, in that it edits out unease and incompatibility, rewriting actual friendship as literary myth.

The *Stanzas*, then, are a sustained attempt to dissolve growing strains between the two friends, and to rebuild their old intimacy. Both poets are made to resemble Thomson's indolent poet-companions, yet both are shown to be exempt from the charge of wasting time. (As in 1798, a contemplative withdrawal from real life is justified by creativity.) They have their shared delights and their shared occupations. Their roles in the castle are complementary: Wordsworth as the lovesick poet, driven crazy by the power of his imagination, Coleridge as the cheerful consoler: a sort of magician of fancy. Features borrowed by one poet from the other, and roles dramatically exchanged, are there to show the merging of their identities, as though an earlier closeness and interdependence were still possible. Artificially, and with a self-deception that one sees in many of the 1802 lyrics, Wordsworth is attempting to reconstruct the past.

He does not succeed, and the reasons become obvious as soon as one puts the *Stanzas* alongside past poems they are intended to resemble. *The Foster Mother's Tale* and *Frost at Midnight* had also offered composite portraits of Wordsworth and Coleridge. So too, though in a less integrated way, had *The Pedlar*. The poets' allusive practices had differed considerably—Coleridge tending to absorb, Wordsworth to define

---

[41] Much more, for instance, than there had been in the stanza from the Christabel Notebook (DC MS 15) that is written (or adapted) for the 'Ballad-Michael', and which contains an affectionate joke at Coleridge's expense:

> Deep read in experience perhaps he is nice,
> On himself is so fond of bestowing advice
> And of puzzling at what may befall
> So intent upon baking his bread without leaven
> And of giving to earth the perfection of heaven
> That he thinks and does nothing at all.

See Stephen Parrish, '*Michael* and the Pastoral Ballad', *BWS*, 72–3 for a discussion of these lines.

[42] Milton Teichman, 'Wordsworth's Two Replies to Coleridge's Dejection: an Ode', *PMLA*, 86, 5 (October, 1971), 988.

himself by a subtle process of differentiation. But neither had been concerned with deliberately obscuring the contrasts on which their interaction had relied. Disparity, in *Frost at Midnight*, had been openly acknowledged, in the Wordsworthian childhood enviously projected by Coleridge for his son; and in *The Pedlar*, it had been the source of lively juxtapositions within the poetry, as well as of the position from which Wordsworth defined his own peculiar strengths. A mixing and merging of identities had taken place, in other words—but naturally, as the two poets got to know each other, rather than artificially, as they drew apart. In the *Stanzas*, on the other hand, the whole process of creating a composite portrait has become self-conscious, and it is this that works against the poets' purpose. Divergence is worrying, and must be hidden; yet the very fact of concealment is a recognition of change. Idealizing Coleridge entirely in his own terms, Wordsworth fails to accommodate or conceal the differences that are growing between them. His self-projection is such that it merely accentuates the things that can no longer be shared. Inevitably, because of his own rather limited values in 1802, and the confidence that is his alone, he turns out to have written two self-portraits.

Retrospectively, the year at Alfoxden comes to stand, in both poets' minds, for perfect friendship. Difference, it seems, could at this time be allowed; and mutual influence could take place without possessiveness or anxiety:

> For Hope grew round me, like the climbing Vine,
> And Leaves & Fruitage, not my own, seem'd mine!
>
> (*Letter to Sara*, 236–7)

If *The Foster Mother's Tale* and other poems provide evidence that such unanxious intertwinings could actually happen, they do so at least partly by contrast with the poetry of 1802, and under the influence of our own (as well as the poets') backward gaze. A degree of scepticism should be maintained. It is to be remembered that very soon after the period of his closest collaboration with Southey, Coleridge was able to write to him, with savage resentment: 'To your Lectures I dedicated my whole mind & heart—and wrote one half in *Quantity*—; but in Quality, you must be conscious, that all the Tug of Brain was mine: and that your Share was little more than Transcription.' (Griggs, i. 172) The same kind of repudiation is implied (with what degree of justice one can never know) by a claim he makes, under different circumstances, in July 1802: 'Wordsworth's Preface is half a child of my own Brain | & so arose out of

Conversations, so frequent, that with few exceptions we could scarcely either of us perhaps positively say, which first started any particular Thought . . .' (Griggs, ii. 830). If generosity and freedom of exchange can give way so readily to resentment, doubt is cast on the equality which has supposedly been left behind.

Such doubt is never acknowledged, by either Wordsworth or Coleridge, in their creative writing—no matter what they choose to say in private correspondence and conversation. For the poets themselves, the compatibility of the Alfoxden period becomes something to draw strength from in times of change: the one fixed certainty, when divergence seems most painful. For the reader, by contrast, doubts are less easy to keep at bay. The lost paradise comes increasingly to appear a nostalgic fiction, and the devices for regaining it consequently doomed to fail.

Wordsworth, in *The Pet Lamb*, unconsciously offers a parody of his own and Coleridge's wishfulness. There is, it seems, a generosity of spirit in the poet which wishes to see private creative impulses as something shared:

> As homeward through the lane I went with lazy feet
> This song to myself did I oftentimes repeat
> And it seemed as I retrac'd the ballad line by line
> That but half of it was hers, and one half of it was mine.
>
> Again, and once again did I repeat the song,
> 'Nay' said I, 'more than half to the damsel must belong,
> For she looked with such a look, and she spake with such a tone,
> That I almost receiv'd her heart into my own!
>
> (*The Pet Lamb*, 61–8)

Such generosity operates in art to counter the equally natural but opposite tendency (demonstrated above, in the quotations from Coleridge) which takes place in real life. In its highest form, as here in Browning's address to Shelley, the ideal of sharing offers an apocalyptic submergence of the self:

> The air seems bright with thy past presence yet,
> But thou art still for me as thou hast been
> When I have stood with thee as on a throne
> With all thy dim creations gathered round
> Like mountains, and I felt of mould like them,
> And with them creatures of my own were mixed,
> Like things half-lived, giving and catching life.
>
> (*Pauline*, 161–7)

It is, however, in the nature of equality to seem suspect in practice and far removed as an ideal. Mergings of the kind suggested by *The Pet Lamb* and *Pauline* take place, not in reality but—like the Alfoxden relationship—in an imagined past. They are the constructs and strategies of myth.

5

'A something given':
Two Versions of *The Leechgatherer*

'William and I sauntered a little in the garden', writes Dorothy in her
Journal entry for 21 April 1802. 'Coleridge came to us and repeated the
verses he wrote to Sara.' Her sympathy for him, immediate and heartfelt,
is interestingly allusive: 'I was affected with them and was on the whole,
not being well, in miserable spirits. The sunshine—the green fields and
the fair sky made me sadder; even the little happy sporting lambs seemed
but sorrowful to me.' (*DWJ*, 113) She identifies with Coleridge via
Wordsworth, echoing *Intimations*, but with a careful adjustment of its
meaning:

> Now while the Birds thus sing a joyous song
>   And while the young lambs bound
>   As to the tabor's sound
> To me alone there came a thought of grief
> A timely utterance gave that thought relief
>   And I again am strong . . .
>
> (ll. 19–24)

The disappearance of Wordsworth's 'visionary gleam' had left him with a
sense of loss; but this had not affected his capacity to acknowledge a
'joyous song' which continued outside him. He could see the young lambs
bounding, even if he could not share their joy. Dorothy, by contrast, lets
the sadness of her mood alter the external world. The lambs, instead of
displaying a joy she cannot share, reflect back her own sorrow. The
dejection of the *Letter* has retrospectively coloured her reading of
Intimations. In her sympathy for Coleridge she has adopted his way of
seeing.

This Journal entry offers a pattern of response and backward allusion
which Wordsworth must, to some extent, have shared with his sister, and
toward which they were guided by the deliberate echoes in Coleridge's
lines:

> These Mountains too, these Vales, these Woods, these Lakes,
> Scenes full of Beauty & of Loftiness
> Where all my Life I fondly hop'd to live—
> I were sunk low indeed, did they *no* solace give;
> But oft I seem to feel, & evermore I fear,
> They are not to me now the Things, which once they were.

(ll. 290–5)

Where Wordsworth differs from Dorothy—and the difference is crucial—is in holding out against the effect that Coleridge's poem has had upon him. She highlights her reaction by playing allusive games in the *Letter*'s own terms; he takes precautions to obscure his response altogether. Fancy as employed in the 1802 lyrics is defensive twice over: it protects Wordsworth from his own sense of loss, and it prevents the doubling of loss which the *Letter* might cause in his writing.

There is no evidence to suggest that he was actually hostile to the claims his friend had made. But to a poet mourning the loss of joy, the central lines of the *Letter* offer little comfort:

> O Sara! we receive but what we give,
> And in *our* Life alone does Nature live.

(ll. 296–7)

Whatever distinctions one might wish to make between childhood perception and creative power, this claim would sound to Wordsworth like an echo of his own elegy—a confirmation of his deepest fears. He could not avoid the obvious connection between his own lament for vanished glory and Coleridge's paralysis of feeling. What he *could* resist was the implication that Coleridge's poem deprived him of his only consolation: joy's continuity outside the fallible and finite mind. It is with an instinct for self-preservation that he writes *The Leechgatherer*. Not, as some critics have supposed, from the desire to console or sympathize with Coleridge, but with the need to assert an alternative way of seeing.

The first version of this poem (3–9 May), though imaginative rather than fanciful, belongs unmistakably to 1802. 'It represents', as one critic has put it, Wordsworth's 'disillusionment with the romantic imagination considered as an end in itself'.[1] To be more precise, it shows Wordsworth defending himself against Coleridge's solipsism, by defining a source of joy outside the self. The second version (14 June–15 July), though the first eight stanzas are identical, offers the reverse. Here Wordsworth breaks

---

[1] Conran, 66.

through his defensive resistance, not into Coleridgean imagination but into his own kind of symbolic vision. In this breakthrough, he finds not only a way of replying to the *Letter*, but a poetic language which is the perfect answer to all the unvoiced criticisms of his friend.[2] Both poems, in their relation to Coleridge, are broadly revisionist, rather than locally or verbally allusive. The first is defiant in its opposition—arriving, therefore, at an extreme and precarious self-definition. The second is more subtle in the differentiation it offers, achieving as a result a stronger and more stable Wordsworthian mode. I hope in this chapter to demonstrate the major change which takes place in Wordsworth's thinking while he makes his alterations to the text, and to suggest that this change marks not only a turning point in the relationship with Coleridge, but a new stage in the development of his art.

The Leechgatherer begins, in both its versions, not with a landscape or a train of thought, but with an atmosphere:

> There was a roaring in the wind all night
> The rain came heavily and fell in floods
> But now the sun is rising calm and bright
> The Birds are singing in the distant woods
> Over his own sweet voice the stock-dove broods
> The Jay makes answer as the magpie chatters
> And all the air is fill'd with pleasant noise of waters

(ll. 1–7)

Atmosphere in *The Leechgatherer* does not mean mood. The scene is not presented as a projection of Wordsworth's mental state; nor is the weather a barometer for his feelings. The poet claims to be observing a world that exists and endures outside his own mind: a world of substantial, literal, and animate things, which have their own energies—their own processes of growth and change.[3] Without explicitly challenging his friend, Wordsworth is evoking a quality of response that is alien to his way of thinking. Where Coleridge in the *Letter* had misread the moon's stillness as a sign of his own fixity, Wordsworth is imaginatively alive. He receives feeling from what De Quincey would call 'perplexed combinations of

---

[2] For the nature of these unvoiced criticisms, see Chapter Four, Part One.

[3] W. W. Robson emphasizes the deliberate artlessness of the poetry: 'There is, we feel, no arranging; the objects of delight simply presented themselves so, freshly and naturally, in their innocent irresponsibility' (*Interpretations*, ed. John Wain (1955), 120). The catalogue effect is something achieved also in the shorter lyrics of the spring (see above, p. 103). There is some evidence to suggest that it is based on Chatterton's style in *An Excelente Balade of Charitie* (particularly ll. 29–35). See Conran, 68–9.

concrete objects',[4] and is capable of responding fully to an actual world. This does not mean we should be literal ourselves, reading the language as description. Wordsworth only seems to be making a catalogue of real sights and sounds. Every detail of the scene is put there for a purpose: to declare that this poet, unlike Coleridge, can see *and* feel how beautiful they are,[5] and that he knows this beauty is not projected.

The first two lines seem less ingenuous if one thinks back to the opening sequence of the *Letter*, where Coleridge had frustratedly yearned for the storm that might release him from his mood. Wordsworth has chosen to highlight the difference between them by starting with a scene of fulfilment and reconciliation. It is a difference which emerges more clearly (perhaps, even, with tacit aggression) in the line, 'Over his own sweet voice the stock-dove broods'. The allusion is parodic: Milton's brooding Holy Spirit created the universe; Coleridge's dove made 'all Things live from Pole to Pole' (*Letter to Sara*, 335); Wordsworth's pigeon is content with the sound of its own voice. As the 1815 Note makes clear, it is this self-involved, self-perpetuating activity that fascinates the poet, not the analogy with God: 'the bird reiterates and prolongs her soft note, as if herself delighting to listen to it, and participating of a still and quiet satisfaction, like that which may be supposed inseparable from the continuous process of incubation.' (*Prose Works*, iii. 32) The dove is not a source of the life going on around her; she is merely a participant in it, and her cooing is non-productive.[6] Here, as with the 'parent hen' passage in *Prelude*, Book Five,[7] Wordsworth gets (and gives) pleasure by cutting Coleridge's symbol down to size. Turning Holy Spirits into farmyard fowls is an affectionate and playful kind of satire. It makes fun of Coleridge's solemnity, and of his analogy between imagination and God; but it also brings one effectively back to the world of literal things.

Wordsworth's description of the hare, in the following stanza, is equally allusive:

> All things that love the sun are out of doors
> The sky rejoices in the morning's birth
> The grass is bright with raindrops: on the moor
> The Hare is running races in her mirth
> And with her feet she from the plashy earth

---

[4] Ward, 130.

[5] Contrast the *Letter to Sara*, 43.

[6] Far-fetching the allusiveness, one might claim that there is a message here to the Coleridge of the *Letter*: 'Nothing is produced from brooding but the brooding itself.'

[7] *1805*, v. 246–60. See Chapter Three for connections with the *Letter to Sara*.

Raises a mist which glittering in the sun
Runs with her all the way wherever she doth run.

(ll. 8–14)

Like the dove, the image of the mist comes from Coleridge,[8] and once again it is his solemn thoughts on imagination that Wordsworth has in mind:

> Ah! from the Soul itself must issue forth
> A Light, a Glory, and a luminous Cloud
> Enveloping the Earth!

(*Letter to Sara*, 302–4)

What the echoic language claims is that the hare (no more, nor less, than man himself) is capable of producing her own 'luminous Mist' (*Letter to Sara*, 311). Like the child Hartley Coleridge, with his 'breeze-like motion' and his 'self-born carol', she lives in a world of her own making, accompanied 'wherever she doth run' by the mist of raindrops her feet produce. She belongs with the best of Wordsworth's writing in 1802.[9] Neither a manifestation of the One Life, nor a type of the poet's creative power, she exists to prove that there is life, and even joy, outside what Stevens calls 'the make of the mind.'[10] She is enviable and removed. Confronted with her, who could believe that 'in *our* Life alone does Nature live'?

To emphasize that the external world has a 'Voice, of it's own Birth', Wordsworth keeps out of the poem as long as he can, describing the scene as though there was no one to observe it. When he does introduce himself, it is merely as a passer-by:

[8] It possibly also contains a more submerged reference to Milton's description (at the end of *Paradise Lost*) of the cherubim, descending 'in bright array', and

> on the ground
> Gliding meteorous, as evening mist
> Risen from a river o'er the marish glides,
> And gathers ground fast at the labourer's heel,
> Homeward returning.

(*PL*, xii. 628–32)

[9] Compare for instance, *To a Butterfly*: 'I've watch'd you now a full half hour | Self-poized upon that yellow flower' (ll. 1–2), and *The Green Linnet*: 'A Life, a Presence like the air, | Scattering thy gladness without care, | Too blessed with any one to pair, | Thyself thy own enjoyment.' (ll. 21–4) In both these poems, Wordsworth is seen responding to the self-sufficiency of the animal world, which seems to have an independent supply of joy. There is a degree of envy apparent in his response, which can be explained, perhaps, in terms of the contrasting sense he has of his own dependency on others (see particularly *The Leechgatherer*, 36–42).

[10] *To an Old Philosopher in Rome*, 7.

I was a Traveller upon the moor
I saw the hare that rac'd about with joy
I heard the woods and distant waters roar
Or heard them not, as happy as a Boy
The pleasant season did my heart employ
My old remembrances went from me wholly
And all the ways of men so vain & melancholy

(ll. 15–21)

'I *was* . . . I *saw* . . . I *heard*': all the emphasis falls on the verbs, which change, not on the subject, which remains the same. One notices the shift of tenses, as the narrative past intrudes on the descriptive present. This heightens the disjunction between poet and scene, as though he is time-bound in a permanence beyond him.

Holding off, for as long as possible, from the despotism of the 'I', Wordsworth lets himself believe in the convenient logic of chance. If it is by coincidence that he is a 'Traveller upon the moor' at this particularly vital moment, and by chance that his mood corresponds for a while with the life around him, then it can only be accidental that his temper changes:

But as it sometimes chanceth from the might
Of joy in minds that can no farther go
As high as we have mounted in delight
In our dejection do we sink as low
To me that morning did it happen so
And fears and fancies thick upon me came
Dim sadness & blind thoughts I knew not nor could name

(ll. 22–8)

The tone of casual acceptance deflates the solemnity and self-pity of Coleridge's mental state. 'Dejection' is no more than a passing mood, which 'sometimes chanceth', or which 'happen[s] so'. But a moment later, one is faced with bewilderment—'Dim sadness & blind thoughts I knew not nor could name'—and Wordsworth seems suddenly defenceless. The joy which had seemed inherent in the natural world vanishes, as if it were nothing more than a mood of the mind. Halted by a sense of loss, the poet can no longer hold at bay his deepest fears:

I heard the sky lark singing in the sky
And I bethought me of the playful hare
Even such a happy child of earth am I
Even as these happy creatures do I fare
Far from the world I live & from all care
But there may come another day to me
Solitude pain of heart distress & poverty.

> My whole life I have liv'd in pleasant thought
> As if life's business were a summer mood:
> Who will not wade to seek a bridge or boat
> How can he ever hope to cross the flood?
> How can he e'er expect that others should
> Build for him, sow for him, and at his call
> Love him who for himself will take no heed at all?
>
>   (ll. 29–42)

Confronted by his own wasted potential, but knowing that a life dedicated solely to imagination is dangerous, he sinks deeper into perplexity. The heroes of this mood are not the strong precursors of a distant past, who managed both their living and their writing, but the difficult, controversial figures of the moment, Chatterton and Burns:

> I thought of Chatterton the marvelous Boy
> The sleepless soul who perished in his pride
> Of Him who walked in glory & in joy
> Behind his Plough upon the mountain's side . . .
>
>   (ll. 43–6)

Wordsworth's language is for the moment entirely heroic. Chatterton, the gifted, precocious, temperamental forger, who (having spent most of his short life doing hackwork) killed himself in 'distress & poverty' at the age of seventeen, is 'deified' by popular myth and by the poet's imagination. He becomes a hero of Romantic sensibility—broody, melancholic, inspired (in short, thoroughly Coleridgean)—who is doomed to a tragic early death, but whose reputation is 'sleepless' as his life had been.[11] And Burns, the people's poet, who led (according to Currie) a life of drunken debauchery towards the end,[12] emerges in Wordsworth's mind as a Christ-like figure, complete with plough and mountain (not to mention 'glory' and 'joy'), preaching Wordsworthian values in the language of real life. There is a sense of exhilaration in both descriptions which makes one temporarily believe that admiration is unqualified. But the word 'pride'

---

[11] For a discussion of Coleridge's identification with Chatterton, and of the myth which grew around the boy-poet, see Dekker, 61–8.

[12] When Currie's *Life* came out in 1800, Coleridge called it a 'masterly specimen of philosophical Biography' (Griggs, i. 607), but Wordsworth was badly shocked by the picture it offered of a drunken and profligate Burns who died of his own excesses. 'I well remember', he writes, in his *Letter to a Friend of Robert Burns* (1816), 'the acute sorrow with which, by my own fire-side, I first perused Dr. Currie's Narrative. . . . If my pity for Burns was extreme, this pity did not preclude a strong indignation, of which he was not the object.' (*Prose Works*, iii. 118)

sounds as a warning note. Chatterton, it implies, was too involved in poetry to take care of himself. He lived incompetently and was trapped in the end by the material things he had scorned. His death—a glorious waste of the talents he had too exclusively fostered—is a warning of the dangers involved in being a poet and nothing else.

Picking up the suggestion of hubris in Chatterton's 'pride',[13] Wordsworth continues, with a mixture of exultation and bitterness:

> By our own spirits we are deified
> We Poets in our youth begin in gladness
> But thereof comes in the end despondency and madness.
>
> (ll. 47–9)

The phrase 'We Poets' is especially appropriate if one thinks of Chatterton and Burns as prototypes of Coleridge and Wordsworth.[14] The poet is placing himself in a tradition of over-reachers: men whose imaginations make them godlike, and who, for a short while in their youth, can sustain themselves as gods; but who reach their peak too early, and are faced with a fall that is more painful for the glory that precedes it. We are back with the earlier lines: 'As high as we have mounted in delight | In our dejection do we sink as low' (ll. 24–5). If Wordsworth is an example of 'the might | Of joy in minds that can no further go', Coleridge is a painful reminder that 'genial Spirits fail'—that the imagination burns itself out, leaving only despondency and madness.

---

[13] 'Pride' might also mean 'prime' (*NED*, 9).

[14] Wordsworth identified with Burns as strongly as Coleridge with Chatterton. See *PW*, iii. 441–2, and *EY*, 256 for comments which imply a correspondence between their poetic processes; and *Biographia*, i. 81–2, for Coleridge's acknowledgment of their similarity. The identification deepened as a result of Currie's *Life*. Dorothy describes in her *Recollections of a Tour made in Scotland* (1803) the 'melancholy and painful reflections' with which she and Wordsworth looked at Burns's grave, and adds: 'some stories . . . respecting the dangers his surviving children were exposed to, filled us with melancholy concern, *which had a kind of connexion with ourselves.*' (*Journals*, i. 202; my italics) 'There is no thought', she writes, 'surviving in connexion with Burns's daily life that is not heart-depressing.' (ibid., 200) The tension between Wordsworth's fervent idealization of Burns and his nagging suspicion that Currie is right, produces the ambiguous figure we see in *The Leechgatherer*: a poet who aspires to godhead and then falls. By 1839, Wordsworth can openly acknowledge that Burns 'faultered, drifted to and fro, | And passed away.' (*Thoughts suggested the day following*, 5–6); but the hero-worship still triumphs:

> Through busiest street and loneliest glen
> Are felt the flashes of his pen;
> He rules 'mid winter snows, and when
>   Bees fill their hives;
> Deep in the general heart of men
>   His power survives.
>
> (ll. 43–8; *PW*, iii. 68)

It is at this point, when Wordsworth's fear of disintegration is at its most intense, that he meets with the leechgatherer. If one has been reading the poem as a kind of oblique commentary on the *Letter*, one is prepared for this as a moment when something essentially Wordsworthian will emerge:

> Now whether it was by peculiar grace
> A leading from above, a something given
> Yet it befel that in that lonely place
> When up & down my fancy thus was driven
> And I with these untoward thoughts had striven
> I to the borders of a Pond did come
> By which an Old man was, far from all house or home [15]
>
> (ll. 50–6)

Commenting on this passage a month later, in his defensive letter to the Hutchinson sisters, Wordsworth suggests that 'A person reading this Poem with feelings like mine will have been awed and controuled, expecting almost something spiritual or supernatural'. But 'What is brought forward?', he asks:

'A lonely place, a Pond' 'by which an old man *was* far from all house or home'—not stood, not sat, but '*was*'—the figure presented in the most naked simplicity possible.

(*EY*, 366)

What Wordsworth finds moving is not the 'peculiar grace' through which this figure so unexpectedly appears; nor the nature of his appearance, nor the details of his life. He is fascinated by the quality of the man's presence in the landscape: a quality which makes him seem to exist, as an organic and permanent part of the things around him, instead of being present as a spectator of the scene. The poet's repeated emphasis, in his letter, on the verb 'was' supports a distinction between being as mere presence and being as existence. The leechgatherer has always been there: this is no case of projection, but of 'something given'.[16]

There is no reason to think that Sara Hutchinson was immune to the direct, literal power of this Wordsworthian moment. When she wrote of the 'tediousness' of the first version of the poem, it was probably the

---

[15] The last words here, 'far from all house or home', echo Chatterton's first description of the beggar in *An Excelente Balade*: 'He had ne housen theere, ne anie covent nie.' (l. 21)

[16] One could, if one wished, read the phrase 'something given' as a refutation of the claim that 'we receive but what we give' (*Letter to Sara*, 296).

remaining thirteen stanzas she had in mind.[17] When the leechgatherer
starts speaking, the mystery of his presence goes. He is more garrulous and
matter-of-fact than the narrator of *The Thorn*:

> Now I am seeking Leeches up & down
> From house to house I go from Barn to Barn
> All over Cartmell Fells & up to Blellan Tarn . . .

> (ll. 131–3)

He clings to the palpable, and Wordsworth clings to him, because what he
offers is reassurance. Not just in the form of palpable things, which can be
grasped (like stones) to pull the poet back from his abyss, but in the form
of practical wisdom, which steers clear of the dangers inherent in
imagination, and asserts the simple necessity of coping with life. The
poem degenerates, from this moment on, into a cautionary tale, and we are
asked to believe that the poet draws strength for his own endeavours from
the thought of the old man:

> I could have laugh'd myself to scorn to find
> In that decrepit man so firm a mind
> God said I be my help & stay secure
> I'll think of the Leech-gatherer on the lonely Moor.

> (ll. 137–40)

All the fears, anxieties, and reservations which Wordsworth has been
feeling can be 'laugh'd . . . to scorn', because here, in the face of extreme
hardship, is an emblem of resolution and independence.

The first version of *The Leechgatherer* ends, as it began, in opposition to
Coleridgean values; and that is how it remains in Wordsworth's mind as
he writes to Sara Hutchinson:

> this I can *confidently* affirm, that, though I believe God has given me a strong
> imagination, I cannot conceive a figure more impressive than that of an old Man
> like this, the survivor of a Wife and ten children, travelling alone among the
> mountains and all lonely places, carrying with him his own fortitude, and the
> necessities which an unjust state of society has entailed upon him.

> (*EY*, 366–7)

As he brings factual details to his defence, one feels the assurance of his
argument giving way. The words 'by which an Old man was' had achieved
their effect through literalness; but matters of fact about the man's life—

---

[17] The letter does not survive, but Sara's views are clear in the Wordsworths' reply. See
EY, 364–70.

the children he had once had, the wrongs society had done him—seem not merely tedious but intrusive. Wordsworth cannot acknowledge this, yet the defensiveness of his letter conveys unease.

A short time after writing to Sara, Wordsworth turned back to the poem, presumably (in the first instance) to put his mind at rest. In a blank-verse fragment of 1799 he had written about a moment when he was forced into admitting the inadequacy of his own language:

> I deemed that I had adequately cloathed
> Meanings at which I hardly hinted, thoughts
> And forms of which I scarcely had produced
> A monument and arbitrary sign.
>
> (*Peter Bell* MS2, Fragment (a),
> 10–13; Norton *Prelude*, 495)

It must have been with the same feeling that he confronted *The Leechgatherer*, and acknowledged that Sara had been right: literalness, despite its occasional power, could not be sustained at a compelling level. One should not underestimate the importance of this moment, or the extent of the changes which are introduced into the poem. It is not just, as Curtis puts it, that the 'language of men' is replaced by 'the language of vision' (98). It is that the resistance to Coleridge on which all the fanciful lyric writing of 1802 depends has collapsed under Sara's criticism. Wordsworth in the new version is not so much altering his poem to suit his audience, as devising for himself a quasi-symbolic mode which conveys the power and strangeness of his imaginative experience. He is unlikely to have been aware of it, but in making his revisions he is defining his own kind of 'Hebrew' poetry:[18] that of the creative and transforming mind.

The first thing he does, with a ruthless logic, is to cut the words he most admires—'By which an Old man was'—and to put in their place the less powerful couplet:

> I spied a Man before me unawares;
> The oldest Man he seem'd that ever wore grey hairs.[19]

One feels there has been loss, not gain, but it is the only moment in Wordsworth's revisions when one does so. The change, moreover, has a

---

[18] For Coleridge's use of the term 'Hebrew' to describe the imaginative sublime, see Chapter Four, above.

[19] *Resolution and Independence*, 55–6. I have now switched to the second version of the poem, which belongs to 14 June–5 July 1802, and is transcribed from the Beaumont papers by Jared Curtis in *Experiments with Tradition*, 187–95 (parallel text). All further references will be made to *R & I*.

purpose. It presents the man as one whose significance lies in being spied
by an observer. The emphasis falls on what he seems, not on what he is,
and it is even implied that his hairs look like clothing.[20] At the back of
Wordsworth's mind, throughout his reworking, is *The Discharged Soldier*
of 1798. It is fascinating to watch how he at once draws upon, and reverses,
the situation of his earlier poem. On first encountering the soldier, he had
seen him in terms that were inappropriately imaginative:

> While thus I wandered step by step led on,
> It chanced a sudden turning of the road
> Presented to my view an uncouth shape
> So near that, stepping back into the shade
> Of a thick hawthorn, I could mark him well,
> Myself unseen.
>
> (ll. 36–41)

The poet had not only divested the man of his humanity (turning him into
a shape, an object), but also made the further literary connection with
Paradise Lost and Milton's 'shape'—'If shape it might be called that shape
had none' (*PL*, ii. 667)—at the gates of Hell.[21] In his resemblance to
Death, the soldier had taken on a fantastic, obsessional quality. Ghost-
like, motionless, and 'propp'd' (as though with no life of his own) he had
been a haunting projection of the imagination:

> I think
> If but a glove had dangled in his hand
> It would have made him more akin to man.
>
> (ll. 65–7)

> still his form
> Kept the same fearful steadiness. His shadow
> Lay at his feet & moved not.
>
> (ll. 71–3)

To allow the man his humanity, the poet had to be disabused of his
fantasies, made to recognize what was actually there:

---

[20] Wordsworth and Coleridge frequently use clothing metaphors when writing about the
conferring power of imagination. See, for instance, *The Ancient Mariner*: 'Within the shadow
of the ship | I watch'd their rich attire' (ll. 269–70); the *Sonnet Composed on Westminster
Bridge*: 'This City now doth like a garment wear | The beauty of the morning' (ll. 4–5);
Intimations: 'The earth and every common sight | To me did seem | Apparrel'd in celestial
light' (ll. 2–4); and *The Letter to Sara*: 'Our's is her Wedding Garment, our's her Shroud'
(l. 298). When Wordsworth says the old man *wears* his hairs, instead of growing them, he is
using a kind of poetic shorthand. He may even be doing so playfully.

[21] See Chapter One, Part (iii), for a more detailed discussion.

> & when erelong
> I asked his history, he in reply
> Was neither slow nor eager, but unmoved,
> *And with a quiet uncomplaining voice,*
> *A stately air of mild indifference,*
> *He told a simple fact . . .*

(ll. 94–9; my italics)

Resolution and Independence is at the other extreme. The old man starts in obstinate actuality, is altered under the poet's altering eye, and ends as Wordsworthian symbol, or what Curtis has called 'myth' (110). There is no sudden access of imaginative power, which then has to be tempered because it is intrusive. Instead, there is a gradual process of transformation, which itself comes to be valued more highly than fact.

As in *The Discharged Soldier*, the poet meets the old man unawares ('himself unseen') and has time for his spying. Instead of transforming him at once, he is watchful, and considers. The pause is marked by a stanza in which Wordsworth hesitates before allowing his imagination its full power:

> My course I stopp'd as soon as I espied
> The Old Man in that naked wilderness;
> Close by a Pond upon the hither side
> He stood alone: a minute's space, I guess,
> I watch'd him, he continuing motionless.
> To the Pool's further margin then I drew,
> He all the while before me being full in view.

(*R & I*, 57–63)

Tricks of suspense from *The Discharged Soldier* are repeated;[22] but with a difference. The language is bare; the details are offered factually, and the figure is treated as a distant object.[23] This is a moment of protracted

---

[22] '. . . stepping back into the shade | Of a thick hawthorn, I could mark him well, | Myself unseen' (ll. 39–41); 'Long time I scanned him with a mingled sense | Of fear and sorrow.' (ll. 68–9); 'I wished to see him move, but he remained | Fixed to his place' (ll. 77–8); 'Not without reproach | Had I prolonged my watch . . .' (ll. 83–4).

[23] The phrase 'before me being full in view' is echoed by Wordsworth, two years later, in the dream sequence of *Prelude*, Book Five:

> He heeded not, but with his twofold charge
> Beneath his arm—before me full in view—
> I saw him riding o'er the desert sands
> With the fleet waters of the drowning world
> In chace of him . . .

(*1805*, v. 133–7)

resistance, before the poet can finally let go of the palpable, and allow
re-creation to affect literal presence. The language of fact offers temporary
reassurance, but as the next stanza proves, the mind's usurpation is
inevitable:

> As a huge stone is sometimes seen to lie
> Couch'd on the bald top of an eminence,
> Wonder to all that do the same espy,
> By what means it could thither come & whence;
> So that it seems a thing endued with sense,
> Like a Sea-beast crawl'd forth, which on a shelf
> Of rock or sand reposeth, there to sun itself.
>
> Such seem'd this Man, not all alive nor dead,
> Nor all asleep . . .

(R & I, 64–72)

These famous lines have frequently been used as the centrepiece for
discussions about imagination. What has been ignored is their connection,
at a deeper level, with the revisionary nature of the writing itself. Frank
Kermode comments helpfully that 'the poem is never asking you to attend
directly to the old man, but to its own transfiguration.'[24] He does not see
this transfiguring process in terms of the poet's textual alterations, but it
makes good sense to do so. In the stanza that precedes this one,
Wordsworth appears to be spying not just on the old man, but on his
former poem. The pause in his narrative exactly corresponds to a
hesitation in the revising process. In the development of the simile, this
self-watching and self-imaging continues. The 'huge stone', lying on its
eminence, corresponds with the old man in all his obstinate actuality—
corresponds, in effect, with the moment when Wordsworth had written
'by which an Old man was'. But as the simile unfolds, the man and the
early poem are 'endued with sense': subjected, that is, to the poet's
transforming imagination.

Critics have too readily assumed that this is the imagination described
by the poet himself in his 'Preface' to *Poems*, 1815:[25]

In these images, the conferring, the abstracting, and the modifying powers of the
Imagination, immediately and mediately acting, are all brought into conjunction.
The stone is endowed with something of the power of life to approximate it to the
sea-beast; and the sea-beast stripped of some of its vital qualities to assimilate it to
the stone; which intermediate image is thus treated for the purpose of bringing the

[24] Kermode, 171.
[25] See, for instance, *Borders of Vision*, 3; Heffernan, 180–1.

original image, that of the stone, to a nearer resemblance to the figure and condition of the aged Man; who is divested of so much of the indications of life and motion as to bring him to the point where the two objects unite and coalesce in just comparison.

(*Prose Works*, iii. 33)

The passage, though eloquent and plausible in its own terms, is far from being accurate about the poetry. One sees nothing, in the unfolding simile, of what Wordsworth calls the 'abstracting' power of imagination.[26] The sea-beast is *not* stripped of its vital qualities; it is simply asleep—with 'all [its] functions silently sealed up';[27] and the old man is not *divested* of life and motion; he is seen in a kind of statuesque trance—caught between stillness and movement, death and life. No 'abstracting' takes place; instead, one watches as the stone, the old man, and the poem are given the strange vitality of the sea-beast. Once the conferring power is released, which it is the moment one sees the stone as 'couch'd',[28] there can be no abstraction, no reversal of the process.

During the next twelve stanzas, we are given, not the tale of the old man (as it existed in the first version) but the poet's response to him in his further stages of transformation. As the narrative continues, a twofold process is seen to be taking place: he is distanced, assimilated into the landscape and given a strange otherness; but he is also taken into the mind, allowed his status as metaphor. The process begins with his being 'Motionless as a cloud' (l. 82)—as Anthon Conran points out, not a cloud that might 'scud across a summer sky', but one of 'The great cumulus heaps [that] will lie around the hilltops for hours, almost as permanent in appearance as the peaks themselves.'[29] Invested with grandeur, he is gradually dehumanized. Not gothically (as the soldier had been) but by a process which allows him to become 'a power like one of Nature's' (*1805*, xii. 312), and to resemble the permanence he is in. The Discharged Soldier had seemed a disturbance to his setting—'more than half detached | From his *own* nature' (ll. 59–60; my italics), and from that outside him. The leechgatherer is at odds neither with his surroundings nor with himself. If he moves, it is 'altogether', like a cloud. This easy and

[26] That is, the power of taking from an object some of the properties it possesses (see *Prose Works*, iii. 32).

[27] See *MS Drafts and Fragments 3(a)*, 70 (*Norton Prelude*, 498).

[28] 'Couched', when used of animals, can mean 'lying down' (*NED* 1) or 'crouching' (*NED* 2) or 'lying hidden, lurking' (*NED* 18; Johnson, 3), but on a metaphorical level, it can also mean 'included secretly' (Johnson, 5) as when applied to the hidden meaning of words.

[29] Conran, 73.

single-minded motion, contrasting strongly with the 'meagre stiffness' of
the Discharged Soldier,[30] is a sign of grandeur and independence. The
man is complete in himself, even the pack he carries *cleaving* to him (l. 91)
like a leech or part of his own body.

Having invested him with autonomy, Wordsworth sets up a dramatic
exchange which makes the poet himself seem inept:

> And now such freedom as I could I took
> And, drawing to his side, to him did say,
> "This morning gives us promise of a glorious day."
>
> (ll. 96–8)

It is a silly, inconsequential comment—as intrusive, in its way, as the
questions asked of the Discharged Soldier—but it gives to the
leechgatherer's own speech an impressiveness one is not expecting:

> A gentle answer did the Old Man make
> In courteous speech which forth he slowly drew . . .
>
> (ll. 99–100)

Again, the poet interrupts him:

> "What kind of work is that which you pursue?
> This is a lonesome place for one like you."
>
> (ll. 102–3)

And again we respond to his comic ineptness—for the leechgatherer is at
one with the 'lonesome place', whereas the poet (who clearly feels he has a
monopoly on loneliness) is an intruder. As if to remind him of this, the
leechgatherer speaks with dignity:

> Choice word & measur'd phrase, beyond the reach
> Of ordinary men, a stately speech . . .
>
> (ll. 109–10)

His language is different, in degree if not in kind, from that of ordinary
men. It is 'plainer and more emphatic' than poetic diction, as theirs is,[31]
and it has its roots in passion and the Bible: 'a stately speech, | Such as
grave livers do in Scotland use, | Religious Men who give to God & Man
their dues.' (ll. 110–12) But it is also 'beyond [their] reach', having a
solemnity and 'stateliness' which the language of 'native passion' cannot

---

[30] 'There was in his form | A meagre stiffness. You might almost think | That his bones
wounded him.' (ll. 43–5)

[31] Preface to *Lyrical Ballads* (1800). See *Prose Works*, i. 124.

have.[32] In making these distinctions, Wordsworth is clearly attributing to the leechgatherer the qualities of a poet: one who 'has thought long and deeply', and is possessed of 'more than usual organic sensibility'.[33] And while the old man takes over this role, Wordsworth himself is left, foolish and inarticulate, with nothing but small talk to offer.

The self-mockery one sees here is part of a dramatic device which goes back to Chaucer's Dream-Vision poems.[34] Wordsworth has used it before, in *Anecdote for Fathers* and *We are Seven*, to suggest a wisdom beyond the reach of intellect, and in *The Discharged Soldier* to poke fun at the poet's imaginings. In each case, the poet within the poem questions and re-questions his subject, receiving each time he does so an answer he neither expects nor understands but which is, none the less, imaginatively right. In reusing this device, Wordsworth is making a similar point, and there is a special appropriateness in the comedy. It is as though the Wordsworth of Alfoxden wanders about in the new poem, asking his hearty bullying questions, and watching in a kind of perplexity as the leechgatherer, and the poem itself, take on a grandeur they did not originally possess:

> The Old Man still stood talking by my side,
> But soon his voice to me was like a stream
> Scarce heard, nor word from word could I divide,
> And the whole body of the man did seem
> Like one [wh]om I had met with in a dream;
> Or like a Man from some far region sent
> To give me human strength, & strong admonishment.

> (ll. 120–6)

As the figure is assimilated into the landscape, his voice becoming 'like a stream | Scarce heard', he is also internalized ('Like one [wh]om I had met with *in a dream*'), and made to seem more distant than ever—'from some far region sent'. It is the poet's perplexity (his inability to understand answers) which gives to the leechgatherer this threefold power, and

---

[32] See Wordsworth's description, in Book Twelve of *The Prelude* (1805), of men 'Who are their own upholders, to themselves | Encouragement, and energy, and will, | Expressing liveliest thoughts in lively words | As native passion dictates' (*1805*, xii. 261–4).

[33] 'For all good poetry is the spontaneous overflow of powerful feelings; but though this be true, Poems to which any value can be attached, were never produced . . . but by a man who being possessed of more than usual organic sensibility had also thought long and deeply.' (Preface to *Lyrical Ballads*, 1800; *Prose Works*, i. 126)

[34] Conran, 66, claims that it 'has far more in common with the comedy of Chaucerian dream-allegory than we commonly realize'. He presumably has the *Hous of Fame* and *The Book of the Duchesse* in mind, but in fact Wordsworth had been reading and translating a range of Chaucer's poems during 1801–2.

permits him to retain his original shape (his 'whole body') as he is taken into the mind. Such perplexity has been seen before, in *There was a Boy*, where it was 'a gentle shock of mild surprize' that carried 'far into his heart the voice | Of mountain torrents', and allowed the visible scene to 'enter unawares into his mind' (ll. 19–22). And it is seen again, in the 'Crossing of the Alps', where Wordsworth and his companion—cheated of their expected epiphany—interrogate the peasant with a sort of bemusement, while the imagination is preparing its sublime recompense for what has been missed.[35] One should not be surprised, therefore, to find Wordsworth in *The Leechgatherer* exploiting his perplexity several times before allowing the old man his transformation. While the questioning poet descends, once again, into dejection—'My former thoughts return'd, the fear that kills, | The hope that is unwilling to be fed' (ll. 127–8)—the writer gathers strength to mount again. As the second half of *Intimations* shows, it is in apparent loss—'fallings from us', 'blank misgivings'—that imaginative power is hidden. The writer watches his former self, in the last moments of clinging to the palpable, asking his obstinate questions: "How is it that you live? & what is it you do?" (l. 133) But he is so far from wanting reassurance that he woos perplexity, allowing the man, in his final shape, the right and the power to disturb:

> While he was talking thus the lonely place,
> The Old Man's shape & speech all *troubl'd* me;
> In my mind's eye I seem'd to see him pace
> About the weary Moors continually,
> Wandering about alone and silently,
> While I these thoughts within myself pursu'd,
> He, having made a pause, the same discourse renew'd.
>
> (ll. 141–7; my italics)

In *The Statesman's Manual*, Coleridge writes that symbols are 'consubstantial with the truths, of which they are the *conductors*' (*CC*, vi. 29). A symbol 'always partakes of the Reality which it renders intelligible; and while it enunciates the whole, abides itself as a living part

[35] See *1805*, vi. 520–4. It is only on one level that the recompense is seen as occurring while the poem is written. Wordsworth's language, in the lines immediately following the anticlimax, deliberately blurs past and present: 'Imagination!—lifting up itself | Before the eye and progress of my song | Like an unfathered vapour, here that power, | In all the might of its endowments, came | Athwart me.' (vi. 525–9). The effect of the past tense is to suggest that the recompense he feels is experienced at the moment of anti-climax—that strength lies hidden, in other words, actually *within* the sense of loss. See Chapter Six, below, for the wider significance of this pattern in Wordsworth, and particularly for its expression in *Intimations*.

in that Unity, of which it is the representative.' (*CC*, vi. 30) It is, in other words, sacramental: containing and evoking God. For Wordsworth, this is never so, even when Coleridge's influence is at its height.[36] For him, a symbol is closer to an epiphany than to an icon or a sacrament: the reality it renders intelligible is other than God's. The contrast can be quickly exemplified, by putting the stone and sea-beast simile alongside a Notebook entry of Coleridge's, belonging also to spring 1802: 'The rocks and Stones seemed to live put on a vital semblance; and Life itself thereby seemed to forego its restlessness, to anticipate in its own nature an infinite repose, and to become, as it were, compatible with Immoveability.' (*Notebooks*, i. 1189) The two passages are, on the face of it, about the same process, whereby 'qualities pass insensibly into their contraries, and things revolve upon each other' (*Prose Works*, ii. 53). But they take very different routes. Wordsworth's stone is 'endued with sense' by imagination. It takes on the vitality of the sea-beast and is left, in its transformed state, to stand for the process it has undergone. Everything is done by suggestion; the poetry is its own commentary. In the Notebook entry, a very different process is at work. Seeming to have their own volition, the rocks and stones 'put on a vital semblance,' whereupon not just the scene they are in, but *Life itself* 'anticipate[s] . . . an infinite repose'. The language is exalted and abstract. Not just movement and stillness, but flux and permanence, are being invoked; and one senses that the 'infinite repose' is God's. This is not the simple conferring power of imagination, but Coleridge's Berkeleyan relationship with the One Mind.

Again by contrast, the old man's final transformation in *Resolution and Independence* is entirely Wordsworthian. The leechgatherer does not merely offer comfort, he reminds the poet of what he himself might become. To see him simply as the emblem suggested by the title is to miss the 'trouble' he creates in Wordsworth's mind. Wandering about, 'alone and silently', he is a reflex of the poet's deepest fears. For all his strength and humanity, he is nearly absorbed by the 'visionary dreariness' of this scene. And though he is to be admired—even perhaps envied—for his

---

[36] Contrast, for instance, the 'secret ministry' of Coleridge's frost, which has inescapable religious implications, with the speargrass image at the end of *The Ruined Cottage*:

> I well remember that those very plumes,
> Those weeds, and the high spear-grass on that wall,
> By mist and silent rain-drops silver'd o'er,
> As once I passed did to my heart convey
> So still an image of tranquillity . . .

(MSD, 513–17; Butler, 75)

sense of purpose (the word 'pace', as Bloom and Curtis both point out, suggests deliberation),[37] yet his aloneness is a source of fear. He continues to 'admonish', even as the poem ends.

In James Joyce's *The Dead*, there is a moment of epiphany, when Gabriel Conroy looks up at his wife, standing on the stairs, and hears a voice in the distance, singing:

He stood still in the gloom of the hall, trying to catch the air that the voice was singing, and gazing up at his wife. There was grace and mystery in her attitude as if she were a symbol of something. He asked himself what is a woman standing on the stairs in the shadow, listening to distant music, a symbol of. If he were a painter he would paint her in that attitude . . . . *Distant Music* he would call the picture . . .[38]

It is the willingness to ask the question, 'Now what is that a symbol of?', and leave it unanswered, that one associates with Wordsworth at his greatest. And it is the power to write in this way, without either an opposition to Coleridge, or a submission to his views, that emerges in the course of reworking *The Leechgatherer*. In assimilating the old man into the scene, and at the same time taking him into 'the mind's eye', the poet allows him both a literal and a symbolic power. He leaves one with a sense of questioning—Joyce's 'as if'-ness—which his own perplexity heightens.

Edmund Burke had seen uncertainty as an essential ingredient of the sublime, because it left the mind reaching for something beyond comprehension.[39] Wordsworth himself, in *The Pedlar* and *Tintern Abbey*, had evolved a language of indeterminacy in which to make his most challenging claims.[40] And two major twentieth century writers, as if with Joyce in mind, use his phrase to open new imaginative worlds: Wallace Stevens, in *To an old Philosopher in Rome*: 'He stops upon this threshold, | *As if* the design of all his words takes form | And frame from thinking and is realized', and Virginia Woolf, in the last sentences of *To the Lighthouse*: 'With a sudden intensity, *as if* she saw it clear for a second, she drew a line here, at the centre. It was done, it was finished. Yes, she thought, laying down her brush in extreme fatigue, I have had my vision.' The penultimate stanza of *Resolution and Independence*, like these passages, belongs to a tradition of epiphanic rather than strictly symbolic writing. Its greatness lies in the questions it leaves one with, not in the

---

37 Harold Bloom, *The Visionary Company* (1962), 166; Curtis, 110.

38 James Joyce, *Dubliners*, ed. Robert Scholes (1967), 240.

39 *A Philosophical Enquiry into the Origin of our Ideas of the Sublime and Beautiful* (Oxford, 1958), 59.

40 See Chapter Two, above, for a discussion of this language, and especially of its non-Coleridgean qualities.

truths it embodies. Wordsworth has found a way of heightening his original perception—'By which an Old man was'—and he has discovered a language in which to do so.

A postscript is needed, though, if only because the poem itself contains one. Of the last stanza, Kermode has written that it 'could pass as the end of a simpler, even of a bad poem'.[41] Which it is. With a curious indiscriminateness, Wordsworth has left unaltered the verse with which the original *Leechgatherer* had ended, so that one moves in a moment from the sublime to the inept:

> And now with this he other matter blended
> Which he deliver'd with demeanour kind,
> Yet stately in the main, & when he ended
> I could have laugh'd myself to scorn to find
> In that decrepit Man so firm a mind;
> 'God,' said I, 'be my help & stay secure.'
> 'I'll think of the Leech-gatherer on the lonely Moor'

> (ll. 148–54)

It is an indiscriminateness which he quite frequently shows: in the Goslar *Prelude*, for instance, where material from *The Pedlar* is inserted (*1799*, ii. 446–64), at a moment when celebrating the 'One Life' is inappropriate; or in *Prelude* Book Seven (696–705), where lines composed in 1800, and entirely out of keeping with the book as a whole, are grafted on as its supposedly logical conclusion. The willingness to use old material alongside new, without seeming to notice the difference, goes hand in hand with the poet's confidence in his present, revisionary self—the self who makes radical alterations, occasionally (as here in *The Leechgatherer*) to good effect, but frequently on a random basis, and with destructive results. At a deeper level, though, it is evidence of the nostalgia with which this book is centrally concerned, for it is Wordsworth's craving for continuity that makes him blind to the sharpness and suddenness of changes in his writing.

[41] Kermode, 171.

Part Three:

'A Power is Gone'

6

The Little Actor and His Mock Apparel

'Where had we been, we two', Wordsworth writes in Book Five of *The Prelude*, addressing the 'belovèd friend' for whom the poem is written,

> If we, in lieu of wandering as we did
> Through heights and hollows and bye-spots of tales
> Rich with indigenous produce, open ground
> Of fancy, happy pastures ranged at will,
> Had been attended, followed, watched, and noosed,
> Each in his several melancholy walk,
> Stringed like a poor man's heifer at its feed,
> Led through the lanes in forlorn servitude;
> Or rather like a stallèd ox shut out
> From touch of growing grass . . .
>
> (*1805*, v. 233–43)

Wordsworth is not writing literally, about a rural landscape, or pretending that Coleridge was actually free to wander, like himself, through 'open ground'. He is suggesting that as children they experienced the same imaginative freedom, and browsed—without constraint or guidance—among fairy tales, romances, books that cultivated and did not curb their childhood dreams. But there is something inappropriate in his choice of simile. With *Frost at Midnight* in the background, one can hardly fail to notice the parallel between Coleridge, 'pent' in his London schoolroom, and the ox, 'shut out | From touch of growing grass'. The intention, presumably, is benign enough: Wordsworth is compensating for difference by calling attention to equality—as he had done, more crudely, at the end of *1799* Part Two:

> Thou, my friend, wast reared
> In the great city, mid far other scenes,
> But we by different roads at length have gained
> The self-same bourne.
>
> (ll. 496–9)

Tropes of this kind, however, have an alarming tendency to subvert themselves. By their very obviousness they invite deconstruction.

There is no way of measuring aggression, nor of assessing the degree of intention it contains. But like wishfulness, to which it is so often nearly related, it can be observed. Coleridge, hearing *The Prelude* read aloud, must on one level have been affronted by the simile in Book Five. Even taking self-deception into account, it reads like an extended reminder of a past that could not be shared. It draws attention, also, to the 'special privilege' which is Wordsworth's alone—a privilege which, by excluding Coleridge, ensures his own mastery.

Allusion and metaphor have it in common that they provide a screen for tactlessness, where ordinary language would not. Chapter Seven of this book deals with such screening in *The Prelude* as a whole. What I want to explore here is not aggression itself but the wishfulness from which it grows. Wordsworth and Coleridge, to sustain closeness, looked always for symbols that transcended disparity, drawing on values and experience that they held in common. But it was impossible (as the Book Five address reveals) to escape the fact that their early lives were different. This made two at least of their symbols—the city and childhood—vulnerable to the kinds of interpretation discussed above. I have looked elsewhere at the importance of the city, in the poetry of 1797–1801.[1] This chapter explores the child as symbol from 1802–4.

One child in particular serves as a focus. Hartley Coleridge, from the moment of his birth, offers Coleridge the chance of overcoming his past— of living, vicariously, a Wordsworthian childhood. His existence, furthermore, gives both poets the hope that shared ideals might bear fruit, not just in poetry, but in the actual development of a child. As Hartley grows up, however, problems arise, and there is an increasing disjunction between myth and fact. The poetry written about him—largely by Wordsworth, who sees him as his earlier self—reflects an awareness of such disjunction. And, as part of a dialogue with Coleridge, it reveals much else besides.

To H.C., Six years old has always been thought to belong to 1802, the year in which Hartley was indeed six.[2] Influenced partly by the resemblances to *Intimations* VI–VIII, two recent scholars have argued

---

[1] See my article, '"In City Pent": Echo and Allusion in Wordsworth, Coleridge and Lamb, 1797–1801' *RES*, New Series 32, 128, pp. 408–28.

[2] Helen Darbishire, in her edition of *Poems in Two Volumes* (*1807*), had no hesitation in asserting that the poem was composed in 1802. And Herbert Hartman, in his excellent article, 'The Intimations of Wordsworth's Ode' *RES*, 6, no. 22 (April, 1930), 129–48, follows suit.

for 1804,[3] but they missed an important piece of evidence, proving that the poem was already in existence by October 1803. 'Hartley is what he always was', writes Coleridge to Thomas Poole on the fourteenth of that month: 'a strange strange Boy—"*exquisitely wild*"!'[4] and yet the affinities with *Intimations*, which are extremely close, remain. I should like to begin by taking a closer look at them, and then to suggest that although the stanzas from *Intimations* are indeed connected with the earlier poem, we should be looking for a different kind of relationship.

In *To H.C.*, Wordsworth sees the young Hartley Coleridge, in his largely unfallen state, as a symbol of imaginative response:

> O Thou! whose fancies from afar are brought;
> Who of thy words dost make a mock apparel,
> And fittest to unutterable thought
> The breeze-like motion and the self-born carol;
> Thou Faery Voyager! that dost float
> In such clear water, that thy Boat
> May rather seem
> To brood on air than on an earthly stream . . .
>
> (ll. 1–8)[5]

'Suspended in a stream as clear as sky' (l. 9), Hartley has the capacity for imaginative trance, and belongs more to the air than to the earth. His suspended motion is not a sign of fixity, but a proof of his creative stillness, his dove-like 'brooding'. What he resembles most is Wordsworth's butterfly, 'self-poized upon [a] yellow flower' (*To a Butterfly*, 2), waiting for the breeze that will 'call [him] forth again' (l. 9).

Hartley is articulate—or, to put it another way, he has undergone the fall into language—but he maintains still, in his 'breeze-like motion and . . . self-born carol', an immunity to its adult implications. He is like the green linnet, who pours forth an intuitive song:

> *As if it pleas'd him to disdain*
> *And mock the form which he did feign,*
> While he was dancing in the train
> Of Leaves among the bushes.
>
> (*The Green Linnet*, 37–40; my italics)

---

[3] See Mark Reed, *The Chronology of the Middle Years*, ii. 180, and Jared Curtis, *Poems in Two Volumes*, 100. Reed's argument depends to some extent on a misdating of *The Language of the Birds*, corrected by Robert Woof in 'A Coleridge–Wordsworth manuscript and "Sarah Hutchinson's Poets"', *SIB*, 19 (1966), 226–31. More recently, Hodgson, 173, has argued that the poem dates between 4 March 1801 and 4 April 1802, possibly as late as 3 May 1802.

[4] Griggs, ii. 1014. The quotation is from *To H.C.*, 12.

[5] Text from *Poems in Two Volumes* (*1807*), ed. Helen Darbishire (Oxford, 1914), 71–3.

The child's words are a mockery of the adult world he 'disdains', and a protective covering against it. He is closer to original harmony than the adult can ever be, except in his highest moments of imaginative perception:

> Ah! from the Soul itself must issue forth
> A Light, a Glory, and a luminous Cloud
>   Enveloping the Earth!
> And from the Soul itself must there be sent
> *A sweet & potent Voice, of it's own Birth,*
> Of all sweet Sounds the Life & Element.
>
> (*Letter to Sara Hutchinson*, 303–7)

Hartley has this 'Voice, of it's own Birth', this 'self-born carol'. Like Sara, he both possesses and symbolizes imagination.

There is of course nothing new in Wordsworth's claim. From the first, Hartley has been thought of, and written about, in such terms. In *Frost at Midnight* (February, 1798), Coleridge promises him the Wordsworthian childhood he himself has missed, and shows him to be intuitively in touch with the symbol language of God (ll. 63–9). In *The Nightingale* (composed two months later), Hartley is seen responding to the nightingale's 'choral minstrelsy' (l. 80)—one of those sounds in God's 'eternal language' that are only 'intelligible' to the gifted (ll. 91–6). And in the conclusion to *Christabel*, Part Two, Hartley (aged five) is symbolic of intuitive joy:

> A little child, a limber elf,
> Singing, dancing to itself,
> A fairy thing with red round cheeks,
> That always finds, and never seeks,
> Makes such a vision to the sight
> As fills a father's eyes with light . . .
>
> (ll. 656–61)

The opposition of finding and seeking (perhaps, at first sight, a denial of imagination) is in fact a redefinition, in less solemn terms, of the *Frost at Midnight* claim: 'he shall mould | Thy spirit, and by giving make it ask' (ll. 68–9). Coleridge is saying that Hartley does not have to seek, in an effortful, adult way, in order to get answers. He 'finds' (reaches deeper truths) unconsciously, as does the primary imagination.

The claims made in *To H.C.* may not be new, but they are made this time by Wordsworth, and have an urgency never felt before. In the first part of *Intimations* (composed 27 March 1802), Wordsworth had mourned the loss of his own childhood vision—a 'celestial light' that had 'apparrel'd' the ordinary world. Now he turns to Hartley, who, with his protective 'mock-apparel', embodies perpetual joy. What chance, Wordsworth asks, has *he* of surviving?

> O Blessed Vision! happy Child!
> Thou art so exquisitely wild,
> I think of thee with many fears
> For what may be thy lot in future years.
>
> (ll. 11–14)

Hartley becomes vulnerable because too much is at stake in his continuing to live. He must be protected, at all costs, from the pain that adulthood brings, and be preserved not just in symbolic, but in actual joy.

As in many lyrics of 1802, affirmation is not far from pain. In the opening line of the second stanza, 'I thought of times when Pain might be thy guest', one hears the rhythms of Wordsworth's troubled meditation in *The Leechgatherer*:

> I thought of Chatterton the marvelous Boy
> The sleepless soul who perished in his pride . . .
>
> (ll. 43–4)

As *To H.C.* continues, the parallels of mood, feeling, and language become more obvious:

> I heard the sky lark singing in the sky
> And I bethought me of the playful hare
> Even such a happy child of earth am I
> Even as these happy creatures do I fare
> Far from the world I live & from all care
> But there may come another day to me
> Solitude pain of heart distress & poverty.
>
> (*The Leechgather*, 29–35)

Wordsworth's fear for Hartley—of 'what may be [his] lot in future years'—is just as strongly a fear for himself. It is related to his own anxiety about prolonging to the last the sense of being 'a happy child of earth', privileged in his withdrawal from real distress and poverty. But what, in himself, comes too near to being irresponsible is, in Hartley, a birthright and a consolation:

> Nature will either end thee quite;
> Or, lengthening out thy season of delight,
> Preserve for thee, by individual right,
> A young Lamb's heart among the full-grown flocks.
>
> (ll. 21–4)

There is a forced bravery in these lines which is out of keeping with the fragile recompense they offer. Wordsworth's allusion to *Intimations* ('A young Lamb's heart among the full-grown flocks.') inevitably reminds one of the adult's exclusion from pastoral joy. The immortality before death that the poet seeks for Hartley is impossible, given life's unflinching rigour. Better that Nature should 'end him quite' than subject him to the slow encroachment of adult dreariness.

As the poem continues, it is Hartley's fragility that emerges as the deepest consolation. In the background, but close to the rhythms and language of the poetry, is Marvell's *On a Drop of Dew*:

> See how the Orient Dew,
> Shed from the Bosom of the Morn
> Into the blowing Roses,
> Yet careless of its Mansion new;
> For the clear Region where 'twas born
> Round in its self incloses:
> And in its little Globes Extent,
> Frames as it can its native Element.
> How it the purple flow'r does slight,
> Scarce touching where it lyes,
> But gazing back upon the Skies
> Shines with a mournful Light;
> Like its own Tear,
> Because so long divided from the Sphear.
> Restless it roules and unsecure,
> Trembling lest it grow impure:
> Till the warm Sun pitty it's Pain,
> And to the Skies exhale it back again.

(ll. 1–18)[6]

Wordsworth's description of Hartley as 'a Dew-drop, which the morn brings forth' draws on Marvell's 'Orient Dew, | Shed from the Bosom of the Morn'; and the tender protectiveness of his observations recalls the tone of Marvell's 'Trembling lest it grow impure'. The dew-drop in each case has an intrinsic purity that is threatened by earthly things. It slights them, 'Scarce touching where it lyes' and 'gazing back upon the Skies',

[6] Text from *The Poems & Letters of Andrew Marvell*, ed. H. M. Margoliouth (2 vols., Oxford, 1971), i. 12–13. Marvell's poems were not reprinted in Robert Anderson's *The Works of the British Poets* (13 vols., Edinburgh, 1792–5), which was normally Wordsworth's source for seventeenth-century poetry; but they were available in Capt. Edward Thompson's *Poems of Marvell* (1776). It is certain that Wordsworth was reading Marvell quite closely in 1802, since his complete transcription of the *Horatian Ode* in MS W. was made—almost certainly—at the end of that year (see Reed, ii. 642).

but is still vulnerable to degradation. Death is an act of pity: it removes the threat of soiling, and allows the dew-drop to return to its original harmony. In Marvell, it is clear from the first that the harmony is heaven, and that the dew-drop (or soul) spends a short lifetime preparing for its destined return:

> How loose and easie hence to go:
> How girt and ready to ascend.
> Moving but on a point below,
> It all about does upwards bend.

(ll. 33–6)

In Wordsworth, there is no sense of preparation, and no absolute assurance of return, to the place of origin. Perhaps *because* Marvell is in the background, one thinks of the 'Faery Voyager' as 'Remembering still [his] former height' (*Drop of Dew*, 22), and yearning to regain it. But as the poem closes, one cannot be sure what has happened. The child is simply

> A Gem that glitters while it lives,
> And no forewarning gives;
> But, at the touch of wrong, without a strife
> Slips in a moment out of life.

(ll. 30–3)[7]

There are no 'intimations of immortality' here; but the finality of death insures Wordsworth against the possibility of Hartley's fall. The intensity of childhood vision can for the moment be preserved.

When Wordsworth in February 1804 composes the second half of *Intimations*[8] he is more preoccupied with the lot of humanity in general

---

[7] Wordsworth was probably unconscious of the pun, but when he wrote the final lines of *To H.C.* he was echoing the first stanza of *We are Seven* as Coleridge had originally composed it:

> A little child, dear brother Jem,
> That lightly draws its breath,
> And feels its life in every limb,
> What should it know of death?

(Grosart, iii. 18)

There may be a submerged consolation in the echo.

[8] The remaining eight stanzas were composed (alongside much of the Five-Book *Prelude*) for inclusion in MS M, which Coleridge took with him to Malta. On 8 February, Coleridge wrote to Wordsworth from London, 'We talk by the long Hour about you & Hartley, Derwent, Sara, and Johnnie . . . I wish, you would write out a Sheet of Verses for them . . .'

than with Hartley as an exception to any rule. He finds in the idea of pre-existence, not something he can literally believe, but a myth which presents the loss of joy as an inevitable part both of growing up and of being human:

> Our birth is but a sleep and a forgetting
> The soul that rises with us our life's star
>> Hath had elsewhere its setting
>> And cometh from afar
>> Not in entire forgetfulness
>> And not in utter nakedness
>> But trailing clouds of glory do we come
> From God who is our home.

(ll. 58–65)[9]

Wordsworth's thoughts seem to pull in opposite directions, but are not incompatible. He clings to his earlier faith in childhood joy, while portraying that joy as itself a falling away from something more. The echoes from *To H.C.* reinforce this tension. On the one hand, the soul that 'cometh from afar' in *Intimations* is like Hartley's fancies, which 'from afar are brought' (*To H.C.*,1), suggesting a preserved contact with original harmony. On the other hand, the word 'trailing' has more threatening associations:

(Griggs, ii. 1060). His request was probably never granted, but it could have been this that prompted Wordsworth into thinking once again about *To H.C.* and the sequence of Hartley poems to which it belonged. The close relationship between *To H.C.* and Stanzas Seven–Eight of *Intimations* suggests that he intended at some point to incorporate the first into the larger structure of the second.

[9] (All references are to the transcription of MS M in Curtis, 166.) Wordsworth's use of the Platonic myth has a private appropriateness, for the earliest poem about Hartley—a sonnet, composed by Coleridge on the day of his birth—centres on the notion that 'We liv'd ere yet this *fleshly* robe we wore.' (Griggs, i. 246) Coleridge's explanations for using the myth are in terms of feeling rather than conviction. To Thomas Poole he comments: 'Almost all the followers of Fenelon believe that *men* are degraded Intelligences, who had once all existed, at one time & together, in a paradisiacal or perhaps heavenly state.—The first four lines express a feeling which I have often had. The present has appeared like a vivid dream or exact similitude of some *past* circumstances.' (Griggs, i. 246) And to Thelwall, a month later, he writes: 'Now that the thinking part of man, i.e. the Soul, existed previously to it's appearance in it's present body, may be very wild philosophy; but it is very intelligible poetry' (Griggs, i. 278). His position, here, is remarkably close to that of *Intimations*—and closer still to Wordsworth's Fenwick Note (Grosart, iii. 194–5).

> Thou art a Dew-drop, which the morn brings forth,
> Not doom'd to jostle with unkindly shocks;
> *Or to be trail'd along the soiling earth . . .*
>
> (ll. 27–9; my italics)[10]

Affirmation is qualified, in this way, by underlying fears: suggestions that the clouds might be transient, or that the trailing might soil their glory.

As the fifth stanza continues, the fears implied in *To H.C.* can no longer be held at bay. Despite a wish to reaffirm the value of childhood vision, it is the fall into adulthood that triumphs:

> Heaven lies about us in our infancy
> Shades of the prison-house begin to close
> Upon the growing Boy
> But he beholds the light and whence it flows
>   He sees it in his joy
> The Youth who daily farther from the East
>   Must travel, still is Nature's Priest
> And by the vision splendid
>   Is on his way attended
> At length the man beholds it die away
> And fade into the light of common day
>
> (ll. 66–76)

On one level, Wordsworth finds consolation in the myth. If mankind in general is subjected to this inevitable fall, then why should he mourn for himself or Hartley in particular? He cannot, however, prevent the sense of individual loss from coming through. The prison-house metaphor may in

---

[10] Coleridge had used the metaphor of clothing for the body in his sonnet on Hartley's birth (l. 6). In doing so, he was of course drawing on a well-established tradition in seventeenth century poetry. Of particular relevance to Wordsworth's trailing and soiling imagery is a passage in Vaughan's *Ascension-Hymn*, describing the effects of the Fall on man's appearance:

> Man of old
> Within the line
> Of *Eden* could
> Like the Sun shine
> All naked, innocent and bright,
> And intimate with Heav'n, as light;
>
>   But since he
> That brightness soil'd,
> His garments be
> All dark and spoil'd . . .
>
> (ll. 19–28)

fact be a reference to Hartley's having at this period to be sent to school,[11] and Hartley is present again in the fostering image of the next stanza:

> Earth fills her lap with pleasure of her own
> Yearnings she hath in her natural kind
> And even with something of a Mother's mind
>   And no unworthy aim
> The homely nurse doth all she can
> To make her foster child her Inmate Man
>   Forget the glories he hath known
> And that imperial palace whence he came . . .
>
> (ll. 77–84)

Most obviously the metaphor of fostering links the child of the Ode to Wordsworth himself (the famous lines 'And I grew up | Fostered alike by beauty and by fear' had been inserted in *The Prelude* within the previous two or three weeks),[12] but behind this reference lies another, to *The Foster Mother's Tale*. Coleridge had quoted the poem in a letter of summer 1802 describing Hartley (Griggs, ii. 804)[13] and there is no doubt the association would have been in Wordsworth's mind as well. Though happy in his relationship with fostering Nature, the child of Coleridge's poem is weaned away by education and adulthood. *Intimations* takes the process back a stage further. Thinking rather along the lines of Blake's *Vala*, Wordsworth sees Nature as seducing man away from an original glory. Instead of offsetting the damage caused by formal education, she is in league with education against the child. With two such opponents, who could survive?

It is this question that Wordsworth pursues in the central section of the

---

[11] In December 1803, after five years of being a 'most unteachable' child (see *The Foster Mother's Tale*, 29), Hartley suddenly learnt to read—making, in a single month, 'more progress than in all his former life' (Griggs, ii. 1022.) A year later, in a letter written to his wife on 19 February 1804, Coleridge refers to the question of Hartley's schooling as though it has been raised by her. He agrees somewhat reluctantly that the child should go to the Town school (meaning Keswick) during his absence, but writes rather wistfully: 'O may God vouchsafe me Health, that he may go to School to his own Father.' The letter continues, 'I exceedingly wish, that there were any one in Keswick who would give him a little instruction in the elements of Drawing.' (Griggs, ii. 1070)—a hint which, if followed up by Mrs Coleridge, may shed light on the 'little plan or chart' which Hartley 'frames' in stanza seven. Biographical details should not of course be taken too far, but it seems likely that Wordsworth observed Hartley's educational progress as carefully as did his father.

[12] *1805*, i. 305–6. The dating of Book One is established in the *Norton Prelude*, 516.

[13] Coleridge uses the phrase 'a pretty Boy' to describe his son, referring to a passage from *The Foster Mother's Tale*: 'And so the babe grew up a pretty boy, | A pretty boy, but most unteachable' (ll. 28–9). At this stage, it was still possible to believe in Hartley as absolutely opposed to the principles of education. A year later the situation is dramatically altered.

Ode, with Hartley still in mind. Stanza Seven opens abruptly with a command: '*Behold* the Child among his new-born blisses', and continues with repeated directions in the same tone: '*See where* mid work of his own hands he lies'; '*See* at his feet some little plan or chart' (ll. 85, 87 and 90). The reader is being asked to look at the child as an emblem, or epitome, of human life. Wordsworth is again alluding, as he had done two years earlier in *To H.C.*, to the rhetorical opening of Marvell's *On a Drop of Dew*, with its more subdued commands and its consistent allegorical meaning:

> *See how* the Orient Dew,
> Shed from the Bosom of the Morn
>   Into the blowing Roses,
> Yet careless of its Mansion new;
> For the clear Region where 'twas born
>   Round in its self incloses . . .
> *How* it the purple flow'r does slight . . .
>
> (ll. 1–6; 9)

The echoes are clear and significant. Wordsworth is borrowing the rhetoric and language of Marvell's ode to describe a process that is its exact opposite. The central part of stanza seven reads like an antithetical (or parodic) version of Marvell's myth:

> See at his feet some little plan or chart
> Some fragment from his dream of human life
> Shaped by himself with newly learned art
>   A wedding or a festival
>   A mourning or a funeral
> And this hath now his heart
> And unto this he frames his song
>   Then will he fit his tongue
> To dialogues of business love or strife . . .
>
> (ll. 90–8)

Marvell had used the word 'frame' in a positive sense, to describe the soul's preservation of innocence, and its preparation for Heaven:

> And in its Globes Extent,
> Frames as it can its native Element.
>
> (ll. 7–8)

Wordsworth uses it to describe a creative urge that is entirely misdirected: not a preparation for Heaven, but a precocious adaptation to adult ways of thinking, seeing, and speaking. If the word 'frame' is a reversal of Marvell, the word 'fit' ('Then will he *fit* his tongue | To dialogues') implies a denial of lines that he himself had written:

> O Thou! whose fancies from afar are brought;
> Who of thy words dost make a mock apparel,
> *And fittest to unutterable thought*
> *The breeze-like motion and the self-born carol* . . .

(To H.C., 1–4; my italics)

At the stage represented by *To H.C.* Hartley was already speaking, but his fall into language was not yet complete. He had exploited adult words as a 'mock apparel', or disguise, behind which the more shadowy workings of 'unutterable thought' could be preserved. 'Thought' was non-linguistic; instead of being clothed in words, it was 'fitted' with 'motion' and 'carol'—the child's private spontaneous expressions of joy, which were a true incarnation of feeling. At the later stage of *Intimations*, when the fall into language has happened, 'fitting' has other associations. Like 'framing' it is a wilful imposing of order on spontaneity and freedom:[14] Hartley is present in the poetry (as he always was) in both an actual and a symbolic sense. His 'pigmy size', as Derwent Coleridge points out in his *Memoir*, is a matter of fact.[15] By coincidence, or a private pun of outstandingly bad taste, he is 'fretted' by sallies of his Mother [Sally]'s kisses,[16] and the light that falls on him 'from his Father's eyes' is taken straight from the conclusion to *Christabel*, Part Two:

> A little child, a limber elf . . .
> Makes such a vision to the sight
> As fills a father's eyes with light;

(ll. 656; 660–1)

But the most important allusion of all is not to another poem, but to a private biographical fact:

> See at his feet some little plan or chart
> Some fragment from his dream of human life

---

[14] Contrast, for instance, Wordsworth's musical metaphor in *It is the first mild day of March*, 35–6: 'We'll frame the measure of our souls, | They shall be tuned to love.'

[15] 'The singularity of [Hartley's] appearance,' writes his brother, 'by which he was distinguished through life, and which, together with the shortness of his stature, (possibly attributable in some measure to his premature birth,) had a marked influence upon his character, was apparent from the first . . .' (*Poems by Hartley Coleridge*, with a memoir of his life by his brother, in two volumes (1851), i. xxiii).

[16] Coleridge frequently used 'Sally' as a nickname for his wife—on one unforgettable and unforgivable occasion even descending to 'Sally Pally!' (Griggs, ii. 888)

> Shaped by himself with newly learned art
> A wedding or a festival
> A mourning or a funeral . . .

> *(Intimations, 90–4)*

On 19 February 1804, Coleridge had written to his wife, encouraging her to find a drawing master for Hartley, and less enthusiastically agreeing he should be sent to school. Both arrangements, envisaged as a way of sustaining the child in his father's absence, were probably made before he set sail at the end of March.[17] The 'little plan or chart' that Hartley 'shapes' is not a free imaginative expression, but a mechanical demonstration of his 'newly-learned art'.[18] All the patterns it might take ('a wedding or a festival | A mourning or a funeral') are connected with adult ceremonies he can scarcely distinguish, let alone comprehend, and foisted on him by a conventional 'dream of human life'. Wordsworth is lamenting in actual, symbolic, and mythical terms, Hartley's fall into education. What the child learns, with increasing 'joy and pride', is how to imitate empty stereotypes of adulthood. He becomes expert: a 'little actor',[19] with a wardrobe of costumes or disguises, which he puts on and takes off at appropriate moments in life's comedy, as though with an innate knowledge of what is fitting. As the dressing-up becomes a habit, his

[17] See Chapter 6, note 10, above. According to Derwent Coleridge, 'It was the summer of the year 1808, that my brother and myself were placed as day-scholars under the care of the Rev. John Dawes . . .' (*Poems by Hartley Coleridge*, liv). But he is clearly referring to a time when they went to school *together*, at Ambleside; and it seems likely that Hartley attended school much earlier at Keswick.

[18] Derwent Coleridge, in his memoir of Hartley, describes how his brother invented a country called Ejuxria, complete with 'nations, continental and insular, each with its separate history, civil, ecclesiastical, and literary', etc. He claims that 'an elaborate map of the country was once in existence', but that 'no written record remains', and that 'the details have gradually faded from [his] memory'. As he recreates these details, the language of *Intimations* is very clearly in his mind: 'the Ejuxrian world presented a complete analogon to the world of fact, so far as it was known to Hartley, complete in all its parts; furnishing a theatre and scene of action, with *dramatis personae*, and suitable machinery, in which, day after day, for the space of long years, he went on evolving the complicated drama of existence . . . . Whatever . . . struck his fancy in reading . . . he thought to reproduce in little in his own playground . . . . These were his "future plans", as he called them—an ominous name.' (*Poems by Hartley Coleridge*, xlii–iii; xlv–xlvi)

[19] Very possibly an allusion to Marvell's 'Horatian Ode': 'That thence the *Royal Actor* born | The *Tragick Scaffold* might adorn' (ll. 53–4). (For Wordsworth's transcription of the *Horatian Ode* at the end of 1802 see ch. 6, n. 5, above.) The 'humorous stage' of l. 103, as De Selincourt points out, is from the 'Prologue' to Daniel's *Musophilus*: 'I do not here upon this hum'rous stage | Bring my transformed verse apparelled | With others passions, or with others rage.' (ll. 1–3) Wordsworth's conflation of 'Tragick Scaffold' and 'humorous stage' gives a sense, perhaps, of his tragi-comic vision, which is confirmed by the background presence of Jacques, describing the seven ages of man (*As You Like It II.* vii. 139–66).

identity is insidiously taken over by the disguises he puts on. Aged six, he had borrowed a 'mock apparel' of words to protect himself from adult interference; aged eight and onwards, he makes the 'apparel' his own. Instead of the 'self-born carol' of his private language, he speaks the adult 'dialogues of business love or strife'. Instead of dancing with a 'breeze-like motion', he is involved in a prolonged and sterile adoption of adult roles,

> As if his whole vocation
> Were endless imitation
>
> (ll. 106–7)

The relentlessness with which he lapses is a reminder of Coleridge's own, equally wilful, rejection of the natural self:

> For not to think of what I needs must feel,
> But to be still & patient all I can;
> And haply by abstruse Research to steal
> From my own Nature all the Natural Man—
> This was my sole Resource, my wisest plan!
> And that, which suits a part, infects the whole,
> And now is almost grown the Temper of my Soul.
>
> (*Letter to Sara*, 265–71)

In each case, imagination is first 'infected', then displaced, by an alien 'plan'.[20] Hartley's 'endless imitation' is a repetition of his father's fall.

The tones of Stanza Seven are consistently difficult to gauge. One is disarmed by touches of indulgence ('new-born blisses', 'four year's darling', 'little actor') but shocked by the satirical overtones that work against them. Again and again one is reminded of the other portrait of a child (this time consistently satirical) which belongs to the same period: the prodigy of *Prelude* Book Five:

> Let few words paint it: 'tis a child, no child,
> But a dwarf man; in knowledge, virtue, skill,
> In what he is not, and in what he is,

[20] In *Dejection: an Ode*, Coleridge alters the final lines of the passage to read:

> Till that which suits a part infects the whole,
> And now is almost grown the *habit* of my soul.
>
> (ll. 92–3; my italics)

It is tempting to think that he has perceived the analogy between Hartley and himself. The word 'habit' can be read as a pun, continuing the metaphors of clothing that have surrounded Hartley from the first, and accentuating the idea of disguise which is so prominent in *Intimations*. The verb 'suits' in *Dejection* may even contain a subdued reference to the fitting of clothes.

The noontide shadow of a man complete . . . .
He is fenced round, nay armed, for ought we know,
In panoply complete; and fear itself,
Natural or supernatural alike,
Unless it leap upon him in a dream,
Touches him not. Briefly, the moral part
Is perfect, and in learning and in books
He is a prodigy. His discourse moves slow,
Massy and ponderous as a prison door,
Tremendously embossed with terms of art.
Rank growth of propositions overruns
The stripling's brain; the path in which he treads
Is choked with grammars . . . .
All things are put to question: he must live
Knowing that he grows wiser every day,
Or else not live at all, and seeing too
Each little drop of wisdom as it falls
Into the dimpling cistern of his heart.
Meanwhile Old Grandame Earth is grieved to find
The playthings which her love designed for him
Unthought of—in their woodland beds the flowers
Weep, and the river-sides are all forlorn.

(ll. 294–7; 314–25; 341–9)[21]

The 'dwarf man' is a repellant version of the pigmy child, based this time on fantasy, not fact, and described with a pictorial sense of the macabre. The parallel continues in 'the noontide shadow of a man complete', which draws attention not just to the child's mimicry of adult actions, but his resemblance to a stunted replica of the grown man.[22] Again the metaphor of 'panoply complete' contains a double allusion to Hartley. The protective 'mock apparel' of *To H.C.* (which became, in *Intimations*, a series of disguises) is transformed here into impenetrable armour. All that was originally valued in Hartley for its vulnerability is missing in the prodigy.

[21] Wordsworth's language is heavy, rhetorical, and cluttered with literary allusions. In the background of 'tremendously embossed with terms of art' (l. 322), one hears *Othello*: 'horribly stuffed with epithets of war' (I. i. 14); and behind the 'Rank growth of propositions' (l. 323) is of course Hamlet's description of the world as 'an unweeded garden, | That grows to seed; things rank and gross in nature | Possess it merely' (I. ii. 135–7).

[22] On 1 November 1796, soon after the birth of Hartley, Coleridge wrote to Thomas Poole saying 'David Hartley Coleridge is stout, healthy, & handsome. He is the very miniature of me' (Griggs, i. 243).

The relation between Stanza Eight of *Intimations* and Book Five is more difficult to determine:

> O Thou whose outward seeming doth belie
> > Thy Soul's immensity
> Thou best philosopher who yet dost keep
> Thy heritage thou eye among the blind
> That deaf and silent read'st the eternal deep
> > Haunted for ever by the eternal mind
> > Thou mighty Prophet Seer blest
> On whom those truth[s] do rest
> Which we are toiling all our lives to find . . .
> > > > (ll. 108–16)

The child of the Ode reads the deep, just as the prodigy 'can read | The inside of the earth, and spell the stars' (*1805*, v. 332–3), and he too possesses truths which are beyond his years. Wordsworth in this case is clearly envious (they are truths which 'we are toiling all our lives to find'), but his envy does not make comprehensible his grandiose claims. It is of course Coleridge who reacts most violently against the language. 'We will merely ask', he writes in *Biographia*,

what does all this mean? In what sense is a child of that age a *philosopher*? In what sense does he *read* "the eternal deep?" In what sense is he declared to be "*for ever haunted*" by the Supreme Being?[23]

The obtuseness of his response cannot easily be explained. One takes it that the objections are genuine, but why the vehemence? Is he merely resentful that Wordsworth should prefer a child's wisdom to formal philosophy? Or does he react at some level against the way in which Hartley is transformed, distorted—turned to something uncomfortably like the prodigy?

Wordsworth in both poems is overloading the child with adult significance—precociousness in Book Five; prophetic vision in the Ode[24]—both of which are distortions. As Stanza Eight continues, the negative tone becomes strident, bringing the portraits more closely together:

---

[23] *Biographia*, ii. 138.
[24] See *To H.C.*, 5–10. The phrase 'seer blest' comes from *PL*, xii. 553, and links the child Hartley Coleridge with the archangel Michael. For the numerous Miltonic echoes and allusions in *Intimations*, see Paul McNally, 'Milton and the Immortality Ode', *WC*, 11, 1 (winter, 1980), 28–33. For the invocation to Hartley, see particularly p. 31.

> O Thou on whom thy immortality
> Broods like the day a Master o'er a Slave
> A presence which is not to be put by
>   Thou unto whom the grave
> Is but a lonely bed without the sense or sight
>   Of day or the warm light
> A living place where we in waiting lie
> Why with such earnest pains dost thou provoke
> The years to bring the inevitable yoke
> Thus blindly with thy blessedness at strife

(ll. 117–26)

The passage divides clearly in two: first exalting childhood ('What does it know of death?'), then lamenting the child's fall. The poetry, though, is consistently threatening. Immortality broods—not creatively, like Hartley's sky-boat in *To H.C.*, but restrictively, like a master's surveillance of his slave.[25] And the place of waiting, intended as an innocent child's eye view of the grave, is so dark and lonely as to be terrifying. Coleridge, who exclaims in *Biographia* against 'the frightful notion of lying *awake* in [the] grave!' (*Biographia*, ii. 141) does so, presumably, because the 'living place' is like the Mariner's Life-in-Death. The violence of his response speaks also of a private understanding of Wordsworth's metaphor that he cannot openly acknowledge. As Wordsworth confers upon the child first prophetic wisdom, then an inhuman indifference to death, what Coleridge sees is a sort of desperate over-compensation, which heightens the inevitable fall:

> Why with such earnest pains dost thou provoke
> The years to bring the inevitable yoke
> Thus blindly with thy blessedness at strife
> Full soon thy soul shall have her earthly freight
> And custom lie upon thee with a weight
> Heavy as frost and deep almost as life.

(ll. 124–9)

Read with Hartley in mind, they are disturbing lines. He had floated, once, in a canoe, joyfully poised between earth and heaven (*To H.C.*, 1–8); now an 'earthly freight' weighs him down, and he is doomed, by implication, to be 'trail'd along the soiling earth' (*To H.C.*, 29). Custom

[25] In contrast to the costumes and disguises which the 'little actor' of stanza seven uses and then discards, this is a 'presence which is not to be put by'. Its permanence is powerful and threatening.

lies heavily upon him, deadening joy, and obliterating the memory of his 'former height'. Immune no longer, he is exposed to the rigour of experience, and is seen—to quote a line from Book Five of *The Prelude*— 'Bending beneath our life's mysterious weight | Of pain and fear' (*1805*, v. 442–3).

The oddest word, here, is 'frost'. Given the allusiveness of the Ode, one can scarcely ignore the connection with *Frost at Midnight*. Wordsworth is again writing negatively about Hartley's alteration. He takes the 'secret ministry' of frost and transforms its silent, beneficent qualities into insidious, destructive ones. Instead of growing into harmony with Nature (moulded' by God's spirit) Hartley is frozen, prematurely, in his adult stance. Coleridge could hardly not read the passage as pointing out the failure both of his original blessing—'*thou*, my babe! Shalt wander, like a breeze'—and of the shared ideals which Hartley at Alfoxden had seemed to embody.

It would be interesting to know how much of this Wordsworth intended. Perhaps, having written this stanza, he became aware of what his allusions could imply, for in the opening of the next he makes amends, as it were, on the same allusive level:

> O joy that in our embers
> Is something that doth live
> That nature yet remembers
> What was so fugitive
> The thought of our past years in me doth breed
> Perpetual benedictions; not indeed
> For that which is most worthy to be blest
> Delight and liberty the simple creed
> Of childhood whether fluttering or at rest
> With new-born hope for ever in his breast,
> > Not for these I raise
> > The song of thanks and praise
> But for those blank misgivings of a Creature
> Moving about in worlds not realized . . .

> (ll. 130–43)

This time the reference to *Frost at Midnight* is positive. The 'something that doth live' is not a phoenix, rising from the ashes; it is Coleridge's 'stranger', fluttering upon the embers in a 'low-burnt fire' (l. 14). As in *Frost at Midnight* its motion symbolizes regenerative process—returning, through association, to sources of power. Adult strength does not depend on recollections of exuberance, though the 'fluttering' of childhood

(l. 139) is clearly connected with the stranger's movement.[26] It feeds, paradoxically, on 'blank misgivings'—those moments of bewilderment, or perplexity, when the real world falls away, leaving one stranded in the 'abyss of idealism'. As in the 'spots of time', Wordsworth is suggesting that the mind in 'nourished and invisibly repaired' by such experience. The bafflement of early childhood becomes a source of adult power.

Outside the Ode itself, Wordsworth finds this belief less easy to sustain. In Book Five of *The Prelude*, pausing in his discussion of literature's influence on imagination, he begins, with a sort of triumph, to assert the power of childhood vision:

> Dumb yearnings, hidden appetites, are ours,
> And they must have their food. Our childhood sits,
> Our simple childhood, sits upon a throne
> That hath more power than all the elements.
>
> (*1805*, v. 530–3)

But the grandeur cannot last. First he retreats into evasiveness, shrugging off the questions that excite him in *Intimations*:

> I guess not what this tells of being past,
> Nor what it augurs of the life to come,
> But so it is . . .
>
> (ll. 534–6)

Then he resumes his claim for 'simple childhood', this time with an undersense of mourning:

>   in that dubious hour,
> That twilight when we first begin to see
> This dawning earth, to recognise, expect—
> And in the long probation that ensues,
> The time of trial ere we learn to live
> In reconcilement with our stinted powers,
> To endure this state of meagre vassalage,

---

[26] Hartley, at the end of *Frost at Midnight*, echoes the movement of the stranger:

> then make thee shout,
> And stretch and flutter from thy mother's arms
> As thou would'st fly for very eagerness.
>
> (ll. 83–5)

Wordsworth may have these words at the back of his mind when he writes 'the Babe leaps up in his Mother's arm' (*Intimations*, 49), and there is possibly a submerged connection in his mind as he writes of the fluttering of childhood.

> Unwilling to forego, confess, submit,
> Uneasy and unsettled, yoke-fellows
> To custom, mettlesome and not yet tamed
> And humbled down—oh, then we feel, we feel,
> We know, when we have friends.
>
>   (ll. 536–47)

Betrayed by the over-assertiveness of his language,[27] he laments, yet again, his loss of vision. More even than in *Intimations*, one gets the sense of age bringing its 'inevitable yoke' to subdue and repress imagination.[28] The child has no real immunity, but is granted his probation ('time of trial') by Nature herself, who is working against him. Well before he is finally 'tamed | And humbled down', he feels mastered by custom, acknowledging—even anticipating—the time when he will live 'In reconcilement with [his] stinted powers'.

It is all expressed much more personally in another passage, composed at the same moment (February 1804), and designed for the Five-Book *Prelude*, to form a bridge between the two climactic 'spots of time'. In its original form, the passage reads:

> Oh mystery of man, from what a depth
> Proceed thy honours! I am lost, but see
> In simple childhood something of the base
> On which thy greatness stands—but this I feel,
> That from thyself it is that thou must give,
> Else never canst receive. The days gone by
> Come back upon me from the dawn almost
> Of life; the hiding-places of my power
> Seem open, I approach, and then they close;
> Yet have I singled out—not satisfied
> With general feelings, here and there have culled—
> Some incidents that may explain whence come
> My restorations, and with yet one more of these
> Will I conclude.[29]

In mood and feeling, the lines are utterly different from the last part of *Intimations*. There, Wordsworth could rely on the power of recollection to sustain him, if vulnerably, in the present; now he writes pure elegy.

---

[27] Compare the rhetoric of *Home at Grasmere* (especially ll. 646–58) which is full of grand claims that cannot be sustained.

[28] The restrictions imposed on the prodigy in Book Five are closely connected with the 'inevitable yoke' of age that tames down Hartley's breeze-like freedom. See particularly *1805*, v. 355–63.

[29] *Norton Prelude*, 517. For further details of composition, see ibid., 516–17.

Recollection seems oddly ineffectual ('the hiding places of my power | Seem open, I approach, and then they close'), so that childhood vision is 'fugitive' twice over—because it has passed, and because, as a source of adult power, it is hidden and removed. As a result, the claim that can be made for mankind is diminished and uncertain:

> I am lost, but see
> In simple childhood *something of the base*
> On which thy greatness stands . . .

A 'base', humble in itself and dimly made out through years of 'pain and abasement' is all that remains of the regal 'throne' in Book Five, which had a 'power more than all the elements', and was associated with the 'imperial palace' of man's origins. In the same way, the grandeur of an 'abundant recompense' has dwindled into the comfort of possible 'restorations' suggestive of transience and repeated need.

It is odd, given the reserve and humility of his language, that Wordsworth should refer to Coleridge's *Letter to Sara* (or to the shorter published text of *The Morning Post*) as though it qualified his claim. If he had been writing triumphantly, a half-apologetic aside might have seemed appropriate; as it is, the allusion reads like a non-sequitur:

> but this I feel,
> That from thyself it is that thou must give,
> Else never canst receive.

It is clearly not enough to say that these lines—*The Prelude's* most specific reference to the *Letter*—are Wordsworth's way of expressing sympathy for Coleridge in the intensity of his loss. Beyond this fellow-feeling, there are deeper connections. Returning to the 'spots of time', and attempting to explain why they should give him 'restorations', Wordsworth is forced to define more closely the origin of their creative strength. His allusion is, in effect, a way of acknowledging that the nourishment they provide can only be 'received' by an active imagination, 'giving' in its turn. They must be sustained by the power they are sustaining, and their strength remains hidden when the poet needs it most: 'I approach, and then they close'. Expanding the passage, in April 1805, Wordsworth makes this clearer:

> I see by glimpses now, when age comes on
> May scarcely see at all; and I would give
> While yet we may, as far as words can give,
> A substance and a life to what I feel:
> I would enshrine the spirit of the past
> For future restoration.
>
> (*1805*, xi. 337–42)

There is something moving and heroic in the poet's tone of acceptance ('I see by glimpses now . . .') almost as though he were describing Miltonic blindness; but his language, after the first impressive claim, loses power. The royal 'we', and the gesture about the inadequacy of words, prepare one for a less than honest conclusion. When it finally comes—'I would enshrine the spirit of the past | For future restoration.'—one is left feeling even more unease. A shrine is a place of worship, but also very frequently a memorial. To 'enshrine the spirit of the past' is to take it out of nature, but not in the Yeatsian sense. The golden bird of *Sailing to Byzantium* is eternal: it sings, not of mortality ('Whatever is begotten, born and dies'), but of perpetual flux: 'what is past, or passing, or to come'. It is lifted beyond time, but still in touch with our human sense of transience, and for this reason it communicates fulness, possibility, what is yet to be.[30] Wordsworth's 'enshrining' is not so positive. It makes childhood permanent, but it also freezes the past, removing it from flux, and therefore from possibility. What it does, in effect, is to create a sort of death. The shrine, like the epitaph, has a ghostly permanence.

Another passage, composed in November 1804 and belonging to Book Seven of *The Prelude*, has exactly this quality. It centres on two human figures—a mother with her child—both of whom are transformed into emblems. They are placed in a symbolic setting, outside a theatre, where they are caught up in the pantomime of London and the larger masquerade of life. The mother, with her 'painted bloom' (l. 374), is like an actress, compromised by Experience, and assimilated into the fallen world that London represents. The child, only a year old, 'in face a cottage rose | Just three parts blown' (ll. 381–2), stands for an innocence which remarkably survives, despite an environment that is depraved. Wordsworth is careful to heighten the child's immunity by extending the theatrical metaphor:

> Upon a board,
> Whence an attendant of the theatre
> Served out refreshments, had this child been placed,
> And there he sate environed with a ring
> Of chance spectators, chiefly dissolute men
> And shameless women . . .
>
> (ll. 383–8)

Placed on his miniature stage, surrounded by onlookers, the child has ample opportunity to become a 'little actor'. But the fall of *Intimations* is

[30] Yeats, *Sailing to Byzantium*, 25–32.

postponed. He adopts no roles, is unaffected by the adult world he could by copying, and stays immune—

> Among the wretched and the falsely gay,
> Like one of those who walked with hair unsinged
> Amid the fiery furnace.
>
> (ll. 397–9)

The child is a version of Hartley, but in his unfallen state, well before the stage represented by the Ode. As the description continues, the parallels grow:

> He hath since
> Appeared to me ofttimes as if embalmed
> By Nature—through some special privilege
> Stopped at the growth he had—destined to live,
> To be, to have been, come, and go, a child
> And nothing more, no partner in the years
> That bear us forward to distress and guilt,
> Pain and abasement; beauty in such excess
> Adorned him in that miserable place.
>
> (ll. 399–407)

There is something uncanny in the whole sequence. Following through the fantasy of *To H.C.*, Wordsworth brings out all that it contained of the macabre. Hartley's 'individual right' to prolonged innocence becomes, in Book Seven, a 'special privilege', and one that is deeply questionable. 'Stopped at the growth he had', this child reminds one of the stunted effigy in Book Five. He is removed not only from the distress and guilt of future years, but from the flux and plenitude of life. He is 'embalmed', just as the past in Book Eleven is 'enshrined', though not by Nature. It is the imagination, craving symbols of its own permanence, that prevents the child from growing, and memorializes the past.

One sees here, on a small scale and in symbolic terms, the embalming process which allusive language tends increasingly to enact. Meanwhile the myth of Hartley Coleridge lived on. Years later—long after he had fallen into Experience (and disrepute)—Hartley composed a sonnet himself that forms a poignant comment:

> Long time a child, and still a child, when years
> Had painted manhood on my cheek, was I,—
> For yet I lived like one not born to die;
> A thriftless prodigal of smiles and tears,
> No hope I needed, and I knew no fears.

But sleep, though sweet, is only sleep, and waking,
I waked to sleep no more, at once o'ertaking
The vanguard of my age, with all arrears
Of duty on my back. Nor child, nor man,
Nor youth, nor sage, I find my head is grey,
For I have lost the race I never ran:
A rathe December blights my lagging May;
And still I am a child, tho' I be old,
Time is my debtor for my years untold.[31]

The poem, for all its elegance, is painful. Not in showing the failure of an illusion ('I find my head is grey'), but in revealing that Hartley is trapped by the myth of himself. He lives out his life in the poetic roles that are chosen for him, 'like one not born to die', 'destined to have been, come, and go, a child'. And when he wakes from his Wordsworthian enchantment, to find that he is aging, the myth (ironically) continues to hold true. He is metaphorically still a 'child', retarded in his growth, and mocked by a potential he will never be able to fulfil. His sonnet is a protest against being embalmed. There is pathos both in his acceptance of a symbolic role, and in his not growing beyond it.

[31] *Poems by Hartley Coleridge*, i. 13.

7

'A Strong Confusion':
Coleridge's Presence in *The Prelude*

Coleridge's presence in *The Prelude* is deceptive, even at first sight. As an account of Wordsworth's life, the poem does not come up to date, and is concerned with experiences the two poets never shared. Again and again, however, their friendship is introduced as part of the unfolding story:

> O friend, we had not seen thee at that time,
> And yet a power is on me and a strong
> Confusion, and I seem to plant thee there.
>
> (*1805*, vi. 246–8)

Misremembrance is deliberate, and factual narrative gets left behind.[1] Coleridge, treated in this way, becomes a continuous being, permanently absorbed into a life that is not his own:

> But thou art with us, with us in the past,
> The present, with us in the times to come . . .
>
> (*1805*, vi. 251–2)

The knowing self-deception here is typical, and alerts us to further and deeper problems. Not only is there the obvious contradiction between *The Prelude*'s design and Coleridge's role; there is also a struggle between Wordsworth's personal quest and the wish to pay homage to his friend. 'Points have we all of us within our souls', he writes, 'where all stand single' (*1805*, vi. 186–7). In its various stages, *The Prelude* is a record of 'singleness'. It finds in childhood memories the origins of imaginative power; and it explains special privilege, not (as with *The Pedlar*) in the context of the 'One Life', but in private Wordsworthian terms. On more wishful and idealizing levels, however, it still remains the 'Poem to Coleridge': a tribute to his powers, and a memorial to the vanished Alfoxden relationship. The result is poetry of a peculiarly divided kind:

---

[1] For a brief discussion of Wordsworth's deviation from actual chronology in *The Prelude*, see Lindenberger, 170; and for an explanation of the more disconcerting aspects of confused time, see Baker, 41–5.

on the one hand logically moving toward assertions of self-sufficiency and independence; on the other withdrawing guiltily, as though the quest for origins can be valid only if shared, and life without Coleridge would be unthinkable.

Complicating matters further, there is the fact that *The Prelude* really ought to be *The Recluse*. Wordsworth's obligation to Coleridge (who had foisted the scheme on him in spring 1798) means that he should be writing a public poem, a philosophical poem, a poem of redemption for mankind. What he finds himself writing, instead, is something which looks by comparison both limited and self-involved. Different kinds of excuse are offered: 'I am not yet ready to write that poem; let this one stand in its stead'; 'this poem is a preparation for writing the other one; is indeed part of it'. But the best excuse is no excuse at all; it is a plea: 'this is not the poem you expect, I know, but it is a *better* poem, and one more appropriate to me. You, Coleridge, of all people, can appreciate its importance.' These, however, are strategies for dealing with a problem which refuses to go away. Wordsworth's triumph in *The Prelude* rests not just on his inability to write *The Recluse*, but on his refusal to do so. And if he succeeds in asserting his independence, he must accept the guilt involved. I want in this chapter to look at the various complications to which this guilt gives rise. And I want to argue that there are, in effect, two Coleridges in *The Prelude*: one mythologized beyond recognition, and needed by Wordsworth to support the values of his past; the other more flawed and human, but used by him merely as a foil. On the conflict between these two figures, the formal addresses turn. I hope, by looking at them in detail, to establish that *The Prelude*—disguised by Wordsworth as a 'joint labour', to pay homage to his friend—is in fact a solitary quest, to which friendship itself is finally irrelevant.

The reference to *Frost at Midnight*, in the opening of the Two-Part Poem, claims companionship and support for a journey into the past:

> For this didst thou,
> O Derwent, travelling over the green plains
> Near my 'sweet birthplace', didst thou, beauteous stream,
> Make ceaseless music through the night and day . . .?
>
> ,   (*1799*, i. 6–9)

Coleridge's priority, in discussing the imaginative function of childhood memory, is firmly established in the tribute-paying quotation. But there is an irony implied, of which both poets would have been aware. Wordsworth is attempting to imply similarity, where it is difference that is most apparent. *Frost at Midnight* had turned on the contrast between Wordsworthian and Coleridgean childhoods. The memory of his 'sweet birthplace', and of church-bells ringing 'all the hot fair-day' had been Coleridge's nearest approximation to a spot of time, and his only imaginative release, when 'pent mid cloisters dim' in the 'great City'. It was a fragile, isolated memory, of an entirely nostalgic kind.[2] Wordsworth's recollection of the Derwent has more power. The music it made was ceaseless, through both night and day; it also singled him out, and remained with him throughout boyhood. Difference, then, is accentuated by friendly quotation. *The Prelude* begins with Coleridge's childhood being quietly trumped.

When, at the end of Part One, Wordsworth attempts to justify having written over four hundred lines about himself, he does so in terms of *The Recluse*. Referring back to the question—'Was it for this . . .?'—with which, in October, he had begun writing, he claims that his movement into the past had been intended as a self-reproach. The assertion, perfectly designed to persuade Coleridge, is prefaced, first by a guilty acknowledge-ment that the past is tempting in its own terms (*1799*, i. 443–6)—and, second, by an expression of confidence in Coleridge's approval which is full of unease (ll. 447–9). When it comes, the poet's justification in terms of *The Recluse* seems less than entirely honest:

> Meanwhile my hope has been that I might fetch
> Reproaches from my former years, whose power
> May spur me on, in manhood now mature,
> To honourable toil.

> (ll. 450–3)

It is only in the last resort, and with a great deal of uncertainty, that he comes to define the purpose of his writing in its own terms. 'Yet should it be | That this is but an impotent desire', he writes, quoting himself, at his most vulnerable, in *Tintern Abbey*,[3] then continues, with another echo:

> . . . need I dread from thee
> Harsh judgements if I am so loth to quit
> Those recollected hours that have the charm
> Of visionary things . . .

> (ll. 458–61)

At the back of his mind are the 'rash judgements' and the 'sneers of selfish

<hr/>

[2] See *Frost at Midnight*, 23–43.

[3] For a discussion of the unconfidence implied by the line 'If this | Be but a vain belief' (*Tintern Abbey*, 50–1), see Chapter Two, Part (iii) above.

men' which, only months before, had made up the 'dreary intercourse' of daily life' (*Tintern Abbey*, 130, 132), and which now, the echo might suggest, Wordsworth fears in his friend. *The Recluse*, planned jointly the previous spring, has become his sole responsibility. Can so private an enterprise as *The Prelude* be justified at all? The unconfidence with which Part Two begins would suggest that Wordsworth's own answer to this question was 'no'. There is no scope, here, for considering the two false starts of *1799* in which, openly apprehensive, he longs for the cheering voice of his friend.[4] I want to turn instead to the lines leading into the famous passage about the Infant Babe. Here, more than anywhere in Part One, Wordsworth begins his double dealings with Coleridge:

> Who knows the individual hour in which
> His habits were first sown even as a seed?
> Who that shall point as with a wand, and say
> 'This portion of the river of my mind
> Came from yon fountain'?

> > (*1799*, ii. 245–9)

The distinction between habits 'sown' in childhood, and those planted at a later stage is strategically blurred; and it is Coleridge who, as a prophet of 'unity', presides over the poet's rearranging of time:

> Thou, my friend, art one
> More deeply read in thy own thoughts, no slave
> Of that false secondary power by which
> In weakness we create distinctions, then
> Believe our puny boundaries are things
> Which we perceive, and not which we have made.
> To thee, unblinded by these outward shews,
> The unity of all has been revealed . . .

> > (*1799*, ii. 249–56)

It might at first seem, as Jonathan Wordsworth has claimed, that a contrast is being made between Coleridge's 'unified vision' and 'a tendency in the poet himself to categorize, impose distinctions'.[5] But as the passage continues, Wordsworth too moves into a higher sphere, counting himself, *with* Coleridge, as one of the elect:

> And thou wilt doubt with me, less aptly skilled
> Than many are to class the cabinet

---

[4] Both belong to *c.* May 1799, and are quoted in full in the notes to the Norton edition, pp. 13–14.

[5] See Jonathan Wordsworth, 'The Two-Part *Prelude* of 1799', *Norton Prelude*, 575.

> Of their sensations, and in voluble phrase
> Run through the history and birth of each
> As of a single independent thing.
>
> (*1799*, ii. 257–61)

The 'unity of all' which is said to have been 'revealed' to his friend is not merely an envious reference to Unitarianism, though Wordsworth would no doubt value the stability that such faith implies. His choice of language is highly strategic: on the one hand, it suggests to Coleridge that the 'One Life' remains his ideal. On the other, it justifies his quest for personal, secular origins by defining unity in broader terms. 'Hard task', he writes, quoting not just Raphael in Book Five, but Adam in Book Eight, of *Paradise Lost*:

> Hard task to analyse a soul, in which
> Not only general habits and desires,
> But each most obvious and particular thought—
> Not in a mystical and idle sense,
> But in the words of reason deeply weighed—
> Hath no beginning.
>
> (*1799*, ii. 262–7)

Adam had been faced with genuine problems: 'For man to tell how human life began | Is hard; for who himself beginning knew?' (*PL*, viii. 250–1); Wordsworth is only rhetorically unsure of what he is doing.[6] Miltonic authority corroborates his claim that there can be no beginnings, only the search for them; and this, in its turn, gives stature to his quest. Despite the apparent contrasts with which the passage opens, Wordsworth succeeds in using Coleridge to support himself. 'The unity of all', he implies, will be 'revealed' as *The Prelude* unfolds.

Having obtained Coleridge's approval for the study of origins, Wordsworth turns to a subject on which Coleridge rarely touches—the relationship between mother and child (*1799*, ii. 267 ff.). With the ending of *Frost at Midnight* in mind, he describes the earliest stages of imaginative life, at once taking his friend into account, and radically modifying his views. Unity had been 'revealed' to Coleridge—and, within the poem, to his son Hartley—by God. Wordsworth sees it emerging as an aspect of maternal love which the child instinctively absorbs (ll. 274–80).

---

6 Compare the artful inadequacy of words at *1799*, i. 320–2: 'I should need | Colours and words that are unknown to man | To paint the visionary dreariness . . .' Lindenberger, 51–61, discusses the rhetorical strategy of wordlessness under the heading 'The struggle toward definition'.

The patriarchal world of *Frost at Midnight*—in which Hartley had wandered about, reading God's (and his father's) sign-language—has been replaced by a Wordsworthian universe, in which the mother counts above all else. Instead of 'A motion and a spirit, that impels | All thinking things, all objects of all thought' (*Tintern Abbey*, 101–2), there now exists, for the child, 'A virtue which irradiates and exalts | All objects through all intercourse of sense' (*1799*, ii. 289–90). Leavis saw the echo, but treated it as though the process of replacement were a matter of course.[7] In effect what has taken place is a much more aggressive usurpation. Immediately following the reference to Coleridge as prophet of unity, the passage as a whole corrects any impression of envy we may have received. Paying tribute to his friend gives Wordsworth the right to go one better: deference is followed by an assertive rewriting of Coleridge's terms.

As he brings the 1799 *Prelude* to its climax, with an account of his adolescent growth, Wordsworth moves easily back again, as though no contradiction were involved,[8] into the language of the 'One Life':

> From Nature and her overflowing soul
> I had received so much that all my thoughts
> Were steeped in feeling.

(1799, ii. 446–8)

That he had felt such things as a boy (and in the Pedlar's terms) is palpably untrue. But in any case the passage is deliberately misleading. It suggests that his belief in the 'One Life' (already, by *Tintern Abbey*, diminished and uncertain) lasts through to the present day. And if that can survive, so too can *The Recluse*. Lines 479–96 are a lengthy, versified quotation from Coleridge's letter to Wordsworth of September 1799.[9] They evoke, in a language which is strongly echoic, 'indifference', 'apathy', 'selfishness disguised in gentle names', and 'sneers | On visionary minds'. But they suggest that triumph over 'dereliction and dismay' is possible, through the 'never-failing principle of joy' (l. 495). Despite moving on, in *The Prelude*, to something distinctly his own, Wordsworth manages to present himself as the poet of *The Recluse*.

Rounding off the Two Part *Prelude*, as the poets go their separate ways,[10] he wishes to ensure that values they have had in common should

---

[7] See *Revaluation; Tradition and Development in English Poetry* (1936), 160.

[8] See the end of Chapter Five, above, for an explanation of the poet's indiscriminateness in this respect.

[9] See Griggs, i, 527.

[10] Literally, as well as metaphorically. In November 1799 Coleridge went to London to become a journalist.

be seen to survive. The drama played out in his final address is one, therefore, of difference triumphed over by sameness, and continuity insuring against change:

> Thou, my friend, wast reared
> In the great city, 'mid far other scenes,
> But we by different roads at length have gained
> The self-same bourne.

(ll. 496–9)

Part One had opened with a quotation from *Frost at Midnight*, and fittingly that is how Part Two ends. As before, Wordsworth is claiming his friend's support for the quest he has begun; but he seems more than usually aware of the paradox implied. As he conflates Coleridge's lament for a wasted childhood—'For I was rear'd │ In the great city, pent mid cloisters dim'—with his celebration of Hartley's different future—'thou shalt learn far other lore, │ And in far other scenes!' (*Frost at Midnight*, 56–7; 55–6)—Wordsworth seems at once to be admitting, and rhetorically attempting to conceal, his own unease. The same ambivalence is present in the violent terms used to describe what Coleridge is *not* feeling: 'And from this cause to thee │ I speak unapprehensive of contempt, │ The insinuated scoff of coward tongues . . .' (*1799*, ii. 499–501). Language intended to exorcize the poet's fears allows their presence to be felt. An unsympathetic (even hostile) Coleridge hovers behind the image of him that Wordsworth is trying to present. And in the poem's climax there is the same gap between statement and underlying awareness:

> thou art one
> The most intense of Nature's worshippers,
> In many things my brother, chiefly here
> In this my deep devotion.

(*1799*, ii. 506–9)

On a surface reading the two poets are brothers, fellow worshippers, alike in all things. Beneath, there is unease, growing difference, and the sense of loss.

A short time before writing this farewell, very probably on the actual day of Coleridge's departure (via Sockburn) for London, Wordsworth had composed as a separate effusion what was later to become the 'glad preamble' to *1805*.[11] The two passages grow out of the same event, but are

---

[11] See *Norton Prelude*, 30, *n.* 6.

not alike. While the one anxiously seeks Coleridge's support, and regrets his departure, the other is full of exhilaration:

> O there is blessing in this gentle breeze,
> That blows from the green fields and from the clouds
> And from the sky; it beats against my cheek,
> And seems half conscious of the joy it gives.

> (*1805*, i. 1–4)

At Goslar, working on the Two-Part *Prelude*, Wordsworth had jotted down a series of fragments, expressing the same exalted state of mind.[12] At first sight it is surprising that he should recall and draw on them now. In doing so, however, he links not just two moods that happen to resemble each other, but two moments at which, in the absence of Coleridge, his creativity is suddenly released.[13] Significantly enough, it is not until January 1804, when Coleridge is once again setting out on a journey, that Wordsworth begins his next real burst of activity on *The Prelude* Book Three. Read to Coleridge, 'in the highest & outermost of Grasmere'[14], the moving farewell lines of *1799* must have taken on a new appropriateness: in 'Fare thee well: | Health and the quiet of a healthful mind | Attend thee' (*1799*, ii. 509–11). But as before, Coleridge's departure brings out in Wordsworth a sense of confidence and inner power:

> And here, O friend, have I retraced my life
> Up to an eminence, and told a tale
> Of matters which not falsely I may call
> The glory of my youth. Of genius, power,
> Creation, and divinity itself,
> I have been speaking, for my theme has been
> What passed within me.

> (*1805*, iii. 168–74)

The loftiness reminds one of the 'Prospectus' to *The Recluse*.[15] But

---

[12] See *Norton Prelude*, 494.

[13] Wordsworth and Coleridge had completely different responses to being separated. In Germany, during the winter of 1798–9, Wordsworth moved into his greatest creative period to date. Coleridge on the other hand was crippled by absence (not just from the Wordsworths, but from England) and his two important poems of this period—*Hexameters* and *Lines written at Elbingerode*—are expressions of loneliness and exclusion.

[14] Coleridge *Notebooks*, i. 1801 (4 January 1804).

[15] Compare the most daring of his out-Miltonings:

> Jehovah, with his thunder, and the quire
> Of shouting angels and the empyreal throne—
> I pass them unalarmed.

> (Darlington, 102)

affinities with the 'Preamble' are also there. Wordsworth celebrates a divinity within himself that re-moulds, and in some respects actually discards, Milton's scheme in *Paradise Lost*:

> Not of outward things
> Done visibly for other minds—words, signs,
> Symbols or actions—but of my own heart
> Have I been speaking, and my youthful mind.
>
> (*1805*, iii. 174–7)

He feels no need, when making his biggest claims, to disguise his singleness. The proof of divinity lies in 'the glory of [his] youth', and this neither Milton nor Coleridge can share:

> Points have we all of us within our souls
> Where all stand single; this I feel, and make
> Breathings for incommunicable powers.
>
> (*1805*, iii. 186–8)

As the passage continues, however, apprehensiveness creeps in. Wordsworth feels the need to generalize—'Yet each man is a memory to himself' (l. 189)—and to include all men in his own sense of achievement: 'There's not a man | That lives who hath not had his god-like hours' (ll. 191–2). The claim for universality is moving, and gives the reader a sense of divinity matching the poet's own. But an over-emphatic quality in his language registers unease. Coleridge, by way of compensation for having been excluded, is given in the next paragraph the status of Wordsworth's guide:

> A traveller I am,
> And all my tale is of myself—even so—
> So be it, if the pure in heart delight
> To follow me, and thou, O honored friend,
> Who in my thoughts art ever at my side,
> Uphold as heretofore my fainting steps.
>
> (*1805*, iii. 195–201)

This is a collusive way of sustaining friendship, while at the same time definining a quite private self.

The longest and most emotional of Wordsworth's addresses to Coleridge occurs half way through Book Six. It begins, as this chapter did, with the poet's reordering of his past:

> O friend, we had not seen thee at that time,
> And yet a power is on me and a strong
> Confusion, and I seem to plant thee there.
>
> (*1805*, vi. 246–8)

As the passage continues, the purpose of misremembrance becomes clear. Wordsworth, believing his friend already to have left the country, faces the loss and release which his departure brings. Resigning himself to separation, he seems also to reassure himself of the deeper bonds that will continue, despite everything, to grow:

> But thou art with us, with us in the past,
> The present, with us in the times to come.
> There is no grief, no sorrow, no despair,
> No languor, no dejection, no dismay,
> No absence scarcely can there be, for those
> Who love as we do.
>
> (*1805*, vi. 251–6)

The poetry moves one for its underlying pathos, which emerges because of (not despite) the absoluteness of the claims. Wordsworth seems almost to chant his words—'There is no grief, no sorrow, no despair'—as though they made up a spell to keep such feelings away. 'I too have been a wanderer', he continues, moving into a reaffirmation in which the closing lines of the Goslar *Prelude* are distinctly recalled:

> but, alas,
> How different is the fate of different men,
> Though twins almost in genius and in mind.
> Unknown unto each other, yea, and breathing
> As if in different elements, we were framed
> To bend at last to the same discipline,
> Predestined, if two beings ever were,
> To seek the same delights, and have one health,
> One happiness.
>
> (*1805*, vi. 261–9)

There is evident strain in the notion that two such radically different minds should come together. The words 'framed', 'bend', and 'discipline' all suggest coercion (or at least constriction) whereas the phrase 'breathing | As if in different elements' gives a sense of freedom and natural growth. What the poetry describes is not the reconciliation of opposites, but the temporary binding together of forces that will pull apart. Drawing on a whole sequence of poems in which Coleridge had evolved the myth of his exile from country life, the passage moves deeper and deeper into a world of blatant and unchangeable contrasts:

> Of rivers, fields,
> And groves, I speak to thee, my friend—to thee
> Who, yet a liveried schoolboy in the depths
> Of the huge city, on the leaded roof
> Of that wide edifice, thy home and school,
> Wast used to lie and gaze upon the clouds
> Moving in heaven, or haply, tired of this,
> To shut thine eyes and by internal light
> See trees, and meadows, and thy native stream
> Far distant—thus beheld from year to year
> Of thy long exile.
>
> (*1805*, vi. 274–84)

Coleridge is meant to become the type of a majestic intellect, carrying with him the freedom and space of his origins, who can mentally inhabit the country despite being 'in city pent'. But Wordsworth's sense of his own privilege gives to his quotations from Coleridge's poems—and to his collusion in the myth they represent—an edge of condescension:

> oh, it is a pang that calls
> For utterance, to think how small a change
> Of circumstances might to thee have spared
> A world of pain, ripened ten thousand hopes
> For ever withered.
>
> (*1805*, vi. 292–6)

His belief that he might have protected Coleridge from 'a world of pain'— might, to pick up the Miltonic echo, have prevented his fall[16]—depends upon an assumption of innate superiority. When, at the end of the passage, he attempts to explain, it is in largely moral terms: 'maturer age | And temperature less willing to be moved'; 'calmer habits and more steady voice' (vi. 321–3). But in fact a different kind of explanation has already emerged, in the highly ambiguous portrait which occupies the intervening lines:

> I have thought
> Of thee, thy learning, gorgeous eloquence,
> And all the strength and plumage of thy youth,
> Thy subtle speculations, toils abstruse

---

16 Wordsworth's allusion is to *PL*, ix. 11.

> Among the schoolmen, and Platonic forms
> Of wild ideal pageantry, shaped out
> From things well-matched, or ill, and words for things—
> The self-created sustenance of a mind
> Debarred from Nature's living images,
> Compelled to be a life unto itself,
> And unrelentingly possessed by thirst
> Of greatness, love, and beauty.

(1805, vi. 305–16)

Wordsworth is emphasizing, as he had done earlier on, the power of
Coleridge's 'internal light' which seems at once enviable and
frightening—like the loneliness of the leechgatherer, as he 'paces the
weary moors continually', or the solipsism of the Arab Quixote,
'crazed | By love, and feeling, and internal thought | Protracted among
endless solitudes' (*1805*, v. 144–6). It is surprising, in a Book that takes
the Coleridgean imagination as its central subject, to find lines so
negative in their implications. What Wordsworth fears might result from
Coleridge's imaginative power is the surrender of literal reality—and the
loss, therefore, of a capacity to distinguish between words and things.[17] He
sees, side by side, the potential for inner vastness and the danger of
falseness or anarchy. Occupying a central position in this Book, Coleridge
becomes—like Burns and Chatterton before him—at once an example,
and a warning, of what the mind can do.

The address comes to its close in a way that points up the duality of
Coleridge's role. First, Wordsworth expresses the belief that he could
'with an influence benign have soothed | Or chased away the airy
wretchedness | That battened on [his] youth.' (ll. 324–6) Then, as if to
withdraw the vulnerable picture of Coleridge he has painted, he
transforms him into myth:

> But thou hast trod,
> In watchful meditation thou hast trod,
> *A march of glory, which doth put to shame*
> These vain regrets; health suffers in thee, else
> Such grief for thee would be the weakest thought
> That ever harboured in the breast of man.

(1805, vi. 326–31; my italics)

---

[17] It is a danger he takes seriously—as one sees for instance in his comments on 'Ossian' in
the *Essay Supplementary to the Preface*: 'In nature every thing is distinct, yet nothing defined
into absolute independent singleness. In MacPherson's work, it is exactly the reverse; every
thing (that is not stolen) is in this manner defined, insulated, dislocated, deadened,—yet
nothing distinct. It will always be so when words are substituted for things.' (*Prose Works*,
iii. 77) The passage, both in its content and its phrasing, seems to echo Coleridge's distinction
between Hebrew and Greek poetry. See Chapter Four above.

In the background, but unmistakeably, one hears the rhythms and language of *Samson Agonistes*: '[His] race of glory run, and race of shame' (l. 597). In a passage that is intended not only to bless Coleridge but to glorify him, the echo has a jarring effect. It recalls, of course, the mood of dejection in which Coleridge had last echoed the same passage,[18] and it highlights the ambiguity of Coleridge's status. On one level, he is a hero with the capacity of a God; on the other, he is a human being whose health and vision are frail. The grandeur of his potential accentuates an underlying pathos, just as the extremity of Wordsworth's myth-making reveals the need to compensate for what is flawed.

A short passage in Book Eight brings out the contrasts already implied: 'With an eye so rich as mine was' Wordsworth writes, with a confidence that is surprisingly unselfconscious,

> I had forms distinct
> To steady me. These thoughts did oft revolve
> About some centre palpable, which at once
> Incited them to motion and controlled . . .
>
> (*1805*, viii. 594; 597–600)

'Whatsoever shape the fit might take,' he continues, as though talking about madness,[19]

> And whencesoever it might come, I still
> At all times had a real solid world
> Of images about me, did not pine
> As one in cities bred might do—as thou,
> Beloved friend, hast told me that thou didst,
> Great spirit as thou art—in endless dreams
> Of sickness, disjoining, joining things,
> Without the light of knowledge.
>
> (*1805*, viii. 601–10)

Symbolic opposition is taken to its extreme, as Wordsworth emphasizes (more strongly than at any other time) an unbridgeable gulf between the poets' ways of seeing. The 'grand and lovely region' in which he had grown up becomes at once the embodiment in his eyes of all that Coleridge had missed; the cause of his sense of privilege; and a justification for the

---

[18] See the *Letter to Sara*, 44.
[19] For an assessment of the extent to which Wordsworth was afraid of madness, see John Beer, *Wordsworth in Time* (1979), 24. And for my own earlier criticism of Dr Beer's argument, which I should now like to modify, see *RES* New Series, 32, 126, 230–1.

superiority with which he addresses his friend. The city, on the other
hand—at one time a 'pasteboard symbol' for 'the unintelligible, the
wholly random' element in man's experience[20]—becomes more specifically a setting against which to see the potential anarchy of Coleridge's
mind. 'Debarred from Nature's living images' and 'Compelled to be a life
unto [him]self', Coleridge occupies an insubstantial and chaotic world,
over which he has no control: 'in endless dreams | Of sickness, disjoining,
joining things, | Without the light of knowledge.'

Interestingly, the clearest link that exists between these lines from Book
Eight and the great central address of Book Six is their common
dependence upon Milton. Adam, in Book Five of *Paradise Lost*, has a
theory about dreams:

> know that in the soul
> Are many lesser faculties that serve
> Reason as chief; among these fancy next
> Her office holds; of all external things,
> Which the five watchful senses represent,
> She forms imaginations, airy shapes,
> Which reason joining or disjoining, frames
> All what we affirm or what deny, and call
> Our knowledge or opinion; then retires
> Into her private cell when nature rests.
> Oft in her absence mimic fancy wakes
> To imitate her; but misjoining shapes,
> Wild work produces oft, and most in dreams,
> Ill matching words and deeds long past or late.
>
> (*PL*, v. 100–13)

In Book Six, Wordsworth's echoing of the phrase 'ill matching words and
deeds' in 'things well-matched or ill, and words for things' had drawn
attention to the anarchic potential of Coleridge's thought. The echo in
Book Eight has the same implications. Conflating two separate Miltonic
phrases—'joining or disjoining' as applied to reason, 'misjoining' as
applied to 'mimic fancy'—Wordsworth suggests that a 'counter-spirit' is
at work in Coleridge's imagination, 'disjoining, joining things, | Without
the light of knowledge.' Just as fancy takes over, in Adam's view, when
reason retires, so the counter-spirit triumphs when palpable reality falls
away. The 'light of knowledge' is, by implication, a faculty akin to reason,
which Wordsworth possesses—steadied and controlled, as he is, by
distinct forms—but which Coleridge must do without. Milton's presence

---

[20] John Jones, *The Egotistical Sublime* (1954), 100.

within the language not only sharpens the poet's meaning, it pinpoints an underlying aggression.

If the Coleridge of Books Six and Eight acts essentially as a foil, his role is different in Book Ten. On this occasion the poet sees him in a redemptive capacity: sharing in man's fallen nature, and shouldering the burden of his guilt, but triumphing, none the less, over the degeneracy that surrounds him. The address begins, significantly, at the nadir of Book Ten. Describing his own immediately post-Godwinian phase in 1796, Wordsworth presents his earlier self as someone very like the 'disjoining, joining' Coleridge of Book Eight:

> Thus I fared,
> Dragging all passions, notions, shapes of faith,
> Like culprits to the bar . . .
> *now believing,*
> *Now disbelieving, endlessly perplexed*
> With impulse, motive, right and wrong . . .
>
> (*1805*, x. 888–90, 892–4; my italics)

Rhythmic echo, and subtle verbal reminiscence, connect the moral anarchy of a confused Godwinian reason not only with the 'mimic fancy' of Adam's dreams, but with the dangerous solipsism imaged in the city-dweller's life. And just when Wordsworth is at his most nearly Coleridgean—'Sick, wearied out with contrarieties', yielding up 'moral questions in despair'—it is Coleridge himself who comes to the rescue:

> Ah, then it was
> That thou, most precious friend, about this time
> First known to me, didst lend a living help
> To regulate my soul.
>
> (*1805*, x. 904–7)

Wordsworth is guilty, here, of 'Planting [his] snowdrops among winter snows'[21]—or (to follow his metaphor through, into its later context) of 'seem[ing] to plant' Coleridge where he has no right to be.[22] As the editor of the Norton text points out, the two friends 'corresponded at times' after they met in 1795, and 'can have exerted no great influence upon each other until June 1797'.[23] But by including his friend at his life's most vulnerable point, Wordsworth suggests that he was (and continues to be) indispensable—almost as much the redeemer as Dorothy, who

---

21 *1799*, i. 446.
22 *1805*, vi. 248.
23 *Norton Prelude*, 408.

'Maintained for [him] a saving intercourse | With [his] true self' (*1805*, x. 914–15). That the inaccuracy is intentional cannot be denied: the phrase 'about this time' is sneakily vague. But there is not, here, the same detachment of self-knowledge that one finds in Book Six, where Wordsworth reflects on the wishfulness of memories reconstructed:

> Through this retrospect
> Of my own college life, I still have had
> Thy after-sojourn in the self-same place
> Present before my eyes, have played with times
> (I speak of private business of the thought)
> And accidents as children do with cards,
> Or as a man, who, when his house is built,
> A frame locked up in wood and stone, doth still
> In impotence of mind by his fireside
> Rebuild it to his liking.
>
> (*1805*, vi. 296–305)

In both passages, one poet acts as saviour to the other, and in both cases this involves a rewriting of the past. Where Book Six is concerned, Wordsworth (like Lamb) 'detecting the fallacy, will not part with the wish' (Marrs, i. 265). In Book Eight, strategy can barely be distinguished from self-deception.

Closeness—called into question by Books Six and Eight—has been reconstructed, and Wordsworth moves on a stage in the process of transforming his friend. As he contrasts his own visit to France in 1790— when the Revolution had just begun, and when his optimism was at its height—with the very different circumstances of Coleridge's visit to Sicily, he seems to be begging his friend to demonstrate the continuity of their shared beliefs (*1805*, x. 954–65). There is in his portrayal of Coleridge, living 'among the basest and the lowest fallen | Of all the race of men' (ll. 947–8), an underlying fear of his being contaminated, rather than improved.[24] But countering this anxiety is the Miltonic hope—already expressed in *Tintern Abbey* and *1799* Part Two—that, like Wordsworth, he will triumph

> though fallen on evil days,
> On evil days though fallen, and evil tongues . . .
>
> (*PL*, vii. 25–6)

---

[24] There is even, as one reads this ambiguous line, the strong implication that Coleridge too has undergone a fall: 'A story destined for thy ear, who now, | Among the basest and the lowest fallen | Of all the race of men, dost make abode . . . (ll. 946–8).

Tacitly, Coleridge becomes a mirror image of the poet himself, capable, in
times of 'dereliction and dismay', of retaining

> A more than Roman confidence, a faith
> That fails not, in all sorrow [his] support,
> The blessing of [his] life . . .
>
> (*1799*, ii. 489–91)

and capable, therefore, of transforming the world around:

> Thy consolation shall be there, and time
> And Nature shall before thee spread in store
> Imperishable thoughts, the place itself
> Be conscious of thy presence, and the dull
> Sirocco air of its degeneracy
> Turn as thou mov'st into a healthful breeze
> To cherish and invigorate thy frame.
>
> (*1805*, x. 970–6)

What, though, is to be the basis of Coleridge's faith? It is clear that the
poet's own is formed by mountains; but Coleridge, 'Debarred from
Nature's living images', is surely less well-placed? Who is to say that, left
to its own devices, and in a setting which exactly parallels the barrenness of
the city, his imagination will not become anarchic? Forced into a role not
his own, he is being used rather obviously by the poet, to recreate early
hopes. 'Carrying a heart more ripe | For all divine enjoyment' (l. 598) he
stands in for an older Wordsworth, who feels himself to have matured, and
whose earlier values must be preserved:

> Our prayers have been accepted: thou wilt stand
> Not as an exile but a visitant
> On Etna's top; by pastoral Arethuse—
> Or if that fountain be indeed no more,
> Then near some other spring which by the name
> Thou gratulatest, willingly deceived—
> Shalt linger as a gladsome votary,
> And not a captive pining for his home.
>
> (*1805*, x. 1031–8)

The closing line reminds one for a moment of the real Coleridge who is
concealed behind the myth: a Coleridge who, whether in the city or
abroad, felt himself to be exiled, and whose own 'home'—as Wordsworth
knew too well—was a mockery of that word. But it is against the poet's will
that this reminder comes. The address ends, as it had begun, with self-

deception, and with a trust in Coleridge's happiness that is out of keeping
with the portrait's most imaginative lines:

> A lonely wanderer art gone, by pain
> Compelled and sickness, at this latter day,
> This heavy time of change for all mankind.[25]

Wordsworth not only passes a fiction on himself; he asks his friend also to
be willingly deceived.

The 'Climbing of Snowdon', structurally and symbolically
Wordsworth's climactic spot of time, demonstrates the nature of
imaginative power: a power which is described in evidently Coleridgean
terms, but which (if one takes the chronology of *The Prelude* into account)
is said to precede Coleridge's influence. The address which ends Book
Twelve, then, is needed to prepare the way for this climax, and to
introduce its implications. 'Dearest friend, | Forgive me', Wordsworth
writes, in tones that are formal, apologetic, distanced:

> Forgive me if I say that I, who long
> Had harboured reverentially a thought
> That poets, even as prophets, each with each
> Connected in a mighty scheme of truth,
> Have each for his peculiar dower a sense
> By which he is enabled to perceive
> Something unseen before—forgive me, friend,
> If I, the meanest of this band, had hope
> That unto me had also been vouchsafed
> An influx, that in some sort I possessed
> A privilege, and that a work of mine,
> Proceeding from the depth of untaught things,
> Enduring and creative, might become
> A power like one of Nature's.

> (*1805*, xii. 298–312)

The aspiration itself is moving; but the mock-humility, exaggerated and
misplaced, registers unease. Coleridge, it seems, must be apologized to
because Wordsworth is ambitious. But is this because the poet regards his
friend as being higher up the ladder than himself, or because he assumes
he's not up to competing? Curiously, the language seems to hold out both
alternatives, the extremity of the self-abasement (where else would
Wordsworth dream of calling himself 'the meanest of the band'?) at once

---

[25] Lindenberger, 19–20, points to the impersonal pity of this passage, and links it with
Thomson's address to Lyttleton (*Spring*, 904–14).

rating Coleridge at an absurdly high level, and implying that he is altogether excluded.

As though to confirm this ambiguity, the address continues with a definition of the poet's creative power that seems barely to take his friend into account. Bypassing seven years of intimacy, influence, and exchange, Wordsworth returns to the most complex of his pre-Coleridgean poems (*1805*, xii. 312 ff.). *Salisbury Plain* comes to stand not just for an exalted state of mind, but for a particular quality of Wordsworth's poetic imagination. He sees it as the origin of his greatness—the poem, above all others, on which he would base his claim to have created 'a power like one of Nature's.'—and he sees it, moreover, in completely un-Coleridgean terms:

> The voice of spears was heard, the rattling spear
> Shaken by arms of mighty bone, in strength
> Long mouldered, of barbaric majesty.
> I called upon the darkness, and it took—
> A midnight darkness seemed to come and take—
> All objects from my sight; and lo, again
> The desart visible by dismal flames!
> It is the sacrificial altar, fed
> With living men—how deep the groans!—the voice
> Of those in the gigantic wicker thrills
> Throughout the region far and near, pervades
> The monumental hillocks, and the pomp
> Is for both worlds, the living and the dead.
>
> (*1805*, xii. 324–36)

It is a passage that links back, in atmosphere, language and meaning, with the Boat-Stealing episode in *1799*, Part One:

> In my thoughts
> There was a darkness—call it solitude,
> Or blank desertion—no familiar shapes
> Of hourly objects, images of trees,
> Of sea or sky, no colours of green fields,
> But huge and mighty forms that do not live
> Like living men moved slowly through my mind
> By day, and were the trouble of my dreams.
>
> (*1799*, i. 122–9)

Wordsworth is making of the Salisbury Plain experience a 'spot of time'—moving it back, through the years, so that it takes on the qualities of

childhood trauma, and belongs to a pre-Coleridgean past. With a sort of
apologetic readiness, however, he accepts Coleridge's different (and in
some ways opposite) valuation:

> Nor is it, friend, unknown to thee; at least—
> Thyself delighted—thou for my delight
> Hast said, perusing some imperfect verse
> Which in that lonesome journey was composed,
> That also I must then have exercised
> Upon the vulgar forms of present things
> And actual world of our familiar days,
> A higher power—have caught from them a tone,
> An image, and a character, by books
> Not hitherto reflected.

> (*1805*, xii. 356–65)

Having chosen *Salisbury Plain*, out of all his poems, to represent his claim
to greatness, and having made this claim in un-Coleridgean terms, he then
uses Coleridge's words to congratulate himself.[26] At first, he makes a show
of modesty to hide it: 'Call we this | But a persuasion taken up by thee | In
friendship' (*1805*, xii. 365–7). Confidence returns, however, and Book
Twelve ends with the poet having it both ways—defining his private sense
of power, but appropriating Coleridge's view of him as well:

> in life's everyday appearances
> I seemed about this period to have sight
> Of a new world—a world, too, that was fit
> To be transmitted and made visible
> To other eyes, as having for its base
> That whence our dignity originates,
> That which both gives it being, and maintains
> A balance, an ennobling interchange
> Of action from within and from without:
> The excellence, pure spirit, and best power,
> Both of the object seen, and eye that sees.

> (*1805*, xii. 369–79)

In effect, what Wordsworth manages to suggest is that before even

---

[26] The response here attributed to Coleridge is analogous to his comment in *Biographia*,
quoted at the beginning of this book. The similarity of the two critical positions does not
persuade one that they represent Coleridge's original response, which (as I have argued in
the Introduction) was primarily political. It does, however, suggest that at some stage in the
relationship he may have made a remark of this kind. Unless, that is, one is to take it that *The
Prelude* puts words into his mouth, and the comment in *Biographia* is a confirming form of
quotation.

meeting Coleridge his poetry had reached its height and that, by further implication, he had evolved already his belief in imagination's transforming power. The arrangement of time, as on so many occasions in *The Prelude*, has an unacknowledged purpose. In this instance it is the displacement of Coleridge, which prepares one for Book Thirteen.

There is no scope in this chapter for discussing the Coleridgean implications of the 'Climbing of Snowdon', which are in any case sufficiently well known.[27] My concern here is with the more ambiguous areas of relationship that emerge in the passage immediately following it, and with various strategies the poet uses in rounding off his poem. It is in Book Thirteen that Wordsworth allows the two extremes of his mythologizing process to meet. Here, therefore, we are presented with a final Janus-like image of his friend.

Wordsworth's commentary on the Snowdon episode (the last and greatest of his 'spots of time') concerns itself with the potential not just of ordinary human imagination, but of the creative power that 'higher minds' possess:

> They from their native selves can send abroad
> Like transformation, for themselves create
> A like existence, and whene'er it is
> Created for them, catch it by an instinct.

(*1805*, xiii. 93–6)

No definition of a 'higher mind' is offered, but from the exalted language it is clear that what Wordsworth has in mind is a visionary company of poets—'each with each │ Connected in a mighty scheme of truth'—to which he himself aspires:

> Such minds are truly from the Deity,
> For they are powers; and hence the highest bliss
> That can be known is theirs—the consciousness
> Of whom they are, habitually infused
> Through every image, and through every thought,
> And all impressions . . .

(*1805*, xiii. 106–11)

It is the strength of his aspiration that causes Wordsworth, at this climactic moment in *The Prelude*, to examine his credentials, and to find himself (as one might expect) rather more than 'the meanest of the band'. He bases his claim to be a 'power' on the inviolable strength of his

---

[27] See *Borders of Vision*, 308–39.

character, and the integrity of his imagination: 'I never in the quest of
right and wrong', he solemnly declares,

> Did tamper with myself from private aims;
> Nor was in any of my hopes the dupe
> Of selfish passions; nor did wilfully
> Yield ever to mean cares and low pursuits;
> But rather did with jealousy shrink back
> From every combination that might aid
> The tendency, too potent in itself,
> Of habit to enslave the mind . . .
>
> (*1805*, xiii. 131–9)

It is primarily to education—his 'early intercourse | In presence of
sublime and lovely forms' (xiii. 145–6)—that this integrity can be
ascribed, and there is the strongest of implications that without it
imagination could not have thrived. Where, then, does Coleridge stand?
What is *his* chance, with so different a childhood to look back on, of being
one of the 'higher minds'? And where does Wordsworth place him, as he
brings *The Prelude* to an end?

Love has its place in the poet's scheme of things—

> From love, for here
> Do we begin and end, all grandeur comes,
> All truth and beauty—from pervading love—
> That gone, we are as dust.
>
> (*1805*, xiii. 149–52)

—and one might expect this at least to represent common ground;
especially when the definition that Wordsworth offers is so self-
consciously Coleridgean. 'Thou calls't this love', he writes of sentimental
attachments,

> And so it is, but there is higher love
> Than this, a love that comes into the heart
> With awe and a diffusive sentiment.
> Thy love is human merely: this proceeds
> More from the brooding soul, and is divine.
>
> (*1805*, xiii. 161–5)

But not even the 'brooding soul' image—intended, perhaps, as a gesture of
inclusion[28]—can reverse the significance of the preceding lines. Coleridgean

---

[28] See the dove image of the *Letter to Sara*, which has its own private allusive history,
discussed in Chapter Three, above.

terms may be adopted, and Coleridgean values shared, but the essence of Coleridge the man is somehow left on one side. Wordsworth is unable, for whatever reason, to regard him as an exemplar of imaginative strength. He assembles a visionary company around himself, but carefully ignores his friend.

One might be tempted to think of this process as wholly unconscious, but there is manuscript evidence proving the reverse. In its original form—as part of the Five-Book *Prelude*—the passage quoted above was followed immediately by lines in which, as a note in the *Norton Prelude* puts it, 'Wordsworth turned to consider the factors which in practice conspired to thwart . . . "divine" love'.[29] These lines—originally intended to lead into the 'spots of time' (which formed the climax of the Five-Book poem)—survive in *MSW*, and leave us in no doubt as to Wordsworth's meaning. The factors he writes about seem at first to be universal: 'petty duties and degrading cares' on a mundane level; 'Labour and penury, disease and grief' on a more threatening scale. But as he continues, one particularly thwarting situation looms largest in his thoughts: 'vexing strife | At home', he writes,

> and want of pleasure and repose,
> And all that eats away the genial spirits,
> May be fit matter for another song . . .
>
> (ll. 8–10)

No one reading this passage can fail to connect it with Coleridge. They will hear, in the phrase 'genial spirits', a clear echo of those famous lines from *Dejection*, which are themselves a double quotation from *Tintern Abbey* and *Samson Agonistes*:

> My genial spirits fail—
> And what can these avail
> To lift the smothering weight from off my breast?
>
> (*Letter to Sara*, 44–6)[30]

But they will also recognize a more general reference to Coleridge's domestic predicament: what he painfully calls, in the *Letter to Sara*, 'those habitual Ills | That wear out Life, | When two unequal Minds | Meet in one House, & two discordant Wills' (ll. 243–5).

---

[29] *Norton Prelude*, 468. The passage is printed in full in *MS. Drafts and Fragments*, 3(b) (*Norton Prelude*, 499–500).

[30] For Wordsworth's and Coleridge's very different allusions to the same phrase from Milton's *Samson Agonistes*, and the reason for them, see Chapter Three, above.

Our attention is drawn in this passage, clearly and unmistakeably, to the destruction of Coleridge's imaginative potential. Factors which conspire (in a general and external sense) to thwart 'divine' love have given place to more insidious forces that 'eat away' the spirits from within. Joy, love, imagination—all seen as vital to the moral strength Wordsworth claims as his own—disappear under the pressure of 'vexing strife | At home'. We are given, in this process, the strongest possible reasons for Coleridge's disqualification from the band of 'higher minds': reasons, furthermore, which seem so unambiguous in their application that Wordsworth is forced to edit them out of the poem before going on.

The Five-Book *Prelude*, intended originally as the poem Coleridge would take with him on his travels, may never have reached its final shape. Wordsworth decided at a late stage to set the last book aside for future use and to split the fourth one in two, thus creating *1805*, Books Four and Five. During the first half of March 1804, Coleridge was sent five books of a longer *Prelude* of which Wordsworth himself did not at this moment know the probable length. No convincing explanation has yet been offered for the sudden shelving of a poem which must have been very nearly complete,[31] and it is interesting to speculate whether he abandoned the Five-Book poem because the drafts in *MS W* had taken him into a discussion of Coleridge's inadequacy that was wholly inappropriate. A letter written in March 1804 suggests that he still needs Coleridge, almost desperately, in order to think himself capable of writing *The Recluse*:

> I am very anxious to have your notes . . . . I cannot say how much importance I attach to this, if it should please God that I survive you, I should reproach myself for ever in writing the work if I had neglected to procure this help.
>
> *(EY, 452)*

But he has muddled himself through, in the poetry itself, to seeing his friend as unworthy. The conflict of attitudes is familiar, and in various ways representative of *The Prelude* as a whole; but it amounts in this case to something like a crisis.

A year later, when he makes his second attempt—this time with a poem of thirteen books—to construct an ending, Wordsworth is feeling more honest:

> Imagination having been our theme,
> So also hath that intellectual love,
> For they are each in each, and cannot stand
> Dividually. Here must thou be, O man,

---

[31] See *Norton Prelude*, 517.

> Strength to thyself—no helper hast thou here—
> Here keepest thou thy individual state:
> No other can divide with thee this work,
> No secondary hand can intervene
> To fashion this ability. 'Tis thine,
> The prime and vital principle is thine
> In the recesses of thy nature, far
> From any reach of outward fellowship,
> Else 'tis not thine at all.
>
>   (*1805*, xiii. 185–97)

On two different levels, the passage brings into the open attitudes that
have been previously implied. Seen as a continued address to Coleridge, it
offers some kind of excuse for the poet's abandonment of his friend—for if
the capacity for 'intellectual love' comes from within, and cannot be
acquired, then Coleridge is truly beyond redemption. Seen, on the other
hand, as a dialogue within himself, the passage faces up to a loneliness and
self-sufficiency which are present throughout *The Prelude*, but which the
poet is very frequently at pains to deny. One is reminded, in the solemn
and emphatic repetitions—'No other can divide with thee this work, | No
secondary hand can intervene | To fashion this ability'—of the lines in
Home at Grasmere which most impressively define Wordsworth's
aloofness:

> Possessions have I, wholly, solely mine,
> Something within which yet is shared by none—
> Not even the nearest to me and most dear . . .
>
>   (MS B, 897–9; Darlington, 94)

The stress on a principle which exists 'in the recesses' of man's nature—
'far | From any reach of outward fellowship'—is one that gives
Wordsworth the maximum possible independence from Coleridge. It is
an independence that allows for the possibility of continuing with *The
Recluse*, but that acknowledges (for the first and last time) the
inappropriateness of expecting to be helped. Having, a year earlier,
brought himself by mistake to a confrontation with Coleridge's
inadequacy, Wordsworth now accepts the obvious implications.

But not for long. As he moves into the second part of Book Thirteen, he
becomes worried by the implied withdrawal, and looks anxiously round
for a role to give his friend. This, after all, is the 'Poem to Coleridge': a role
must be found. It is not difficult to fit his sister into his final scheme of
things:

> thy breath,
> Dear sister, was a kind of gentler spring
> That went before my steps.
>
> (*1805*, xiii. 244–6)

But when Coleridge is given the same status as Dorothy, the old unease
returns:

> O most loving soul,
> Placed on this earth to love and understand,
> And from thy presence shed the light of love,
> Shall I be mute ere thou be spoken of?
> Thy gentle spirit to my heart of hearts
> Did also find its way . . .
>
> (*1805*, xiii. 248–53)

It is not that one cannot value, or find credible, the impulse behind these
emotional and moving lines. It is just that the myth-making process is
being asked to do too much. The Coleridge who, again and again in *The
Prelude*, has been seen as a solipsistic figure, shut out from the light of
knowledge, his imagination feeding solely on itself, is transformed here
into an emblem of outgoing love. We are asked to forget a whole sequence
of extremely powerful images:

> Thou, my friend, art one
> More deeply read in thy own thoughts . . .
> (*1799*, ii. 249–50)

> But yet more often living with thyself,
> And for thyself . . .
>
> (*1799*, ii. 512–13)

> The self-created sustenance of a mind
> Debarred from Nature's living images,
> Compelled to be a life unto itself . . .
> (*1805*, vi. 312–14)

> in endless dreams
> Of sickness, disjoining, joining things,
> Without the light of knowledge.
> (*1805*, viii. 608–10)

> A lonely wanderer art gone, by pain
> Compelled and sickness . . .
> (*1805*, x. 983–4)

And not only to forget *them*; but to cancel out any of the more critical attitudes to Coleridge which have emerged, overtly or by implication, earlier in the poem. The reluctant admission, in MS W, of Coleridge's inadequacy, and the honest facing up to independence earlier in Book Thirteen, are both discarded. 'Placed on this earth to love and understand', Coleridge takes on, once again, the redemptive status he had been given in Book Ten. Alongside Dorothy, he becomes the poet's saviour, leading him on, from the 'deep enthusiastic joy' of his early responses, to a perception of

> the life
> Of all things and the mighty unity
> In all which we behold, and feel, and are . . .
>
> (*1805*, xiii. 253–5)

It is a fiction based entirely on need, and it prepares the way for Wordsworth's final address to his friend. 'When thou dost to that summer turn thy thoughts', he writes, retreating nostalgically into Alfoxden and the summer of 1798:

> When thou dost to that summer turn thy thoughts,
> And hast before thee all which then we were,
> To thee, in memory of that happiness,
> It will be known—by thee at least, my friend,
> Felt—that the history of a poet's mind
> Is labour not unworthy of regard:
> To thee the work shall justify itself.
>
> (*1805*, xiii. 404–10)

Wordsworth's mood, in May 1805, as he writes these lines, is one of acute anxiety. With Coleridge expected back from Malta at any time, he is asking himself whether *The Prelude* will be well received, whether his neglect of *The Recluse* will count against him, whether—in any terms— the work can 'justify itself'. The Coleridge whom he sets up as judge of these questions is not the man who left for the Mediterranean, or the one who will return the following August, sadly changed. He is a figure at once creative and sympathetic, belonging to the now distant past.

Behind Wordsworth's evocation of 1797–8 as a 'golden age' lie the threatening memories of a collaborative period when the two writers had not always agreed. Neither *Christabel* nor *The Ancient Mariner* can be mentioned in this context without unease; and—for different reasons— *The Idiot Boy* and *The Thorn* are scarcely more tactful. Wordsworth's references at this climactic moment imply perhaps the hope that he can subdue painful associations. The self-mockery of the allusions to *The Thorn* and *The Idiot Boy* is there to balance the tacit aggression in his treatment of Coleridge; and the hope is that all poems belonging to the 'golden age' will take on the same colouring, pass unpainfully into myth.

Just as the past must be carefully treated, so as neither to reveal the disparities it contained, nor to reflect back the disagreements that have since emerged, so the present must seem of a piece with what has gone before. Under the pressure of 'a private grief | Keen and enduring' (ll. 416–17)—the grief occasioned by the death of his brother, John—Wordsworth anticipates the moment when, in remembrance of the Alfoxden days, he will read aloud his 'Poem to Coleridge':

> a comfort now, a hope,
> One of the dearest which this life can give,
> Is mine: that thou art near, and wilt be soon
> Restored to us in renovated health—
> When, after the first mingling of our tears,
> 'Mong other consolations, we may find
> Some pleasure from this offering of my love.
>
> (*1805*, xiii. 421–7)

The words 'some pleasure' are not mere self-deprecation. No more than in October 1799—'I long to see what you have been doing. O let it be the tail-piece of "The Recluse!" for of nothing but "The Recluse" can I hear patiently' (Griggs, i. 538)—can it be guaranteed that Coleridge the task-master will be mollified by an offering of love. It is for this reason that the poet is heard at this moment talking anxiously to himself:

> Oh, yet a few short years of useful life,
> And all will be complete—thy race be run,
> Thy monument of glory will be raised.
>
> (ll. 428–30)

Once more in Wordsworth's mind is the passage from *Samson Agonistes* to which he and Coleridge have turned so often[32]:

> So much I feel my genial spirits droop,
> My hopes all flat, nature within me seems
> In all her functions weary of herself . . .

only this time it is the final lines of Milton's sentence that matter most:

---

[32] See above, p. 176, for the presence of these lines in Wordsworth's address to Coleridge in Book Six. Presumably Milton is also at the back of the poet's mind when he writes in *Intimations*, 'Another race hath been, and other palms are w[on]' (l. 192).

> My race of glory run, and race of shame,
> And I shall shortly be with them that rest.
>
> (ll. 594–6; 597–8)

Useful life—life that might achieve the writing of *The Recluse*—is dwindling. The poet's race of glory may prove a race of shame. 'Then, though too weak to tread the ways of truth', he goes on,

> This age fall back to old idolatry,
> Though men return to servitude as fast
> As the tide ebbs, to ignominy and shame
> By nations sink together, we shall still
> Find solace in the knowledge which we have,
> Blessed with true happiness if we may be
> United helpers forward of a day
> Of firmer trust, joint labourers in the work—
> Should Providence such grace to us vouchsafe—
> Of their redemption, surely yet to come.
>
> (ll. 431–41)

In December 1799 Wordsworth had brought the Two Part *Prelude* to a close by maintaining his 'more than Roman confidence' in the face of

> indifference and apathy
> And wicked exultation, when good men
> On every side fall off . . .
> To selfishness . . .
>
> (ii. 480–3)

Now, he contemplates whole nations sinking together 'to ignominy and shame',[33] and yet is able—apparently—to think in terms not just of personal confidence but of the redemption of mankind. He and Coleridge, who before were merely brothers in a deep private devotion to Nature, are now 'joint labourers' in a work ordained by Providence. Biblical allusion reinforces the redemptive claims, as Wordsworth (identifying himself, by implication, with St Paul) quotes Philippians, 4:3: 'And I intreat thee also, true yoke-fellow, help those women which laboured with me in the

---

[33] In the background is not just Luke's personal fall in *Michael*—'He in the dissolute city gave himself | To evil courses: ignominy and shame | Fell on him' (ll. 453–5)—but the fall of the vainglorious in *Paradise Regained*:

> But why should man seek glory? who of his own
> Hath nothing, and to whom nothing belongs
> But condemnation, ignominy and shame?
>
> (iii. 134–6)

gospel, with Clement also, and with other my fellow-labourers, whose names *are* in the book of life'.[34]

The tentativeness of Wordsworth's language might anyhow lead us to see anxiety beneath his claims;[35] but beyond the allusions to *1799*, there is an echo even more disquieting. 'I've join'd us', says Rivers to Mortimer in the central scene of *The Borderers*,

> by a chain of adamant;
> Henceforth we are fellow-labourers—to enlarge
> The intellectual empire of mankind.

> (IV. ii. 187–9)

Biblical allusion in this context had been ironic, for it is Pauline assumptions that Rivers overturns. In *The Prelude* no irony is intended, but while conscious biblical parallel pulls in one direction, unconscious self-echo pulls in the other. Wordsworth and Coleridge too are to enlarge the empire of intellect—

> Prophets of nature, we to them will speak
> A lasting inspiration *sanctified*
> *By reason and by truth* . . .
> Instruct them how *the mind of man* becomes
> A thousand times more beautiful than the earth
> On which he dwells . . .

> (xiii. 442–4; 446–7; my italics)

One obvious effect of the echoes is to undermine confidence. As *The Borderers* reminds us, schemes built on the perfectibility of mankind can be misguided, or go badly wrong. More damaging, however, is the implication for the poets' relationship. Rivers binds Mortimer with a chain of adamant by causing him to repeat the crime he has himself committed. There is no way that Wordsworth can be thought of as doing the same to Coleridge; but may not an echo be called to mind by a situation in reverse? Much of the resentment and aggression seen in *The Prelude* invocations stems from the oppressive sense that a task is yet to be completed, an obligation waits to be fulfilled. Coleridge has bound his friend by making him the poet of *The Recluse*.[36] It is indeed a chain of adamant: one that leaves Wordsworth dominated by guilt almost to the end of his life. And it places him, too, in a strange and unreal relation to his tormentor.

[34] I am grateful to Wallace Robson for pointing out this echo.

[35] Onorato, 8–11, gives a full and perceptive account of the unease Wordsworth feels as he brings *The Prelude* to an end.

[36] See Onorato, 90, for Coleridge's creation of Wordsworth as a second and dependent self.

'Triumphal Wreaths': *To William Wordsworth* and *A Complaint*

> Let Eagle bid the Tortoise sunward soar—
> As vainly Strength speaks to a broken Mind.[1]

Coleridge may not have thought of himself as precisely 'embalmed' by *The Prelude*, but *To William Wordsworth*, written after hearing the poem read in January 1807, centres nevertheless on an extraordinary image of his own death:

> Sense of pass'd Youth, and Manhood come in vain;
> And Genius given, and Knowledge won in vain;
> And all, which I had cull'd in Wood-walks wild,
> And all, which patient Toil had rear'd, and all
> Commune with Thee had open'd out, but Flowers
> Strew'd on my Corse, and borne upon my Bier,
> In the same Coffin, for the self-same Grave!
>
> (ll. 75–81)[2]

Poetry which should be hailing the triumph of his fellow labourer has turned to elegy—and elegy which, despite the echoes of *Lycidas*, is not for another poet, but for himself. In the poignant regret for his own past youth, and manhood come in vain, Coleridge is evidently weighing himself (as he had done in the *Letter to Sara*) against the achievements of Wordsworth. It was to be his most bitter complaint, during the quarrel of 1810, that he had given his genius to and for his friend, subordinating his own creative powers and receiving nothing in return.[3] There is no reason to suppose that at the time of *To William Wordsworth* he has articulated such resentment, but equally there can be no doubt that his admiration for *The Prelude* is qualified by bitterness. At the back of his mind, he surely

---

[1] Beer (Coleridge's *Poems*, 304) dates this epigram 1807. It seems to be closely related to *To William Wordsworth* and may well have been composed at around the same time.

[2] All references are to the early text of *To William Wordsworth*, as reproduced in *Norton Prelude*, 542–5.

[3] The best account of this quarrel still remains Mary Moorman's. See *The Later Years 1803–1850* (Oxford, 1965), 187–219.

connects the 'Sense of pass'd Youth' with the 'Sense of intolerable wrong' (*Pains of Sleep*, 19).

It is here, then, that we see Coleridge at his most self-involved, writing not a homage, but a lament for his own wasted powers—not a celebration of friendship, but a rejection of *The Prelude's* central myth. As in the *Letter to Sara*, the soul's flight spirals inward, and it is not long before 'its wings beat against the personal self'.[4] Writing at a Miltonic pitch that recalls *Religious Musings*, but which cannot be sustained, he begins by invoking Wordsworth as 'mighty prophet' (ll. 1–8), then proceeds, in the words of Reeve Parker, to give 'an astonishingly deft critical précis of Wordsworth's poem'.[5] It is not, however, a précis that is neutral, or accurate, or just. Coleridge's method of synopsis is highly selective— giving more prominence to the French Revolution than to any other event in the growth of Wordsworth's mind;[6] but it is also extremely uneven in its responses. On the one hand is political enthusiasm (ll. 28–36), which can be entered into without sham; on the other is a claim for natural landscape (ll. 18–20) which is not only literary ('Hyblaean murmers', 'Lilied Streams') but half-hearted and flat. The most Wordsworthian of Wordsworthian themes is thus played down; and even the subject of imagination—which ought to be given a generous prominence—is dealt with laconically, even dismissively, in four lines:

> Of Tides obedient to external Force,
> And Currents self-determin'd, as might seem,
> Or by interior Power: of Moments aweful,
> Now in thy hidden Life; and now abroad . . .

> (ll. 12–15)

The précis ends (omitting, incidentally, any reference to the climactic vision on Snowdon), with a curious allusion to duty—'chosen Laws controlling choice' (l. 38) which seems almost wilfully unrelated to what *The Prelude* is about.[7] It is only when he turns to envy that Coleridge's interest mounts:

[4] *Notebooks*, ii. 2531. For alternative (and blander) views, see M. H. Abrams' note in *Norton Prelude*, 542; and E. L. Griggs, 'Wordsworth through Coleridge's Eyes', *Wordsworth Centenary Studies*, 69.

[5] Reeve Parker, 'Wordsworth's Whelming Tide: Coleridge and the Art of Analogy', *Forms of Lyric: Selected Papers from the English Institute*, ed. Reuben A. Brower (New York, 1970), 89.

[6] l. 33, referring to 'the Watch-tower of Man's absolute self', clearly alludes to *The Watchman* of 1796, and shows Coleridge thinking back to the political commitment which drew him to Wordsworth in the first place.

[7] There may be a subdued allusion to the *Ode to Duty* (ll. 33–6; 41–4) which accompanied Coleridge to Malta in MS M.

> Ah great Bard!
> Ere yet that last Swell dying aw'd the Air,
> With stedfast ken I view'd thee in the Choir
> Of ever-enduring Men. The truly Great
> Have all one Age, and from one visible space
> Shed influence: for they, both power and act,
> Are permanent, and Time is not with them,
> Save as it worketh for them, they in it.
> Nor less a sacred Roll, than those of old,
> And to be plac'd, as they, with gradual fame
> Among the Archives of mankind, thy Work
> Makes audible a linked Song of Truth.
> Of Truth profound a sweet continuous Song
> Not learnt, but native, her own natural notes!
>
> (ll. 40–53)

His lines recall Wordsworth, at his most apologetically ambitious— 'forgive me, friend | If I, the meanest of this band . . .' (*1805*, xii. 305–6)— asking none the less to be placed among the band of 'prophets, each with each | Connected in a mighty scheme of truth' (*1805*, xii. 301–12). Coleridge, detecting and correcting the false modesty, has no hesitation in acquiescing with the plea. But the corollary of his adulation (as the double implications of Wordsworth's writing have already shown)[8] is that he himself is not included in the 'Choir | Of ever-enduring Men'. He proposes, for the 'truly great' a kind of eternity—they 'Have all one Age and from one visible Space | Shed influence'—and, in so doing, seems to imitate the process by which he had himself been transformed into a God:

> But thou art with us, with us in the past,
> The present, with us in the times to come.
>
> (*1805*, vi. 251–2)

Imitation, in this case, implies reversal. Coleridge is dedicated not just to exposing the fiction of eternity that has been built around him, but to revealing the human inadequacies which make him unfit for such a role. The gratitude he feels for *The Prelude*—'Dear shall it be to every human Heart. | To me how more than dearest!' (ll. 54–5)—is mingled with pain; for he sees in its mythical constructions the figure he might have been mocking the figure he is:

---

[8] See Chapter Seven, above.

> Me, on whom
> Comfort from Thee and utterance of thy Love
> Came with such heights and depths of Harmony
> Such sense of Wings uplifting, that the Storm
> Scatter'd and whirl'd me, till my Thoughts became
> A bodily Tumult! and thy faithful Hopes,
> Thy Hopes of me, dear Friend! by me unfelt
> Were troubles to me, almost as a Voice
> Familiar once and more than musical
> To one cast forth, whose hope had seem'd to die,
> A Wanderer with a worn-out heart,
> Mid Strangers pining with untended Wounds!
>
> (ll. 55–66)

As the allusion in the last line suggests—compare 'And not a captive pining for his home' (*1805*, x. 1038)—it is *Prelude* Book Ten that gives Coleridge his sharpest sense of pain. Reeve Parker is right in drawing our attention to the fact that the book must have stunned Coleridge, because he had 'betrayed Wordsworth's hopes, which came now only to remind him of his continued degeneracy'.[9] But it should be added that the effect of this shock is to strengthen his rejection of *The Prelude*'s myth. More and more strongly, one feels, Coleridge is detecting the doubleness of Wordsworth's portrayal, and preferring to face the reality than to accept the more favourable abstraction. It is as though the private, reluctant portraiture of MS W is in his mind:

> petty duties and degrading cares,
> Labour and penury, disease and grief,
> Which to one object chain the impoverished mind
> Enfeebled and [?], vexing strife
> At home, and want of pleasure and repose,
> And all that eats away the genial spirits,
> May be fit matter for another song . . .[10]

Omitted from Book Thirteen because, as an example of 'the unremitting warfare' waged on intellectual love it had seemed inappropriate, this passage nevertheless remains as a kind of sub-text to the public poem. Which Coleridge (perhaps without seeing MS W) has perceived:

> O Friend! too well thou know'st, of what sad years
> The long suppression had benumm'd my soul,

---

[9] Parker, op. cit. note 5 above, 87.
[10] *Norton Prelude*, 499–500.

That even as Life returns upon the Drown'd,
Th'unusual Joy awoke a throng of Pains—
Keen Pangs of LOVE, awakening, as a Babe,
Turbulent, with an outcry in the Heart:
And Fears self-will'd, that shunn'd the eye of Hope,
And Hope, that would not know itself from Fear:
Sense of pass'd Youth, and Manhood come in vain;
And Genius given, and Knowledge won in vain;
And all, which I had cull'd in Wood-walks wild,
And all, which patient Toil had rear'd, and all
Commune with Thee had open'd out, but Flowers
Strew'd on my Corse, and borne upon my Bier,
In the same Coffin, for the self-same Grave!

(ll. 67–81)

The tones of the passage recall not just the *Letter to Sara*, with its
appalling revelation of married unhappiness—

my coarse domestic Life has known
No Habits of heart-nursing Sympathy
No Griefs, but such as dull and deaden me . . .

(ll. 258–60)

—but *The Pains of Sleep*, with its more dramatic and tortured sense of
unnamable guilt:

Deeds to be hid which were not hid,
Which all confused I could not know,
Whether I suffered, or I did:
For all seemed guilt, remorse or woe,
My own or others still the same
Life-stifling fear, soul-stifling shame.

(ll. 27–32)

With an intensity that matches these earlier poems, Coleridge enacts the
pain of his awakening from death, and confronts us, in an ironic reference
to *Lycidas*, with the picture of himself as the drowned Edward King,
resuscitated against his will.[11] The death of feeling which characterizes his
real existence, and is evoked in the image of a soul 'benumm'd' gives way

---

[11] Whalley, 117, draws attention to a self-echo from *The Ancient Mariner*:

Like one who hath been seven days drown'd
My body lay afloat . . .

(ll. 585–6)

for a moment to unwelcome and over-sentient life, then relapses finally into a ceremonial death of the body and a Death-in-Life of the mind. As the poet, going nearly as far as the speaker of *Maud*,[12] attends his own funeral procession and witnesses his own burial, one becomes aware of the extent to which he is rejecting *The Prelude*'s image of him as somehow embalmed. Better to accept the loss of his former self than to believe with Wordsworth in the fiction of continuity. Better to be dead than preserved.

Becoming suddenly aware of the damaging nature of his protest, he attempts to redress the balance:

> —That way no more! and ill beseems it me,
> Who came a Welcomer in Herald's Guise
> Singing of Glory and Futurity,
> To wander back on such unhealthful Road
> Plucking the Poisons of Self-harm!
>
> (ll. 82–6)

But even this self-rebuke is qualified, as he makes a bitter comparison between his own failure and Wordsworth's success:

> and ill
> Such intertwine beseems triumphal wreaths
> Strew'd before thy Advancing!
>
> (ll. 86–8)

The poetry of celebration gives way to personal lament, as Coleridge pleads with his friend not to accept the blame implied:

> Thou too, Friend!
> O injure not the memory of that Hour
> Of thy communion with thy nobler mind
> By pity or grief, already felt too long!
> Nor let my words import more blame than needs.
>
> (ll. 88–92)

The ambiguity of Coleridge's language is worth noting. If we read 'that Hour' as the time during which *The Prelude* was read aloud, he is acknowledging something in Wordsworth's poem that appeals to his 'nobler mind', and is asking the pain of his own response not to detract from that appeal. The 'pity or grief, already felt too long' simply refers, then, to the time-lapse between hearing *The Prelude* and writing *To William Wordsworth*. If, on the other hand, we take 'that Hour' (as M. H.

---

[12] See Part II. v. 11.

Abrams does in his note) to mean 'during the early association between the two poets, 1797–98' a very different meaning emerges. Coleridge is then asking that the value of early friendship should not be affected by present feelings, and is suggesting, by implication, that the 'pity or grief, already felt too long' are manifested in *The Prelude* itself. The passage that follows seems deliberately to sustain ambiguity: 'Eve following eve' and 'hours for their own sake hail'd' (ll. 97–9) are sufficiently vague to belong anywhere, and an eternal present is evoked which seems also to partake of the past. Into this timeless moment is introduced the reconciling vision of poet as sea (not drowned here, but assimilated), passively responsive to the elements beyond:

> In silence list'ning, like a devout Child,
> My soul lay passive, by thy various strain
> Driven as in surges now, beneath the stars,
> With momentary Stars of my own Birth,
> Fair constellated Foam still darting off
> Into the darkness! now a tranquil Sea
> Outspread and bright, yet swelling to the Moon.

(ll. 101–7)[13]

There are implications here more significant than change of mood. What Coleridge implies, when he writes

> Driven as in surges now, beneath the stars,
> With momentary Stars of my own Birth . . .

(ll. 103–5)

is that the strife of competing with Wordsworth is at an end. His own creative strength is subdued, but in its place there is a passiveness which, he implies, is equally creative. The echo of the *Letter to Sara* in 'momentary Stars of my own Birth'—compare 'A sweet & potent Voice, of it's own Birth' (l. 306)—highlights paradox. Imagination may have been 'suspended', but in the capacity for response there is imagination.

Just as, at Alfoxden, his own and Wordsworth's poems had mingled— 'Leaves & Fruitage not my own, seem'd mine!' (l. 237)—so now the 'stars of [his] own Birth' seem at one with the stars above. Wordsworth is dominant, of course, for in Coleridge's metaphor he is the wind driving

---

13 It is a passage based very closely on a Notebook entry of September 1798, written by Coleridge on the boat going out to Germany as the Alfoxden period came to an end: 'The Ocean is a noble thing by night— | the foam that dashes against the vessel, beautiful. White clouds of Foam roaring & rushing ~~over the sea~~, by the side of the Vessel with multitudes of stars of flame that danced and sparkled & went out amidst it . . .' (*Notebooks*, i. 335).

the waves before him. But somehow, despite the subordination which his
language implies, Coleridge has managed to suggest his own kind of
strength. He has evolved a myth for the present which both echoes and
corresponds to the earlier Alfoxden myth. In doing so, he has arrived at a
saving fiction.

   If Coleridge had ended on such a note, all would have been well. But the
balance of giving and receiving is entirely lost:

> And when O Friend! my Comforter! my Guide!
> Strong in thyself and powerful to give strength!
> Thy long sustained Lay finally clos'd
> And thy deep Voice had ceas'd . . .
> Scarce conscious and yet conscious of it's Close,
> I sate, my Being blended in one Thought,
> (Thought was it? or aspiration? or Resolve?)
> Absorb'd, yet hanging still upon the sound:
> And when I rose, I found myself in Prayer!
>
>   (ll. 108–11, 115–19)

The opening exclamations return us, from a visionary scene, to the action
of one personality on another, and we are inevitably reminded of the envy
and exclusion which Coleridge has earlier felt. Uneasiness increases with
the intrusion of an over-emphatic Miltonic voice, and comes to a climax in
the parenthetical questions. These are used by Coleridge to suggest that
what *The Prelude* gives him is a mounting sense of self-respect. One can
accept the poem's final sentence as a record of imaginative response; but
the over-stressing of resolve (coming so soon after the painful confession
of failure) inevitably strikes a false note.

   The poem ends, then, with self-deception, but not of a kind that was
likely to deceive. In a moving love-poem to Coleridge, written presumably
in January or February 1807,[14] and bearing the title *A Complaint*,
Wordsworth writes a fitting reply:

> There is a change—and I am poor;
> Your Love hath been, nor long ago,
> A Fountain at my fond Heart's door,
> Whose only business was to flow;

---

[14] Reed, ii. 43, argues that the poem was 'Probably composed between 30 Oct 1806 and
early Apr 1807 . . . possibly . . . by 7 Dec 1806'. Despite the evidence of Dorothy's letter
to Catherine Clarkson, quoted on p. 203, it seems unlikely that Wordsworth could have been
so clear-sighted about Coleridge until they had spent a good deal of time together at
Coleorton. A date some time after the reading aloud of *The Prelude* would seem logical; and
in my view the most likely time for the poet to feel this intense disappointment would be just
after the writing of *To William Wordsworth*.

> And flow it did; not taking heed
> Of its own bounty, or my need.
>
> What happy moments did I count!
> Bless'd was I then all bliss above!
> Now, for this consecrated Fount
> Of murmuring, sparkling, living love,
> What have I? shall I dare to tell?
> A comfortless, and hidden WELL.
>
> A Well of love—it may be deep—
> I trust it is, and never dry!
> What matter? if the Waters sleep
> In silence and obscurity.
> —Such change, and at the very door
> Of my fond Heart, hath made me poor.

Disappointment, betrayal, pain: brushing aside the mythologizing strategies of his 'Poem to Coleridge', Wordsworth confronts his inmost feelings and his hitherto unconscious thoughts. It is a poem of clear edges, and of emotions so strong they hurt. Alongside it one should put Dorothy's letter to Catherine Clarkson, written on 6 November 1806, and describing her first meeting with Coleridge after his return from Malta:

We all went thither to him and never did I feel such a shock as at first sight of him. We all felt exactly in the same way—as if he were different from what we have expected to see; almost as much as a person of whom we have thought much, and of whom we had formed an image in our own minds, without having any personal knowledge of him.

(MY, i. 86)

Dorothy's comments are less self-centred than her brother's, but they reveal the same sense of emotional shock, and the same sudden apprehension of the reality behind private myth.

The simplicity of *A Complaint*, reminding one inevitably of Herbert, at once universalizes grief and heightens the intensity of personal loss. Echoes, of a recognizable and verbal kind, have almost disappeared. Instead, as the poet looks back over the years, he allows the single, dominant metaphor of the fountain to absorb and control his associative thinking. Many fountain images come to mind. Traumatic experience, in the Goslar *Prelude*, had been a source of imaginative power:

> All these were spectacles and sounds to which
> I often would repair, and thence would drink
> As at a fountain.

(ll. 368–70)

Memories, in *Intimations*, had been the same:

> those first affections
> Those shadowy recollections
> Which, be they what they may
> Are yet the fountain light of all our day
> Are yet the master light of all our seeing . . .
>
> (ll. 146–50)

For Coleridge, too, the fountain image meant creative power—'I may not hope from outward Forms to win | The Passion & the Life, whose Fountains are within!' (ll. 50–1)—and on occasion the capacity for love, with which it is so closely linked:

> This Love which ever welling at my heart,
> Now in its living fount doth heave and fall,
> Now overflowing pours thro' every part
> Of all my frame, and fills and changes all,
> Like vernal waters springing up through snow,
> This Love that seeming great beyond the power
> Of growth, yet seemeth every more to grow . . .[15]

Using this once-shared symbol, however, Wordsworth does not in *A Complaint* play his own or Coleridge's customary allusive games. The fountain image is not itself turned into a source of power; nor are its occurrences in earlier poetry nostalgically remembered, then elegiacally re-lost.[16] In response to the change that has come over Coleridge, Wordsworth's habits of poetic reference have themselves altered. Verbal echo, of the kind that registers sharing, intimacy, or even unease, has been displaced by a simpler language in which resonance can no longer be pinned down. The 'consecracted Fount | Of murmuring, sparkling, living love' does indeed stand for the poetry (and the Coleridge) of Alfoxden, both of them left behind. But it does so symbolically, and without the allusive connections that might imply either the continuity of self, or the possibility of recovering past feelings.

---

[15] *To Asra*, 5–11.
[16] Contrast, for instance, the allusive language of the *Letter to Sara* or *The Prelude*.

Appendix

'In City Pent': Echo and Allusion in Wordsworth, Coleridge, and Lamb, 1797–1801

For Wordsworth and Coleridge, in the years 1797 to 1801, the opposition between city and country was not a literary cliché. It was a way of alluding to differences that were felt to lie very deep: differences on a personal level between their own childhood experiences, and on a purely symbolic level between states of mind.

John Alban Finch has shown how Wordsworth, writing the Preamble in November 1799, invents a fictitious urban setting—'yon City's walls', (*Prelude* 1805, i. 7)[1]—so as to evoke a sense of release from emotional imprisonment:

Combining allusions to Goslar and London, Wordsworth celebrates in the Preamble something more inclusive and significant than literal escape from either—escape from a deadening way of life into a free and creative existence.[2]

Finch comments on Wordsworth's verbal borrowings from Milton, but not on the way in which he draws on his own and Coleridge's earlier poetry. It is this I intend to examine, since there is during the early period a sustained undercurrent of allusions and cross-references that creates its own pattern of meaning.

In June 1797 Coleridge, writing 'This Lime Tree Bower my Prison', celebrated a moment of great confidence in Nature's regenerative power: a confidence that could only come from his new closeness with Wordsworth. The poem, like Wordsworth's 'Lines left upon a Seat in a Yew-tree' (April–June 1797) is about the imprisonment of self, but it also enacts the breaking free from self that can come through a perception of the One Life. Coleridge shows us, on the one hand himself, 'imprisoned' in his lime-tree bower, excluded from the close companionship of Lamb

---

[1] References are to the 1805 version of *The Prelude*, ed. E. de Selincourt (Oxford, 1926), revised H. Darbishire, 1959; hereafter abbreviated to *1805*. Occasional reference will be made to the two-Part *Prelude* of 1798–9, ed. Jonathan Wordsworth and Stephen Gill, *Norton Anthology of English Literature* (3rd edn., New York, 1974), ii. 196–218; cited below as *1799*.

[2] 'Wordsworth's Two-Handed Engine', *Bicentenary Wordsworth Studies*, ed. Jonathan Wordsworth (Ithaca, NY, 1970), pp. 10–11; cited hereafter as *BWS*.

and the Wordsworths; and on the other, Lamb—who has been 'imprisoned' in the city, and who is feeling released for the first time:

> But chiefly Thou,
> My gentle-hearted CHARLES! thou, who hast pin'd
> And hunger'd after Nature many a year
> In the great City pent, winning thy way,
> With sad yet bowed soul, thro' evil & pain
> And strange calamity.[3]

Coleridge has two important literary sources in his mind: Milton's simile in *Paradise Lost*, Book Nine:

> As one who long in populous city pent,
> Where houses thick and sewers annoy the air
> Forth issuing on a summer's morn . . . (ll. 445–7)

and Young's (derivative) simile in Book Four of *Night Thoughts*:

> As when a Wretch, from thick, polluted Air,
> Darkness, and Stench, and suffocating Damps,
> And Dungeon Horrors, by kind Fate discharg'd,
> Climbs some fair Eminence, where Ether pure
> Surrounds him, and Elysian Prospects rise,
> His Heart exults, his Spirits cast their Load,
> As if new-born, he triumphs in the Change;
> So joys the Soul, when from inglorious Aims,
> And sordid Sweets, from Feculence and Froth
> Of Ties terrestrial, set at large, she mounts
> To Reason's Region, her own Element,
> Breathes Hopes immortal, and affects the Skies.   (1743, p. 151)

Imprisonment within the city and release into Nature are both traditional literary motifs[4]—so too, as Max Byrd has pointed out, is the sym-

---

[3] All quotations from 'This Lime-Tree Bower' refer to the version Coleridge sent to Southey on 17 July 1797, and not to the (much-revised) poem as it was first published in *The Annual Anthology*, 1800. For complete 1797 text, see *Collected Letters of Samuel Taylor Coleridge*, ed. E. L. Griggs (Oxford, 1956–71), i. 334–6.

[4] See, for instance, James Thomson, *The Seasons* (1730), i. 99–102:

> Now from the town
> Buried in smoak, and sleep, and noisom damps,
> Oft let me wander o'er the dewy fields,
> Where freshness breathes . . .

And, in a more symbolic context, *The Seasons* iii. i. 250–3:

> This is the life which those who fret in guilt,
> And guilty cities, never knew; the life,
> Led by primaeval ages, incorrupt,
> When GOD himself, and ANGELS dwelt with men!

bolic association between the city and corruption.[5] With not just the Old Testament but Milton, Thomson, and Cowper behind him, Coleridge moves his city one stage further into the world of metaphor. The city of 'This Lime Tree Bower' represents all that is at enmity with human virtue; but it is also an emotional state, poetic shorthand for the suffering that Lamb has gone through, with his sister's madness and the appalling disasters of 1796.[6] It is interesting that, in combining the symbolic and the personal, Coleridge should use the words 'winning thy way, | With sad yet bowed soul'. Perhaps unconsciously, he is referring back to the apocalyptic lines of 'Destiny of Nations', where 'heavenly Truth' is seen 'from Bethabra northward . . . | With gradual steps, *winning her difficult way* . . .' (ll. 124–5). In Coleridge's imagination, Lamb is assuming for the moment an allegorical role. The apocalyptic undertones implied by the echo are felt to inform its new context, so that the transition ("Ah! slowly sink behind the western ridge; thou glorious sun!') seems less awkward and exaggerated.[7] Lamb's function in the poem is to bridge the gap between the two worlds of imprisoned self and visionary insight. As allegory, he is Truth 'winning [his] way' toward the central theoretical claim of the poem: 'Nature ne'er deserts the wise and pure' (l. 60). And as a symbol, he is like the 'companionable form' of 'Frost at Midnight'—an echo of the self that initiates human response and leads towards imaginative sharing. But behind this dual poetic function there is something much simpler and more

More recent, and better known by Coleridge, were Cowper's lines in Book One of *the Task* (1785), also based quite closely on Milton's simile:

> He does nor scorn it, who, imprison'd long
> In some unwholesome dungeon, and a prey
> To sallow sickness, which the vapours, dank
> And clammy, of his dark abode have bred,
> Escapes at last to liberty and light . . . (ll. 436–40)

[5] Max Byrd, *London Transformed: Images of the City in the Eighteenth Century* (New Haven, 1978), p. 39.

[6] In September 1796, Lamb's sister Mary, in a fit of madness, knifed her mother to death and wounded her father.

[7] Lamb particularly admired these lines from 'Destiny of Nations' and referred to them in a letter to Coleridge (13 February 1797) as 'elegantly' written. See *The Letters of Charles and Mary Lamb*, ed. E. W. Marrs (Ithaca, NY, 1976–8), i. 101 (cited hereafter as Marrs). Wordsworth drew on the same description when he wrote the 'Woman on the Hill' episode in the 1799 *Prelude*, again creating a figure that has a half-allegorical, half-human function:

> A girl who bore a pitcher on her head
> And seemed with difficult steps to force her way
> Against the blowing wind. (*1799* i. 317–19; *1805* xi. 305–7)

For a full account of Wordsworth's allusion here, see Reeve Parker, *Coleridge's Meditative Art* (Ithaca, NY, 1975), pp. 116–19.

personal: although it is not made explicit, one is aware of Lamb as a 'companionable form' because Coleridge feels they share the same childhood experience. And when he writes 'Frost at Midnight', in February 1798, this comes into the foreground. In blessing his son Hartley, Coleridge wishes upon him the imaginative fulness which he sees as coming through communion with Nature. He himself had lacked this:

> it thrills my heart
> With tender gladness, thus to look at thee,
> And think that thou shalt learn far other lore,
> And in far other scenes! (ll. 48–51)[8]

He is echoing the rhythms of 'To the Rev. G. Coleridge' (May 1797) in which he had contrasted his own and his brother's fortunes:

> To me the Eternal Wisdom hath dispens'd
> A different fortune and more different mind . . . (ll. 15–16)

Just as his brother had been privileged, in being allowed to remain in the scenes of his childhood, so Hartley is seen to be elect, nurtured in a way that Coleridge never was. The affection and tenderness of the early poem had verged on the sentimental, but the writing in 'Frost at Midnight' has a new, and very different, power:

> For I was reared
> In the great city, pent 'mid cloisters dim,
> And saw nought lovely but the sky and stars.
> But *thou*, my babe! shalt wander like a breeze
> By lakes and sandy shores. (ll. 51–5)

The highly stylized contrast of two childhoods is made more potent, and more privately meaningful, by the echo from 'This Lime Tree Bower': 'in the great City pent'. Despite the new romantic overtones of 'cloisters dim', one associates this 'great city' with imaginative deadness: Lamb's 'hungering' after Nature, his absence from the very source of the mind's nourishment. By his borrowing from the earlier poem, Coleridge is doing more than tacitly acknowledging his and Lamb's shared deprivation; he is also pulling into the new context all his original faith in a sharing which goes beyond just similarity. If he had achieved vicarious fulfilment before, by imagining Lamb's perception of the One Life, then it would certainly be possible to do so now, through this child:

---

[8] References are to the Everyman edition of Coleridge's *Poems*, ed. John Beer (1974).

> so shalt thou see and hear
> The lovely shapes and sounds intelligible
> Of that eternal language, which thy God
> Utters, who from eternity doth teach
> Himself in all, and all things in himself.
> Great universal Teacher! He shall mould
> Thy spirit, and by giving make it ask.   (ll. 58–64)

As in 'This Lime Tree Bower', perception and release are achieved by wishing them on to someone else. It is only through blessing that Coleridge, like Lamb, can win his way through evil and pain. To take his words from 'The Dungeon', he

> . . . can no more endure
> To be a jarring and a dissonant thing,
> Amid this general dance and minstrelsy;
> But, bursting into tears, *wins back his way*,
> His angry spirit heal'd and harmoniz'd
> By the benignant touch of Love and Beauty.   (ll. 25–30)[9]

'Blessing' meant the same sort of thing to Wordsworth in late February 1798. He was expanding his 'Description of a Beggar' (begun *c*. May 1797) to form 'The Old Cumberland Beggar', which finally found its way into *Lyrical Ballads*, 1800. As he did so, he wrote a blessing on the old beggar that draws on Coleridge not only in mood and feeling, but in very close verbal ways too:

> Then let him pass, a blessing on his head!
> And, long as he can wander, let him breathe
> The freshness of the vallies, let his blood
> Struggle with frosty air and winter snows,
> And let the charter'd wind that sweeps the heath
> Beat his grey locks against his wither'd face.
> Reverence the hope whose vital anxiousness
> Gives the last human interest to his heart.
> *May never House, misnamed of industry,*
> *Make him a captive; for that pent-up din,*
> *Those life-consuming sounds that clog the air,*
> Be his the natural silence of old age.
> Let him be free of mountain solitudes,
> And have around him, whether heard or not,
> The pleasant melody of woodland birds.   (ll. 164–78)[10]

---

[9] All italics are mine, unless it is otherwise stated.
[10] All references are not *Lyrical Ballads*, ed. R. L. Brett and A. R. Jones (Edinburgh, 1963).

Like Hartley in 'Frost at Midnight', the old man is seen as one of the elect, capable of achieving a vital communion with Nature. Instead of captivity, he will experience release. The House of Industry—really a House of Bondage—would be life-consuming; freedom among the 'mountain solitudes' will be a form of imaginative nourishment. Even the wind, with its apparent harshness, will be benignant—like the 'touch of Love and Beauty' in Coleridge's 'Dungeon' (l. 30), which both heals and harmonizes.

As Wordsworth writes this very tender blessing, he draws on Coleridge's 'in the great City pent', and creates another metaphor of imprisonment, the '*pent*-up din' of the House of Industry. It is only a half-echo, probably unconscious; but it implies a pattern of associative meaning which gives a highly emotional, personal charge to his blessing on the old man. Wordsworth is thinking not only of Hartley, but of Lamb, achieving a release which is denied to Coleridge until it is imagined by him. In protecting the old beggar from the house of bondage, Wordsworth is conferring upon him the grandeur of vision which has come to be associated with release from the city. Coleridge's phrase 'in city pent' has developed into a way of conveying the deadness which is opposite to, but which immediately precedes, imaginative fulfilment.

In 'Tintern Abbey', composed four months after these lines from 'The Old Cumberland Beggar', the city is once again symbolic of an alien environment. But this time the sterility and the loneliness are there to be transcended, not escaped from or left behind:

> Though absent long,
> These forms of beauty have not been to me,
> As is a landscape to a blind man's eye:
> But oft, in lonely rooms, and 'mid the din
> Of towns and cities, I have owed to them,
> In hours of weariness, sensations sweet . . .   (ll. 23–8)

So powerful is the mind's ability to retain the 'forms of beauty', and to create, in the act of memory, recurrent pleasure, that the crowded isolation of city life can be overcome. The symbolic 'towns and cities' are there simply as a foil; it is the mind's capacity to triumph that matters. And, by implication, it is *despite* being still in the city (or despite the alienation which the city represents), that Wordsworth arrives at the sublime:

> that blessed mood,
> In which the burthen of the mystery,
> In which the heavy and the weary weight

> Of all this unintelligible world
> Is lighten'd . . .   (ll. 38–42)

Only when the poet is retreating from his full pantheist claim—'We see into the life of things'—does the city take on its more personal significance as a mood, a seemingly inescapable state of mind:

> *If this*
> *Be but a vain belief*, yet, oh! how oft,
> In darkness, and amid the many shapes
> Of joyless daylight; when the fretful stir
> Unprofitable, and the fever of the world,
> Have hung upon the beatings of my heart,
> How oft, in spirit, have I turned to thee
> Oh sylvan Wye! Thou wanderer through the woods,
> How often has my spirit turned to thee!   (ll. 50–8)

The city has lost the generalized quality it had earlier in the poem— 'But oft, in *lonely rooms*, and mid the din | *Of towns and cities*' (ll. 26–7)—and has become detailed, particular, and symbolic in a fully personal way. As a prison, it resembles the House of Bondage in 'The Old Cumberland Beggar' with its 'pent-up din' and 'life-consuming sounds'. But here the detail is not just physical, it is also painful: the life-consuming sounds had clogged the air, but the fever of the world *hangs* upon the beatings of the heart, capable—but for imagination's power—of smothering and denying liberty.[11]

The city in Book Three of Cowper's *The Task* had been nightmarish in its grotesqueness:

> . . . are not wholesome airs, though unperfum'd
> By roses; and clear suns, though scarcely felt . . .
> To be preferred to smoke, to the eclipse
> That Metropolitan volcanoes make,
> *Whose Stygian throats breathe darkness all day long;*
> *And to the stir of commerce, driving slow,*
> *And thund'ring loud, with his ten thousand wheels?*
>
> (ll. 723–3, 736–40)

But Wordsworth's city is haunting because it leaves so much unsaid. Its terrors are ambiguous 'shapes' belonging to the day rather than the night, and they could be either imagined or real. They are frightening

---

[11] The painful external pressures are very precisely contrasted with the 'forms of beauty' in Nature that create 'sensations sweet | Felt in the blood, and felt along the heart' and which pass into the 'purer mind | With tranquil restoration' ('Tintern Abbey', ll. 28–31).

by their very blankness, like the 'huge and mighty forms' of terror in the 'Boat-stealing' episode of *The Prelude*, which move through the child's mind, displacing the 'familiar shapes of hourly objects' and heightening his sense of 'blank desertion'.[12] It is in search of these 'familiar shapes'—which he later calls the 'ballast of familiar life' (*1805* vii. 604)—that Wordsworth turns once again to the river Wye:

> How oft, in spirit, have I turned to thee
> O sylvan Wye! Thou wanderer through the woods,
> How often has my spirit turned to thee!   (ll. 56–8)

As he does so, he echoes Coleridge in 'Frost at Midnight':

> But O! how oft,
> How oft, at school, with most believing mind,
> Presageful, have I gazed upon the bars,
> To watch that fluttering *stranger*!
> (ll. 23–6; Coleridge's italics)

In Coleridge's isolation, the grate on which the film fluttered had taken on the significance of a prison. He had 'gazed upon the bars' and longed for release from the imprisonment of self, and the '*stranger*' had provided him with this by taking him back into the scenes of his childhood. Wordsworth, imprisoned in that part of himself that the city represents, similarly turns to the Wye as a means of release through recollection. The river, like Coleridge's '*stranger*' is a connective image that is both literal and figurative. It connects past with present, and internal feeling with external form—above all, it leads the poet's mind away from emotional imprisonment towards imaginative freedom.[13]

In November 1799, when Wordsworth wrote the Preamble, he was drawing very consciously on the patterns of associative meaning which had evolved during these two preceding years:

> Oh there is blessing in this gentle breeze
> That blows from the green field and from the clouds
> And from the sky: it beats against my cheek,
> And seems half-conscious of the joy it gives.
> O welcome Messenger! O welcome Friend!

---

[12] The passage comes at the end of the Boat-stealing episode; see *1799* i. 119–29.

[13] In the background is the ending of Coleridge's 'Reflections on having left a Place of Retirement', composed in February 1796 as he left Clevedon to work on *The Watchman*:

> Yet oft when after honourable toil
> Rests the tir'd mind, and waking loves to dream,
> My spirit shall revisit thee, dear Cot!   (ll. 63–5)

A captive greets thee, coming from a house
Of bondage, from yon City's walls set free,
A prison where he hath been long immured.   (*1805* i. 1–8)

It is a passage rich in private allusion, carefully designed as both a response and an address to Coleridge in his own idiom. The first line takes on back to the most confident and tender moments of the years which Wordsworth and Coleridge had shared: the 'blessings' which they had given to Lamb, Hartley, the Old Cumberland Beggar, and Dorothy. The 'breeze' had originally been associated with Hartley: 'thou my babe shalt wander like a breeze . . .' ('Frost at Midnight', l. 54) and in Wordsworth's mind had become a formative and joy-giving principle, wished in turn on the Old Cumberland Beggar and Dorothy.[14] Here in the Preamble it is closer to the 'charter'd wind' that beat against the withered cheek of the old beggar than to the 'misty mountain wind' of 'Tintern Abbey' which 'simply blew against' Dorothy. In the same way, the fictitious city of line 7 recalls the beggar's industrial prison rather than the 'cloisters dim' of 'Frost at Midnight'. These strong verbal echoes suggest that Wordsworth has 'The Old Cumberland Beggar' very much at the back of his kind as he writes the Preamble; and this is confirmed by another (equally important) echo further on. In 'The Old Cumberland Beggar' Wordsworth had caught the monotony of the old man's existence in the words:

> . . . *one little span of earth*
> *Is all his prospect*. Thus, from day to day,
> Bowbent, his eyes for ever on the ground,
> He plies his weary journey, *seeing still,*
> *And never knowing that he sees, some straw,*
> *Some scattered leaf* . . . (ll. 50–5)

---

[14] Blessing and breeze were closely associated from the first. In 'The Ancient Mariner', Coleridge had written of the breeze that welcomed him as he returned to his own country:

> It raised my hair, it fanned my cheek
> Like a meadow-gale of spring—
> It mingled strangely with my fears,
> Yet it felt like a welcoming.   (ll. 456–9)

And Wordsworth, in 'Lines written at a small distance from my House; (March 1798), drew on the original Coleridgean context at a moment when he was celebrating joy and love:

> There is a blessing in the air,
> Which seems a sense of joy to yield
> To the bare trees and mountains bare,
> And grass in the green field.   (ll. 5–8)

Wordsworth clearly has both contexts at the back of his mind as he writes the Preamble.

In the Preamble Wordsworth recalls these words and transforms them. Instead of 'one little span of earth', 'The earth is *all* before [him]' (l. 14). And the straw and scattered leaf become a 'twig or any floating thing', which are to guide him in his joyous wanderings:

> *Long months of ease and undisturb'd delight*
> *Are mine in prospect*; whither shall I turn
> By road or pathway or through open field,
> *Or shall a twig or any floating thing*
> *Upon the river, point me out my course?*   (*1805* i. 26–30)

Whether consciously or not, he is identifying in the Preamble with the most extreme, the most downtrodden of all the figures who have received his or Coleridge's blessings. He wills upon himself a future immunity to imaginative deadness by recalling his own address to the beggar:

> May never House, misnamed of industry,
> Make him a captive . . .   (ll. 172–3)

At the same time, he acknowledges that he has experienced such deadness, and his use of the city metaphor is a form of acknowledgement that takes him closer to Coleridge's experience as he sees it. It is a way of arriving at deeply shared feelings, when, in another context, there could only be the underlying sense of difference:

> . . . Thou, my friend, wast reared
> In the great city, 'mid far other scenes,
> But we by different roads at length have gained
> The self-same bourne . . .[15]

Above all, it is a way of pulling into this new context all the confidence that had been implied in his and Coleridge's early blessings. The biblical and Miltonic references in the Preamble imply—even if they do not deliberately invoke—very traditional notions of guidance.[16] But the accumulation of private allusions makes Wordsworth seem 'elect' in a completely different way. He is chosen, like Moses, for the task before him; but he will receive a special sort of nurturing—one that has

---

[15] (*1799* ii. 496–9). Wordsworth's echo of 'Frost at Midnight', 'in far other scenes' (l. 51) is poignant and slightly ironic in its new context. See above, p. 411, for the optimism of Coleridge's original meaning.

[16] The house of bondage (ll. 6–7) is from Exodus 13: 3 and describes Egypt as it seemed to Moses, searching for the promised land under the guidance of God. The words 'The earth is all before me' (l. 15) are drawn from the end of *Paradise Lost*, and describe Adam and Eve as they leave Paradise in search of their new home:

> The world was all before them, where to choose
> Their place of rest, and *Providence their guide*   (*Paradise Lost* xii. 646–7)

intensely personal connotations for him and Coleridge, and has come to
signify their complete sharing with Nature and with each other:

> And let him, *where* and *when* he will, sit down
> Beneath the trees, or by the grassy bank
> Of high-way side, and with the little birds
> Share his chance-gather'd meal, and, finally
> As in the eye of Nature he has liv'd
> So in the eye of Nature let him die.
> ('Old Cumberland Beggar', ll. 184–9)

The voice that Wordsworth adopts in 1800 when talking about the
city is very different from the voice of 1797–9. Quite suddenly there is
a new vehemence in his tone, and it verges at times on the hysterical:

> he truly is alone,
> He of the multitude whose eyes are doomed
> To hold a vacant commerce day by day
> With that which he can neither know nor love—
> Dead things, to him thrice dead—or worse than this,
> With swarms of life, and, worse than all, of men,
> His fellow men, that are to him no more
> Than to the Forest Hermit are the leaves
> That hang aloft in myriads—nay, far less,
> Far less for aught that comforts or defends
> Or lulls or chears. (*Home at Grasmere*, ll. 808–18)[17]

The city is the antithesis to all that Grasmere represents, but it is no
longer felt simply as absence from natural forms of beauty, as it had
been in 'Tintern Abbey'. Instead, it is felt to be actively harmful: capable of reducing human response to 'vacant commerce', making man
himself capable of deadening ('dead things, *to him thrice dead*'), and
obliterating all traces of sympathy or imagination in the mind.

Such vehemence may partly be due to Wordsworth's growing defensiveness about retreating to the seclusion of Grasmere. As his position
becomes more embattled, a strained and exaggerated note enters his
writing, expressing an unbalance that has not been there before. Against
such a background, the tones of his more private and personal poetry
become increasingly difficult to assess. The opening lines of 'To Joanna',
composed in August and addressed to someone he was very fond of, are
particularly puzzling, given their context:

---

[17] The text is from *Home at Grasmere, MS. B*, ed. Beth Darlington (Ithaca, NY, 1977),
pp. 38–106. In the most recent assessment of evidence for dating, Jonathan Wordsworth
argues that *MS. B* belongs almost entirely to 1800. See 'On Man, on Nature, and on
Human Life', *RES* NS xxxi (1980), 17–29.

> Amid the smoke of cities did you pass
> Your time of early youth, and there you learn'd
> From years of quiet industry, to love
> The living Beings by your own fire-side,
> With such a strong devotion, that your heart
> Is slow towards the sympathies of them
> Who look upon the hills with tenderness,
> And make dear friendships with the streams and groves.
> Yet we who are transgressors in this kind,
> Dwelling retired in our simplicity
> Among the woods and fields, we love you well,
> Joanna!   (ll. 1–12)

It is not just that Wordsworth has deliberately distorted Joanna's 'early youth', and consigned her to imprisonment in the city when in fact she grew up in the country with the best of them.[18] It is also that the mock humility ('Yet we who are transgressors in this kind . . .') so uncomfortably does *not* conceal the real condescension of Wordsworth's attitude. He may be writing playfully, and Joanna may not have minded very much, but there is still a seriousness in his tone when he charges her with being 'slow towards the sympathies of them | Who look upon the hills with tenderness'. To say this is in a sense to estrange her from the most central of his values, and to make her representative of all that is unfeeling, impervious to Nature. Back in Alfoxden he had written more seriously about this lack of sympathy:

> Why is it we feel
> So little for each other, but for this,
> That we with nature have no sympathy,
> Or with such things as have no power to hold
> Articulate language?
> And never for each other shall we feel
> As we may feel, till we have sympathy
> With nature in her forms inanimate,
> With objects such as have no power to hold
> Articulate language. In all forms of things
> There is a mind.[19]

---

[18] In an editorial note, Jonathan Wordsworth points out that this distortion is exactly parallel to the one in the Preamble, as an example of 'the city as a symbol'. He goes on to say: 'One is presumably to infer that for WW himself and the members of his circle this sort of poetic licence seemed normal and acceptable' (*BWS*, p. 13).

[19] From the *Alfoxden Notebook* of January–March 1798, transcribed in Wordsworth's *Poetical Works*, ed. E. de Selincourt (Oxford, 1940–7), v. 340.

Though the context has changed, and with it the tones of Wordsworth's voice, these are the claims that he is making once again in 'To Joanna'. At the centre of the poem is a moment of ambiguity which, interpreted in this way, might help to explain the oddity of the opening lines. When Joanna laughs, it is difficult to know quite what is intended:

> . . . such delight I found
> To note in shrub and tree, in stone and flower,
> That intermixture of delicious hues,
> Along so vast a surface, all at once,
> In one impression, by connecting force
> Of their own beauty imag'd in the heart.
> —When I had gaz'd perhaps two minutes' space,
> Joanna, looking in my eyes, beheld
> That ravishment of mine, and laugh'd aloud.   (ll. 45–53)

Given Wordsworth's normal association of laughter with spontaneity and joy,[20] and given also the clear parallel between Dorothy and Joanna—'that wild-hearted maid' (l. 23)—one could very well interpret the laughter as a form of joyous response. But it is not so simple as that. Joanna is clearly laughing *at* Wordsworth's 'ravishment' and to do that is to be insensitive, both to the beauty of Nature and to Wordsworth's enjoyment of it. In terms of the Alfoxden lines, she lacks both forms of 'sympathy': she is detached from Nature and sceptical towards human response. Her laughter is not joyous in Wordsworth's sense because it does not share another's joy. It is uncomprehending and almost scornful. As if admonishing her, the landscape all around takes up her laugh, and becomes joyously alive:

> The rock, like something starting from a sleep,
> Took up the Lady's voice, and laugh'd again:
> That ancient Woman seated on Helm-crag
> Was ready with her cavern . . .   (ll. 54–7)

This laughter is not just a reproof for Joanna's scorn: it is also a proof that Nature is capable of response in a way that she is not. The mountains 'hold no articulate language', yet they communicate with each other and with her. Furthermore, they can transform her scorn into

---

[20] See, for instance, 'The Idiot Boy', where laughter is seen in terms of a communion with Nature that is spontaneous and joyful, even when it seems to be ambiguous:

> And Johnny burrs and laughs aloud,
> *Whether in cunning or in joy,*
> *I cannot tell*; but while he laughs,
> Betty a drunken pleasure quaffs,
> To hear again her idiot boy.   (ll. 387–91)

joy—'In all forms of things | There is a mind'. Joanna's sudden per-
ception of this is not simple perplexity at their defiance, nor is it quite
the 'gentle shock of mild surprise' which in 'There was a Boy' had 'car-
ried far into his heart the voice | Of mountain torrents' (ll. 18–21).
Instead, it is a mingled sense of fear and recognition:

> Now whether . . .
>   this were in simple truth
> A work accomplish'd by the brotherhood
> Of ancient mountains, or my ear was touch'd
> With dreams and visionary impulses,
> Is not for me to tell; but sure I am
> That there was a loud uproar in the hills.
> And, while we both were listening, *to my side*
> *The fair Joanna drew, as if she wish'd*
> *To shelter from some object of her fear.*   (ll. 66, 68–76)

She has been admonished, and Wordsworth's carving of her name in the
rock, like the poem itself, is a commemoration of this moment. If one
interprets the central passage in this way, the opening seems less awk-
ward than it might if one took Joanna's laugh as itself a form of positive response.[21] The central oddity of the poem is still there: Joanna the
close personal friend is juxtaposed with Joanna as the representative of
city life, herself a symbol. But the ambiguous laughter at least offers
some justification for that oddity, and perhaps also for the condescension of the opening lines. Wordsworth sees her as questioning his
assumptions. He consigns her to the prison of the city because in his
terms she is imprisoned by her own lack of response. The tones of the
entire poem are mixed: now light and playful, now serious and thoughtful, but the extremity expressed in Wordsworth's position remains constant. If the city represents a deadening way of life, then those whose
sensibilities are dead might just as well belong to the city.

From this standpoint, it is possible to move into one that is even more
extreme—as he does, for instance, in those lines from the end of *The
Prelude*, Book Seven:

> Oh, blank confusion! and a type not false
> Of what the mighty City is itself
> To all except a Straggler here and there,
> To the whole Swarm of its inhabitants;

---

[21] For a reading of this passage in 'To Joanna' in terms of 'the relationship between
the daemonism of laughter and the daemonism of the sublime', see John Beer, *Wordsworth
in Time* (1979), pp. 100–7.

An undistinguishable world to men,
The slaves unrespited of low pursuits,
Living amid the same perpetual flow
Of trivial objects, melted and reduced
To one identity, by differences
That have no law, no meaning, and no end
                        (*1805* vii. 695–704)

Referring to the London of Book Seven, Herbert Lindenberger writes: 'The city, in short, assumes a consciously symbolic role—and often, indeed, it becomes grotesquely symbolic of hell, or of the whole multitude of evils in the modern world.'[22] The danger of such a view is that it ignores conflicts and paradoxes that arise from the way the Book was put together. It comes as no surprise to find that the lines on 'blank confusion' were written for 'Michael' in 1800 and later grafted (in the form of a summary) on to material composed in 1804.[23] The stridency of Wordsworth's tone, and the intensity of his moral condemnation, seem oddly intrusive—as they do also in the published text of 'Michael', where the 'dissolute city' deadens Luke's moral sensibilities, makes him a prey to vice, and removes him conveniently from the poem.[24] But they are all the more inappropriate in *The Prelude* for coming at the end of a Book that appears so often to be celebrating vitality, excitement, change:

The broad high-way appearance, as it strikes,
On Strangers of all ages, the quick dance
Of colours, lights and forms, the Babel din
The endless stream of men and moving things . . .
                        (*1805* vii. 155–8)

As a whole, Book Seven shows Wordsworth at last accepting the imaginative challenge of London, even while he writes of it as a threat to his sense of order; but at an odd moment, the voice of 1800 intrudes.

---

[22] *On Wordsworth's 'Prelude'* (Princeton, 1963), p. 241.
[23] The lines were written between early October and 19 Dec. 1800. See Mark Reed, *William Wordsworth: The Chronology of the Middle Years* (Cambridge, Mass., 1975), p. 13.
[24]   at length
        He in the dissolute city gave himself
        To evil courses: ignominy and shame
        Fell on him, so that he was driven at last
        To seek a hiding-place beyond the seas. (ll. 452–6)

The lines are described by John Jones as 'typical of Wordsworth's use of the city as a pasteboard symbol of vice and artifice, the home of the unintelligible, the wholly random element in things'. See *The Egotistical Sublime* (1954), p. 100.

At the end of 1800 Wordsworth wrote a passage in the Preface to *Lyrical Ballads* which might be taken as a factual summary of the attitudes expressed during the previous months:

> For a multitude of causes unknown to former times are now acting with a combined force *to blunt the discriminating powers of the mind, and unfitting it for all voluntary exertion to reduce it to a state of almost savage torpor.* The most effective of these causes are the great national events which are daily taking place, and *the encreasing accumulation of men in cities,* where the uniformity of their occupations produces a craving for extraordinary incident which the rapid accumulation of intelligence hourly gratifies.[25]

In effect of course, what the passage offers is a defensive rationalization of the emotional attitude that has underlain his symbol-making. His vague reference to the war with France ('the great national events which are daily taking place') and his generalization about urban growth, offer only a thin factual disguise for prejudices that lie very deep. The emotive quality of his language ('blunt', 'reduce', 'savage torpor', 'craving') reveals the same crazed rejection of city life (its deadness and uniformity) as had come through, at the beginning of the year, in *Home at Grasmere.*

Wordsworth did not go unanswered: during the winter of 1800 and the early months of 1801, Charles Lamb wrote a series of letters to his acquaintances eulogizing London life.[26] The letters are private in some of their references, but otherwise have a self-consciousness of style and intention that makes them seem not just literary but publicly so. They are also remarkably similar in phrasing, as though Lamb is reworking, and slightly embroidering each time, a single body of material. In the *Morning Post*, on 1 February 1802, he wrote an article, 'The Londoner', which drew together the thoughts he had been developing about London life.[27] Material from the letters is recast here in an elegant and

[25] *The Prose Works of William Wordsworth*, ed. W. J. B. Owen and Jane Worthington Smyser (Oxford, 1974), i. 128. Wordworth's attitude here had been briefly anticipated in a letter to Coleridge, written from Germany in February 1799: 'I do not so ardently desire character in poems like Burger's, as manners, not transitory manners reflecting *the wearisome unintelligible obliquities of city-life*, but manners connected with the permanent objects of nature and partaking of the simplicity of those objects.' See *The Letters of William and Dorothy Wordsworth; The Early Years*, revised edn. C. L. Shaver (Oxford, 1967), p. 255; the edition is cited hereafter as *EY*.

[26] The first of these was to Manning on 29 Nov. 1800 (Marrs i. 247–8), the second to Wordsworth on 30 Jan. 1801 (ibid., 265–8), and the third to Robert Lloyd on 7 Feb. 1801 (ibid., 270–1). He made further comments on his feeling for London in a letter to Manning of 27 Feb. 1801 (ibid., 277).

[27] A copy of the article was sent in a letter to Manning on 15 Feb. 1802 (Marrs ii. 55–8).

genially expansive form, but in the process a lot of the subtlety in
Lamb's tone is lost—the tone which, in a private context, could change
from facetiousness to serious polemic at a moment's notice. It is in the
letters, then, that one finds a wholly appropriate response to
Wordsworth's extremity.

In the first of these he is writing to Manning, in November 1800, in
response to his friend's invitation to go and stay with him in Cambridge.
On one side of the page, he writes a mock refusal, couched in 'Romantic'
terms which are deliberately parodic:

I have received a Very kind invitation from Lloyd and Sophia, to go and spend
a month with them at the Lakes. . . . I need not describe to you the expectations which such an one as myself, pent up all my life in a dirty city, have
formed of tour to the *Lakes*. Consider, Grassmere! Ambleside! Wordsworth!
Coleridge! I hope you will.[28]

And on the reverse side, he declares his real preference: 'Hills, woods,
Lakes and mountains, to the Eternal Devil. I will eat snipes with thee,
Thomas Manning. Only confess, confess a *Bite*.' (Marrs i. 248.)
Apparently, Manning was indeed taken in by the initial teasing, and one
can see why it might have been thought genuine. But Lamb's mock-
wonderment is beautifully handled so as to reveal the condescension
implied in Wordsworth's and Coleridge's attitude. And his facetious
echo of 'This Lime Tree Bower' ('pent up all my life in a dirty city')
takes Coleridge's phrase so literally that it succeeds entirely in debunk-
ing him. Lamb is clearly riled not just at the condescension of it all, but
at certain sorts of over-simplification which he finds pretentious. Three
months earlier he had written twice to Coleridge about the same passage in 'This Lime Tree Bower'.[29] In his first letter, the objection he
raised was not just to condescension, but to diction:

For God's sake (I never was more serious), don't make me ridiculous any more
by terming me gentle-hearted in print, or do it in better verses. It did well
enough five years ago when I came to see you, and was moral coxcomb enough
at the time you wrote the lines, to feed upon such epithets; but, besides that,
the meaning of gentle is equivocal at best, and almost always means poor-
spirited, the very quality of gentleness is abhorrent to such vile trumpetings. My
sentiment is long since vanished. I hope my *virtues* have done *sucking*. I can scarce
think but you meant it in joke. I hope you did, for I should be ashamed to think

[28] 29 Nov. 1800 (Marrs i. 247).
[29] Coleridge published 'This Lime Tree Bower My Prison', for the first time, in *The
Annual Anthology* of 1800. Until then it was probably regarded by Lamb as an intensely
private poem. Two versions had been enclosed in letters to Coleridge's friends in July
1797, one to Southey, the other to Lloyd.

that you could think to gratify me by such praise, fit only to be a cordial to some green-sick sonneteer.[30]

The archness of his tone is heightened by the pedantry; he clearly delights in mocking the sentimental side of Coleridge. A week later, he writes about the same line, insisting on realism:

. . . please to blot out *gentle hearted*, and substitute drunken-dog, ragged-head, seld-shaven, odd-ey'd, stuttering, or any other epithet which truly and properly belongs to the Gentleman in question. And for Charles read Tom, or Bob, or Richard, *for more delicacy*.[31]

In Lamb's view, Coleridge dilutes what is real so as to make it endearing. What *he* values—and this is revealed by the exaggerated self-deprecation—is idiosyncrasy, or the oddity of what is 'normal'. By the time he writes to Manning, Wordsworth's and Coleridge's distinctions between the city and the country have come to seem like gross over-simplifications. On the reverse of the letter Lamb abandons facetiousness for a direct confrontation with their views:

For my part, with reverence to my friends northward, I must confess that I am not romance-bit about *Nature*. The earth, and sea, and sky (when all is said) is but as a house to dwell in . . . (Marrs i. 248)

He is being half whimsical, half serious. The question he is really asking is 'What excites the imagination?' and the answer he gives is by no means orthodox:

Streets, streets, streets, markets, theatres, churches, Covent Gardens, Shops sparkling with pretty faces of industrial milliners . . . Lamps lit at night, Pastry cook & Silver smith shops . . . noise of coaches, drousy cry of mechanic watchmen at night . . .

And so it goes on: a long evocative catalogue of details, all minutely recollected, in which the prose-rhythms enact his sense of London's abundance and vitality.[32] One is reminded of the Cowper who wrote excitedly in Book One of *The Task*:

[30] 6 Aug. 1800 (Marrs i. 217–18). The letter reached Coleridge in the month when Wordsworth was writing 'To Joanna'. If Wordsworth saw it, or discussed Lamb's attitude with Coleridge, this might explain the use of 'wild-hearted' as an epithet for Joanna (l. 23). In any case Lamb could well be in Wordsworth's mind as he writes the poem.
[31] 14 Aug. 1800 (Marrs i. 224).
[32] One at least of Lamb's atmospheric details is aimed, very directly and wryly, at Coleridge: the 'drousy cry of mechanic watchmen' refers to his early poem 'The Nightingale' (1795):

Sister of love-lorn Poets, Philomel!
How many Bards in city-garret pent,

> Where has commerce such a mart,
> So rich, so throng'd, so drain'd, and so supplied,
> As London—opulent, enlarg'd, and still
> Increasing, London?   (ll. 719–22)

But Lamb does not distance himself—as Cowper does, for instance, in his formal conclusion to Book Three:

> O thou, resort and mart of all the earth,
> Chequer'd with all complexions of mankind,
> And spotted with all crimes; in whom I see
> Much that I love, and more that I admire,
> And all that I abhor . . .   (ll. 835–9)

He is closer to the city's texture, and he writes in an affectionate manner that makes fun of formality, and teasingly defies all moral judgements:

These are thy Pleasures O London, with-the-many-sins—O City abounding in whores—for these may Keswick and her Giant Brood go hang.

When he wrote to Wordsworth in January 1801, Lamb drew on material from this letter to Manning, but gave it a new sharpness. His cavalier dismissal of 'Keswick and her Giant Brood' turns into whimsicality; but there is also a seriousness in what he is saying:

Separate from the pleasure of your company, I don't mu[ch] care if I never see a mountain in my life.—I have passed all my days in London, until I have formed as many and intense local attachments, as any of you Mountaineers can have done with dead nature.[33]

The claim he is making is that, without friendship, the landscape has no meaning. In personal terms, 'friendship' is the pleasure of the Wordsworths' company. In philosophical terms, it is 'pleasure' itself—'Joy', or the power of the imagination to perceive joyousness in the landscape. With one of his most whimsical statements, Lamb is joining Blake

> While at their window they with downward eye
> Mark the faint Lamp-beam on the kennell'd mud,
> And listen to *the drowsy cry of Watchmen,*
> (Those hoarse unfeather'd Nightingales of TIME!)
> How many wretched Bards address *thy* name.   (ll. 1–7)

There is an obvious appropriateness in Lamb's alluding to the poem that contains Coleridge's earliest usage of the phrase 'in city pent'.

[33] Marrs i. 267.

and taking up an extreme Romantic position: Nature itself is '*dead*'; it is the mind of man that enlivens.[34]

For Lamb, as for Wordsworth, the imagination was nourished by 'intense local attachments'. In talking of London in this way he was not just being defensive; he was taking Wordsworth's ideas as far as they could go:

. . . parsons cheap'ning books, coffee houses, steams of soups from kitchens, the pantomimes, London itself, a pantomime and a masquerade, *all these things work themselves into my mind and feed me without a power of satiating me*. The wonder of these sights impells me into night-walks about her crowded streets, and I often shed tears in the motley Strand from fullness of joy at so much Life.

The rhythms and language of Lamb's prose recall 'Tintern Abbey', with its world of substantial 'things' that become

> sensations sweet,
> Felt in the blood, and felt along the heart,
> . . . passing even into [the] purer mind
> With tranquil restoration . . .   (ll. 28–31)

The idea that the mind can physically be *nourished* is also distinctly Wordsworthian: in 'Tintern Abbey', colours and forms are 'An appetite' (l. 81); the perception of beauty provides 'life and *food* | For future years' (ll. 65–6); and Nature *feeds* 'With lofty thoughts' (ll. 128–9).[35] Lamb perceives the full potential of this 'language of the sense', indeed takes it one step further—'feed me without a power of satiating me'— so that one has an impression of permanent seeking, a whimsical alternative to the 'something evermore about to be'. Lamb's use of the verb 'impel', in 'the wonder of these sights impells me' would surely summon up in Wordsworth's mind 'A motion and a spirit, that impels | All thinking things'. And his 'fulness of Joy at so much Life' is analogous to Wordsworth's early pantheism—his joy at apprehending 'something far more deeply interfused' ('Tintern Abbey', l. 97). Whether con-

[34] In his annotations to Wordsworth's *Poems*, 1815, Blake writes boldly: 'Natural Objects always did & now do Weaken deaden & obliterate Imagination in Me Wordsworth must know that what he Writes Valuable is Not to be found in Nature . . .' (*The Poetry and Prose of William Blake*, ed. David V. Erdman (New York, 1970), p. 655).

[35] Use of the word 'feed' is mocked, very wittily, in a poem from *The Annual Anthology*, 1799. It was probably composed by Southey, and shows an immediate response to the language of *Lyrical Ballads*:

> Then may the enthusiast Youth at eve's lone hour,
> Led by mild Melancholy's placid power,
> Go listen to the soothing Nightingale
> And *feed* on meditation; while that I
> Remain at home and *feed* on gooseberry-pie.   (Sonnet xv, ll. 10–14)

sciously or not, Lamb has couched his plea for the life of London in the language of 'Tintern Abbey'. He is challenging Wordsworth in the Wordsworthian idiom.

As the letter continues, it becomes more whimsical, more obviously designed to tease:

My attachments are all local, purely local—. I have no passion . . . to groves and vallies. . . . have I not enough without your mountains?—I do not envy you. I should pity you, did I not know, that the Mind will make friends of anything.

His tone has become ironically pitying, and his stress has shifted back on to 'friendship', but this time specifically in the philosophical sense: Lamb is implying that it is immaterial whether the poet talks of cities or mountains, since 'Mind' itself is what counts, and 'Mind' will share joy with whatever is readily available. In the last passage of his letter, Lamb takes this position as far as it can go—almost into the realm of absurdity. His eye is continually on the elegance of his own paradox:

I consider the clouds above me but as a roof beautifully painted, but unable to satisfy the mind, and at last, like the pictures of the apartment of a Connoisseur, unable to afford him any longer a pleasure. So fading upon me from disuse, have been the Beauties of Nature, as they have been confinedly called; so ever fresh & green and warm are all the inventions of men and assemblies of men in this great city—. I should certainly have laughed with dear Joanna.³⁶

This picture of himself as an aging art-lover is delightful to Lamb, but not nearly so much as the closing comment. He is making an ally of Joanna because she, like him, is the victim not only of Wordsworth's condescension but of his wrong-headedness. The laughter which, in Wordsworth's poem, had suddenly become frightening to Joanna is triumphant here. It mocks the assumption that 'friendships with the fields and groves' ('To Joanna', l. 8) are all that matter, and seems in its confidence to proclaim that 'the Mind will make friends of anything'. For Lamb there is genuine wonderment to be felt in London—not 'ravishment' at perceiving what is sublime, but the sense of warmth and vitality that comes from things abundantly human: 'so ever fresh & green and warm are all the inventions of men and assemblies of men in this great city.'³⁷ Wordsworth's description of the torpor of city life ('to hold

³⁶ Lamb had just read the second volume of *Lyrical Ballads*, and in addition had received a copy from Wordsworth himself, who ordered it for him when writing to Longman on 18 Dec. 1800 (*EY*, p. 310).

³⁷ As Max Byrd points out, Lamb's London has very deep affinities with Samuel Johnson's: both feel it as 'a fully human city, actual but not unacceptable' (*London Transformed*, pp. 114, 118).

a vacant commerce day by day | With that which he can neither know nor love— | Dead things')[38] is a denial of sensibility, and of the very tenderness towards things inanimate which he appears to offer in the Alfoxden lines.[39] What Lamb succeeds in showing is the inconsistency of Wordsworth's position. If there is indeed a mind 'in all forms of things', then nowhere is this more obvious than in the city, animated as it is by all that is human:

> The wonder of these sights impells me into night-walks about her crowded streets, and I often shed tears in the motley Strand from fullness of joy at so much Life.

It is the word 'motley' which, above all else, indicates Lamb's feeling for London. He uses it not only to evoke a sense of diversity—and even incongruity—but also to suggest the pathos and the humanity of the Fool. He may be rejecting Wordsworthian grandeur, which does not touch him ('I should certainly have laughed with dear Joanna'), but he is not rejecting Wordsworthian tenderness.

The following year Wordsworth was to write his great sonnet on Westminster Bridge:

> Earth has not anything to shew more fair:
> Dull would he be of soul who could pass by
> A sight so touching in its majesty:
> Ships, towers, domes, theatres, and temples lie
> Open unto the fields, and to the sky;
> All bright and glittering in the smokeless air . . . (ll. 1–6)

It is not the motley Strand that touches him—as Dorothy said, London seemed at this moment before dawn to have 'something like the purity of one of nature's own grand spectacles'[40]—but the old antipathy has gone none the less. Lamb at this stage could hardly have claimed a convert, but it was he who later in the summer of 1802 took Wordsworth and Dorothy to visit Bartholomew Fair; and it is the Fair which in *The Prelude* Book Seven shows the poet finally able to enter imaginatively into a world that is the opposite of his chosen tranquillity. The city, for so long a symbol or a foil, had come into its own.

---

[38] Quoted above, p. 417.

[39] I refer to the lines beginning 'Why is it we feel | So little for each other . . .', which are quoted in full above, pp. 418–19.

[40] *Journals of Dorothy Wordsworth*, 2nd edn. Mary Moorman (Oxford, 1971), p. 151.

Index

self-deception:
  in Coleridge 37–8, 85–6, 202
  in Wordsworth 33, 55, 103, 110–13,
      142, 165, 171, 174, 181–2, 190
  see also fiction, myth, wish-fulfilment
self-parody 23, 45, 48, 52, 62–3, 72, 101,
      109, 132–3, 192
  see also echo, self-
self-portraiture 27, 109–16, 150
senses, the 26, 39, 41, 44, 64, 67, 80
Shakespeare, William 10, 12
  Iago 12
  Hamlet 30, 155 n.
  As You Like It 153 n.
  Othello 155 n.
Sheats, Paul D. 4
Sheridan, Thomas Brinsley 9
Sidney, Sir Philip, *Astrophel and Stella*
      67 n.
Sockburn 74
solipsism:
  Coleridge's recognition of, in himself
      71, 79, 85, 93
  portrayed by Coleridge 45, 71
  portrayed by Wordsworth 22–3, 28–9,
      65, 176
  seen by Wordsworth as Coleridgean
      42 n., 109, 118, 178–9, 190
  see also madness, imagination, projection
Song of Solomon, The 104
Sotheby, William 87–9, 91, 94, 96
Southey, Robert 7, 9, 10, 15, 87, 89, 96,
      114
  Fall of Robespierre, The 4
  Joan of Arc 7, 9, 10, 17
  Idiot, The 17 n.
  Ruined Cottage, The 17 n.
Spenser, Edmund, *Epithalamion* 75–6
spontaneity 43, 55
  see also blessing, joy
Stevens, Wallace, *To an Old Philosopher in
      Rome* 86, 121, 136
Stuart, Daniel 33 n.
sublime, the 19, 30, 39, 40, 60, 67 n., 97,
      98, 134, 137, 186
  see also imagination
suffering 5, 6, 10, 12, 14, 15, 18, 29, 101
supernatural, the 34, 47, 50, 125
  see also gothic, the
superstition 93
Swift, Jonathan, *A Tale of a Tub* 18 n.
symbol:
  contrasting attitudes to, in Coleridge
      and Wordsworth 134–7

  definitions of, in Coleridge 94, 96–7,
      134–5
  uses of 19, 26, 83–5, 103, 142, 145,
      153, 158, 162–4, 177, 182, 204
  Wordsworthian 127, 129, 131, 135–7
symbolic language of God 7, 20, 35, 37,
      144, 170
symbolic vision:
  alien to Wordsworth 42–3, 120
  loss of, in Coleridge 63, 65, 72
  see also allegory, Coleridge/Wordsworth
      relations: difference; emblem,
      imagination

tautology 89, 95
Teichman, Milton 113
Tennyson, Alfred Lord, *Mariana* 22,
      Maud 200
Thelwall, John 6, 8, 89 n., 97, 112 n.,
      148 n.
Thompson, Captain Edward, *Poems of
      Marvell* 146 n.
Thomas, James, *Castle of Indolence, the*
      109–15 *passim*; *Seasons, The* 182,
      206 n.
Tobin, James Webbe 49
tragedy 9
trauma, in Wordsworth's spots of time
      35, 203

unconscious, the 77, 115, 158, 181, 187,
      194
  discussed by Milton 178
  role of, in allusion viii–ix
  role of, in associations 69–70, 147 n.
  role of, in primary imagination 43 n.,
      144
Unitarianism 19, 20, 24, 34 n., 83, 169
  see also God, 'One Life', Priestley

Vaughan, Henry, *Ascension Hymn* 149 n.
Virgil 97

Wain, John 119 n.
Ward, Eileen P. 120 n.
Watson, George 88
Wedgwood, Thomas 26 n., 88
Whalley, George 199 n.
will, the 43 n., 95
  see also unconscious, the
wish-fulfilment 27, 32, 38, 53, 71,
      110–16, 142, 165, 180
  see also self-deception
Woof, Robert 4 n., 5, 17 n., 33 n., 143 n.